GLOBAL
SOUTH
ASIA

Padma Kaimal
K. Sivaramakrishnan
Anand A. Yang
SERIES EDITORS

History and Collective Memory in South Asia, 1200–2000

SUMIT GUHA

UNIVERSITY OF WASHINGTON PRESS

Seattle

Printed and bound in the United States of America
Composed in Minion Pro, typeface designed by Robert Slimbach

Cover and frontispiece illustration: A hero-stone with an old Kannada inscription (1286 CE) from the rule of Yadava King Ramachandra at the Kedareshvara temple in Balligavi, Karnataka state, India. Photograph by Dinesh Kannambadi. Courtesy Wikimedia Commons.

23 22 21 20 19 5 4 3 2 1

UNIVERSITY OF WASHINGTON PRESS
www.washington.edu/uwpress

LIBRARY OF CONGRESS CATALOGING-IN-PUBLICATION DATA
Names: Guha, Sumit, author.
Title: History and collective memory in South Asia, 1200-2000 / Sumit Guha.
Description: Seattle: University of Washington Press, [2019] | Series: Global South Asia | Includes bibliographical references and index. |
Identifiers: LCCN/ 2019015554 (print) | LCCN/ 2019981028 (ebook) | ISBN 9780295746227 (hardcover : alk. paper) | ISBN/ 9780295746210 (pbk. : alk. paper)
Subjects: LCSH/: Collective memory—South Asia—History. | Great Britain—Colonies—South Asia—History.
Classification:
LCC/ DS340 .G84 2019 (print) | LCC/ DS340 (ebook) | DDC/ 954.0072—dc23
LC/ record available at https://lccn.loc.gov/2019015554
LC/ ebook record available at https://lccn.loc.gov/2019981028

The paper used in this publication is acid free and meets the minimum requirements of American National Standard for Information Sciences—Permanence of Paper for Printed Library Materials, ANSI Z39.48–1984>.∞

To the memory of Dr. Mrinal Kumar Chatterjee, 1930–2018

Contents

Preface: Revisiting Histories in the Post-truth Era *ix*

Acknowledgments *xi*

A Note on Translations and Diacritical Marks *xiii*

Introduction 3

1 The Construction of Collective Memory: Sites and Processes 9

2 The Many Pasts of the Indian Subcontinent 50

3 Social Structure and Historical Narration in Western India 83

4 History and Memory through the Nineteenth and Twentieth Centuries 118

Conclusion 176

Notes *179*

Bibliography *203*

Index *225*

Preface

Revisiting Histories in the Post-truth Era

Our times are testing the truth of Orwell's bitter aphorism "Who controls the past controls the future; who controls the present controls the past." I was working on an article in 2004 that came to form part of this book when a leading research institute in Pune, India, was invaded and vandalized by a mob that objected to the institute's remote connection to an American scholar who was said to have written disrespectfully of the seventeenth-century King Shivaji. The history wars and the wholesale replacement of truth with "truthiness" might have seemed to be passing phenomena, but they have lasted. This book was completed soon after "post-truth" became the *Oxford English Dictionary*'s word of the year in 2016.[1]

The word had been a decade or more coming. Soon after the launching of the US-led invasion of Iraq in 2003, the Pulitzer Prize–winning political journalist Ron Suskind interviewed a number of the decision-makers involved in that historic blunder. One of them dismissed Suskind's questions about facts and consequences. Suskind was told that he was a mere dweller in the reality-based community, one of the people who accepted things as they were. His interlocutor, on the other hand, dwelt among those whose acts of will made reality for lesser mortals to inhabit and historians to analyze. It is almost as though the anonymous official had read Foucault and decided to mold discourse through power. Postmodern thought had thus been captured by its inveterate critics in the power elite. Reality and knowledge of it (including historical knowledge) were judged but artifacts of the time. According to the unnamed Bush administration official quoted by Suskind in a 2004 *New York Times* piece, "When we act, we create our own reality."[2] Less than twenty years later, even action has become redundant: reality is whatever was last tweeted.

Alongside this, however, is the contradictory concept of history and the past as "monumental," permanent. That is especially so in the United States, where "history" or "our past" is seen as solidly embodied in stone and bronze. Indeed, the concept of historical inquiry as fundamentally complete is so strong as to make the idea of an uncontested and irrefutable history a part of collective "common sense." Any alteration must then be a falsification. In television debates and newspaper editorials alike, "revisionist history" is practically a euphemism for falsehood, or at best, half-truth. Thus recent efforts at removing Confederate monuments from US public spaces have led to protests that these are attempts to erase or deny "history."[3] The narrative is seen as physically lodged in an inanimate object. When debating the fate of a Confederate monument in the city of Georgetown, Texas, real estate broker Jeff Parker said he understood that the statue was offensive to some people but that it should stay because "that's our history."[4] This discourse is also found in the highest office of state. The president of the United States tweeted on August 17, 2017: "Sad to see the history and culture of our great country being ripped apart with the removal of our beautiful statues and monuments."[5]

The monumental and the malleable may, however, be reconciled if we grant the capacity of power to produce "facts"—the claim made by Suskind's anonymous interlocutor. The casting of statues and razing of monuments alike involve the exercise of power. Force can move a monument—can it also change history?

One answer is that it can be changed by the consensus of the profession. In March 2017 the American Historical Association (AHA) sought to define the protocols of historical practice. It did this as part of a statement criticizing a presidential executive order that had cited a few carefully selected facts from recent history. The AHA wrote that it had "applied the discipline's professional standards to the revised directive and found that it does not pass historical muster." The AHA also explained the said professional protocols: "History is a discipline that begins with questions and impartially marshals evidence before generating answers. A compelling argument requires facts presented in context."[6]

The new administration's reply came in a budget proposal that emerged soon after. It planned to eliminate all four federal agencies that fund the arts and humanities, including support for museums and libraries. Nor are such efforts confined to the US. External assault on the community of professional historians has indeed intensified across the world in recent years. Reflecting on these developments made me more keenly aware of how the academy exists only as part of a society. That caused me to look more closely at how academic study and the creation of public knowledge of the past have been enfolded in political and economic systems through the last few centuries, especially in the American academy wherein I dwell and the Indian one whence I came.

Acknowledgments

This book has been many years in preparation. The project commenced with the support of a fellowship from the American Council of Learned Societies in 2003–4. It continued during my years at Rutgers, The State University of New Jersey, and was largely completed during a semester of leave granted by the University of Texas at Austin. I am grateful to these supporting beams of the scholarly frame for affording me the time needed to think and write.

I am indebted to many scholars for their generous response to my inquiries over nearly two decades. Prachi Deshpande shared her research on historical narratives with me for nearly two decades. Ramya Sreenivasan offered valuable comments on many presentations around these themes over the decades. Conversations with Cynthia Talbot on her studies of the historical and monumental traditions of Rajasthan clarified and developed my own thought. Dipesh Chakrabarty, whose book is echoed in much of this one, read parts of it and offered valuable advice. Phillip Wagoner's research on Telugu literature inspired my earliest forays into Marathi histories. Rochona Majumdar helped clarify the status of some Bengali texts, and Michael Dodson guided me to mid-nineteenth-century sources on Indology. Gautam Bhadra shared a copy of a rare Bengali text. Saurabh Dube offered a participant's view of the spread of subaltern studies to the Spanish Americas. Camilla Townsend guided me to valuable sources from that region, and her research on Nahuatl histories in Mexico gave me a deeper understanding of how judicial and political processes shape memories. My colleagues Miriam Bodian, Toyin Falola, Azfar Moin, and Patrick Olivelle were more than collegial in answering my requests for information. Brian Levack led me to a treasure trove of medieval heraldic sources. Deborah Bolnick patiently devoted several hours to clarifying my understanding of contemporary DNA studies and methods, and guided me to the work of Jennifer Pierre and her collaborators. Mary Rader in the University of Texas Library was indefatigable in locating sources and texts. Ajay Skaria permitted me to read his unpublished PhD dissertation. Gayatri C. Spivak offered a valuable clarification of her own early work. Additionally, I am indebted to Nikhil Bellarykar, Ethan Kleinberg, Dilip Menon, William (Vijay) Pinch, Jennifer Pierre, Anupama Rao, Ulrike Stark, and Gary Shaw for their help at various times. Indrani Chatterjee generously shared her books and thoughts and gave me solace and support through the many years this project has taken to complete. The editors at the University of Washington Press have been generous with their time and attention through the several iterations this project has undergone; Richard Isaac has patiently pointed out the many infelicities and omissions in successive drafts.

I thank the various academic institutions that have given me the opportunity to present my work. The critical response of learned audiences has been vital for the development of my ideas. Venues for this have included the American Historical Association annual meetings, Duke University, Columbia University, Wesleyan University, and the University of Chicago. I nonetheless am responsible for any errors or oversights that remain in this book.

Material included in chapters 3 and 4 of this work has previously appeared in the *American Historical Review* and *Modern Asian Studies*. I am grateful to these journals for permission to include parts of those articles.

A Note on Translations and Diacritical Marks

I have translated all non-English sources used in composing this book. As sources in the bibliography are not divided by language, in the few cases in the text where I used translations by others, I have included their names. Book titles in the bibliography and endnotes carry the standard diacriticals found in the texts.

I have tried to minimize the use of diacritical marks for non-English words and names, inserting them only where the reader might otherwise be misled. Widely known names of gods or kings or places are, for example, rendered as they usually are in English—so Vishnu, Shiva, Akbar, Aurangzeb, Delhi, Arya, Samaj, etc.; likewise common nouns such as zamindar, jagirdar, *chaudhuri*, *patil*, and *deshmukh*. Bengali words and names have often been presented in modern hybrid form. For Chinese I have followed the usage in the source where I encountered the name, even though that results in inconsistency. If proper nouns, individual or collective, they are capitalized: Dalit, Kayastha, Sayyid, Brahman, and so on. Many Indian names have acquired widely known English forms, so it would not be useful to write Vasu for Basu, or Kuḷkarṇi instead of Kulkarni. This practice extends to author names in the bibliography as well, so that the form cited in the endnote will match that in the bibliography. I hope readers will overlook the occasional inconsistencies that result from my efforts at simplification.

History and Collective Memory in South Asia, 1200–2000

Introduction

IT IS NOW THIRTY YEARS SINCE THE CHICAGO HISTORIAN PETER Novick published his study of the shaping of the historical profession in the United States. His work won the Beveridge Award from the American Historical Association (AHA) for the best book in American history in 1991. It was centrally an institutional study of the struggle for academic freedom and professional autonomy in the United States. This was needed, so the argument ran, for the pursuit of objective research unimpeded by administrative or political pressure—that was the "noble dream."

The book was concerned with the century-long struggle of the historical profession to establish its place in the emerging American academy. After chronicling how that was achieved, it moved to consider debates among established members of the guild of historians in the United States. Novick's frame narrative was therefore principally focused on intramural disputes in the history departments of leading universities. These were often cushioned by sizable endowments from the dictates of legislatures and protected by their own police from the disruption of the streets.

But already in 1988, Novick thought that the professional independence of US academic historians had been achieved at the cost of abandoning the "aspiration to achieve a dominant position in providing history for the general reading public."[1] Novick, nonetheless, classified himself as an "anti-objectivist," a historian who rejected the search for objective truth as an uninteresting project. He was prepared, though, to coexist with its votaries, since in his view their practice differed little from his own. But he thought that the real threat to history came from outside the profession, in the very demand for an unattainable objectivity. He warned of a "very serious conservative backlash in the academy—massively funded by right-wing foundations, cheered on by the mass media." He saw these changes as a dangerous threat to the hard-won institutional autonomy of the profession, all the more so as they had "increasing support from middle-of-the-road academics."[2] That political change, he thought, threatened the recently secured power of history departments to determine their membership as well as their research methods.

Yet much historical memory worldwide is now shaped outside the academy. In the United States, most mass-market histories are written by nonacademics and are frequently spin-offs from or precursors to TV or film productions. Additionally, there is the growing body of genealogical research based on DNA and miscellaneous records. Many historians are aware of the family history and genealogy branch of their discipline, but they may not realize that its growth is now far outstripping that of professional history. There is today a veritable explosion in the commercial production of genealogical information via sites such as Ancestry.com.[3] This testifies to a growing public interest in a new kind of history: ego-centered rather than religious, national, or lineage-focused.[4]

Nor, perhaps, is the marginalization of academic historians wholly accidental. Novick's 1988 book came after several decades during which historians had turned to consider the institutional practices, epistemological assumptions, and silent exclusions that shaped their own discipline.[5] This resulted in fierce debates across the Anglo-American world. The University of Chicago historian Dipesh Chakrabarty has retrospectively observed that the protagonists in that controversy were more focused on the practices of the profession and less concerned with the public domain beyond. The debate therefore, largely lacked any "sense of the diverse and changing relationship between the cloistered and public lives of the discipline."[6] But as the opening pages have already indicated, nowadays the cloister worldwide, wherever it exists, is increasingly threatened from outside its walls. In India, for example, alternative currents have undercut professional history since 1947, when the new national state was initially able to dominate historical discourse. These largely operate outside the official discipline, often effectively marginalizing it. Political battles around "history" in India now focus not on books but on Bollywood films, such as *Jodha-Akbar* or *Padmavat*.

Chakrabarty's juxtaposition of "cloistered" and "public" is a productive metaphor that I shall frequently invoke throughout this book. Indeed, it gave rise to the project itself. Mine is an effort to view the practice of history through a wider and longer span than historians usually do. I will argue that historical memory—of which history is itself a part—is embedded in and constrained by the social institutions that produce knowledge. That knowledge includes the knowledge of institutions' own production of it.[7] This is reflected in the very metaphor of the "cloister," a protected space separated from the regular life of society. Yet it must be noted that the Christian monastery, the Indic *maṭha* or *vihāra*, the Sufi *dargāh*, the college of temple priests, its successor the Christian cathedral chapter, the office of the Chinese imperial historian, the regius professorship of an English university, and endowed chairs in American universities—all were protected and funded by those outside the cloister. They depended on both passive tolerance and on an active flow of resources to sustain their cloistered lives.

Not every human society has had such protected spaces. Fewer yet have devoted any part of them to harboring those makers of social memory now called historians. Cloisters themselves have both appeared and disappeared in historical time. An encompassing society provided the larger, often regional, social and political frame within which historical practice fitfully appeared through the centuries. Yet these structures of social authority both support and constrain the production and transmission of knowledge. That includes knowledge of the past. Knowledge is not mainly produced by historians; we have always had neighbors and rivals in the cloister, from prophets and astrologers to geoscientists, geneticists, and many others. Our practice of history is but a minor species within the small genus of scholars. I therefore devote a part of chapter 1 to a consideration of these "boundary disciplines"—disciplines that have over time, contributed to the research methods and background knowledge of historians.

At the beginning of the current century, another much-cited book by Dipesh Chakrabarty called for the removal of Europe from its central, normative role in world history in order to make space for alternative historical visions. He suggested an effort to create conjoined and disjunctive genealogies for European categories, history being a key one of the said categories.[8] This book takes a necessarily incomplete step toward such an enterprise. It seeks to recollect the practices of historical memory found in all societies and locate them in their public and also their cloistered frames (when the latter existed). But one cannot provincialize Europe without discussing it too. India's inclusion in the academic hierarchy of the British Empire deeply shaped its scholarly practices, especially history. Furthermore, my academic training within the Anglosphere was a result of the former existence of that empire. It is for that reason that European, and especially British, practices of the early modern to modern era receive considerable attention here.

Two axes therefore transect this study. Both concern the reconstruction of the past by authorized institutions for the production of knowledge in human societies, large and small. One axis traverses space and the other traverses time. Each is centered on the institutional processes that produce and authenticate different types of social or collective memory. These types include clan and family genealogy, legends associated with holy men and sites, and nowadays, the academic processes that produce "history." In these institutions, socially recognized guardians of the past resided and reside, across various part of the world. But, as many academics should remember, those institutions need recurring support.

Of interest here is not only the work of professional historians. The appearance or reappearance of research practices among a handful of scholars in Renaissance Europe and their rise to academic dominance in the nineteenth century is a much-told story. But beyond these small circles of scholars is the lived and contentious domain of collective memory, where struggles over Ayodhya or the Alamo are fought. In past times too, such memory was *the* history that agitated ordinary people. This was true even in the European forges where (according to received Western opinion) the modern historical discipline was wrought into its modern shape.

Scholars have often tended to focus on the high scholarship of past times; we have a natural fellow-feeling for it. I will consider that too but offer a corrective by seeking out folk and popular modes of reconstructing pasts at various scales—from the family estate, the clan, and the village up to the larger imagined communities of ordinary folk and their commonplace and everyday pasts. At various times and places, these occupied the whole space of historical practice: all history was nonprofessional history. It was also then consciously public, directed, for example, to establish present privilege through genteel descent. We must reflect upon the structuring and control of memory in forms such as genealogies, hagiographies, and the practices of commemoration at sites both sacred and secular. Partha Chatterjee in 2003 called on academic historians to recognize the diverse forms of social memory "that continue to shape beliefs, stereotypes, and attitudes in the public sphere."[9] This book seeks to undertake that task by looking at the societal settings within which public memories have taken shape.

If we go back a few centuries, we see that it was only gradually that historical memory centered on claims to sanctity, honor, property, and taxation were displaced by new professional histories—and that was often only in the confines of the formal educational system. Furthermore, just as early science overlapped with astrology and alchemy, so too did heraldic study inflect the matrix of history in Europe. The Clarenceux King of Arms used his earnings to endow a history professorship at Oxford, while centuries-old monastic records were being searched by the royal *juges d'armes* for the authentic history of French noble families. But even societies that did not generate the detailed records of medieval Western Europe needed and produced social memory. I will therefore both locate present-day practice among its other neighbors in the cloister and also survey practices of historical memory across human societies. Without such a review, the invocation of alternatives to Western discourse must remain a mere aspiration, with no concrete meaning. Historiography today is inevitably dominated by the institutionalization of the profession in the imperial West. Historical practices originating there grew to dominate the entire world during the nineteenth and twentieth centuries. But the historical discipline has always had neighbors in the cloister. It has borrowed from some and neglected others. Historians are often unaware of how neighboring practices have, through generations, changed the protocols their discipline takes for granted.

One of these is the separation of history from cosmology, and another its grounding in regions and languages. My own training has been in South Asian history broadly construed. A major historiographic shift occurred with the birth of "New Persian" historiography in Southwest Asia and its simultaneous arrival in the subcontinent. This coincided with the commencement of the "vernacular millennium" in southern Asia.[10] Active practices of social memory grew in the different regional languages that took shape from the tenth century onward. This is the main area that this book surveys. A broad historiographic vision of social memory will present it in a frame comparing what are now the modern states of Maharashtra, Bengal, Rajasthan, and Uttar Pradesh. Chapters 2 and 3 therefore analyze early historical materials from several of these traditions, seeking to establish their character from the time before their encounter with Western tenets—indeed, a time before the tenets themselves existed. As precolonial Maharashtra generated the most active and socially recognized practices of memory, most of chapter 3 concerns that region.[11] The visibility of South Asia in world history today owes much to the international prominence of subaltern studies. We cannot therefore neglect the Marathi-speaking area, the one region where we have good evidence that plebeian and subaltern classes also participated in the enterprise of social memory.[12] But the social frame of collective memory is also subject to decay, and with that, manuscripts perish, inscriptions erode, glyphs are forgotten, and scripts become illegible. That is irretrievable loss, as important for historians as entropy is for physicists. The chapter therefore ends by exploring the place of conscious neglect and irretrievable oblivion in Marathi historical traditions of the Vijayanagara Empire. In passing, we will consider the efforts at fabricating memory to supply British antiquarian searchers at the end of the eighteenth century and Indian nationalists in the twentieth.

Historical memory was structured by the varying sociopolitical organization of eastern, northern, and western India. Claims to land and honor required the control of relevant public narratives. But the resulting "accepted tradition" was differently shaped in different regions: more integrated in some, more fragmented in others. That difference existed before and through imperial rule and was shaped by the structure of social organization and political power across South Asia. The colonial era did not overthrow these patterns. In fact, the introduction of print technology and the creation of a standardized educational system together led to a wider and more contentious public sphere.

Eastern India was the first major cultural zone brought under British colonial rule. Its linguistic regions had, however, distinct institutional histories and therefore came into the colonial domain with different patterns of historical memory. My linguistic competence limits me to a detailed consideration only of key texts from the Bengali literary world. But I have also unearthed a nowadays less-studied upper-caste history of the region, one that resided in the oral traditions and carefully guarded texts of genealogists working as arbiters of rank. As we shall see with the College of Arms in England, this was the history that keenly interested many. Chapter 4 highlights how diverse practices of building the past shaped the historiographic reactions to the British imperial era in India. But the colonial regime also grounded imperial legitimacy in the historical past in a newly assertive way and pushed that vision in its newly established schools. All these changes stimulated history-making outside the cloistered and regimented world of colonial schools and universities. Emerging national, religious, caste, and regional identities of the time all felt the need to ground themselves in the new discipline. Thus the imperial view was imitated and challenged in parallel and autonomous institutions that emerged in reaction to the colonial enterprise. This was especially important for "modernist Hindu" organizations, such as the Arya Samaj. This body successfully built an educational infrastructure within the emerging colonial one and fostered a narrative of the past that fed later into a Hindu nationalist politics.

Despite these efforts, there was a major unification of historical discourses under colonial auspices. This was mainly the unintended consequence of the creation of a centralized educational system and the consequent mass production of textbooks. It was accompanied by the gradual unification of academic historical practice under the institutional impact of the new Western and colonial standards. The rise of competing national projects in the late colonial era intensified the recourse to "history." The afterword, therefore, considers the separate and rival efforts at national unification by the parallel but opposed historical narratives of India and Pakistan after decolonization.

1 The Construction of Collective Memory

Sites and Processes

INVOKING THE MEMORY OF A "HISTORICAL" PAST INVOLVES SEVERAL different usages of the terms "past" and "history" that are often rhetorically conflated. As a result of that conflation of meanings, "the past" is often thought to be a transparent and unproblematic term. Everyday speech refers so readily to "the past" as equivalent to "history" (and many historians do so as well) that this may seem a trivial distinction. But this is a fallacious idea. The idea that the past is constantly extant and therefore known or knowable is an untenable one. We have, at minimum, three pasts: the grammatical past, the narrative past, and the *historical* narration of a past. The grammatical past is a feature of natural language: it is a statement made in a past tense (and there may be more than one such tense). The narrative past is a retelling of events in a past tense—a narration that may be openly imaginary or that may lay claim to reality. If verified by protocols relevant to the world of knowledge of its time, the latter type may graduate to recognition as a historical narration of the past. But that status is always open to revision. Therefore, since "the past" is a reconstruction, so must history also be.[1]

If a defender of the monumental view of the past argues that the possibility of making true statements about "the past" exists, then knowledge of the past exists somewhere, and the true statement is drawn from that stock of knowledge. This implies that there is an entity, a matrix that holds said knowledge of *all* the past—a store increased every instant as the present slides into the past and today slips into yesterday. "The past" is thus implicitly defined as the sum of all such instants. But in our world, no living individual and no single archive or database contains or records such total knowledge. If it indeed does exist, we are already in that matrix and cannot know it.[2] It follows, then, that as far as we humans are concerned, there is no "past" out there somewhere. We have to work to build a narrative of it. Once built, it has to be propagated and replicated; that is what gives us *social memory*. A modern subset of that is *historical memory*, whose institutional construction is the main theme of this book.

Of course, not every statement in the past tense claims to be about a historical past. The historical past must refer to a unique location in time and space. This kind of past is a category (in today's parlance, "a real thing") that exists only once one admits the reality of time. The question of time and its nature was the subject of extensive debate in the Indian philosophical tradition. One stream of that tradition, that of Advaita Vedānta, systematically problematized time in order to maintain the nonduality of true Being. Consequently, it had to reject the ontological existence or reality of a past or future. The strongest defense of the reality of universal time and space came from the Nyāya-Vaiśeṣika school. The historian Anindita Balslev summarizes its view as follows: All events are events *in* time. Time must therefore be granted a separate existence. Causal explanation—or at any rate the tracing of a sequence of causes and effects—is invoked by historical narrative, insofar as it is presented as a sequence of actions and their outcomes. Even in early Indian tradition, the historical past was the subject of *itihāsa* (a term usually translated as history).[3] We shall return to this theme later in this chapter.

Meanwhile, what may be termed "Abrahamic" religious philosophies necessarily developed a linear outlook on time that began with God's creation of the universe. Furthermore, as the span of human time was based on counting generations in the Hebrew Bible, so it had a very short chronology of some seven thousand years from creation to the present.[4] A secularized version of such unitary, God-created time continued to inform much Western philosophical thought, infecting even contemporary metaphilosophical works, like Paul Ricoeur's boldly titled *The Reality of the Historical Past* (1985). This book still began by assuming the existence of a past, if only as a body of past thoughts. Ricoeur proposed that historical study is based on reading "traces" of a past. Historians, he claimed, believe that it is this reading of traces (I would say "documents") that distinguishes their efforts from the imaginative fictions of novelists. Ricoeur then asked, "What does the term 'real' signify when it is applied to the historical past? What do we mean to say when we say that something really happened?" Ricoeur argued that historians work by successively moving from the archive whence they extracted the document to the document itself, to their valuing it as a "trace" of the past. But, he adds, they do not linger over the enigma of how the "trace" connects to the past, or consider the essentially indirect character of the connection. He asks, "Of what exactly are documents the trace? Essentially of the 'inside' of events, *which has to be called thought*." He argues that when historians speak of the surviving trace, that statement is meaningless by itself. The traced past must, he claims, be reconstructed by reenactment. He continues that as the trace was originally a thought, a reenactment thus amounts to rethinking that thought. "All that is finally meaningful is the current possession of the activity of the past."[5] Implicitly, then, there was an unquestionably real past that has left us its thoughts embodied in documents and artifacts.

Ricoeur had a limited understanding of historical evidence, much of which was never the "thought" of any past sentient being. This was, perhaps, because he derived his idea of historical practice solely from the part-time archaeologist and full-time idealist philosopher R. G. Collingwood (1889–1943).[6] Collingwood claimed that archaeologists differed from paleontologists in that the former always interpreted human remains as evidence of the thoughts and intentions of past humans. The latter, on the other hand, dealt with the remains of animals devoid of thought. Archaeology belonged to history, paleontology to nature. All history was the history of human events, and the historian's object was to recover the thought (intention) present in the event. So all history was history of thought. That was why Collingwood claimed that past thought could be recovered only by its reenactment in the mind of the historian.[7]

I agree with Ricoeur and Collingwood that historical assessment of the truth of a narrative set in some past time is based not on direct knowledge but on the evidence, that is to say, the body of relevant traces. Recovering the worldview that is embedded in evidence is often an important procedure. But analyzing evidence is a much larger enterprise than "re-thinking," one by one, the thoughts embodied in each document or "trace." Archaeology offers the clearest example of this. For example, the geographical distribution of Painted Grey Ware pottery across North India in the fifth century BCE enables us to understand the emerging cultural unification of the region. But no individual living in that epoch could have observed that distribution. Similarly, we may now study the varying width of growth rings in long-lived trees as historical evidence of past rainfall fluctuations over periods longer than the life span of any human. Equally, the advance of sister disciplines (X-rays or microscopes, for example) has added to the body of traces of the past available to historians. Historical narrative is an architectural "construction," but it is one constrained by the materials at hand—and the architect does not make bricks or cast pillars.

A more fruitful way of thinking about the constitution of historical memory draws on the pioneering work of the French sociologist Maurice Halbwachs.[8] All historical consideration of the processes that shape memory must start from his analysis. Halbwachs sought to integrate the then-emerging science of social psychology with his concept of community memory. He argued that memory was not something naturally extant but was "reconstructed under the pressure of society."[9] Almost a century of psychological research after Halbwachs has solidly supported his claim. "Remembering" is not an act of retrieval, but of reconstruction. That reconstructive process is where mistakes, such as the implanting of false memories, occur. Experimental psychologists have long known of the phenomenon of false or implanted memory. But obviously, demonstrating falsity depends on our capacity to recover authentic truth. So if the memory claims to be a statement of fact, then it is open to interrogation—even first-person eyewitness narrative may be questioned. Eyewitness testimony has failed scrutiny more than once.[10] Modern psychology has established even more solidly that even recent personal memory is not constantly available to the witness, that it must be reconstructed, and it may be falsified in the effort of recovery. As the forensic psychologists Elizabeth Loftus and James Doyle describe it, "Sometimes information was never stored to begin with. Sometimes interference prevents memory from emerging to consciousness. Sometimes witnesses wish to forget; sometimes they are temporarily unable to retrieve. . . . Moreover, another force, known as a constructive force, is also at work. People seem to be able to take bits and pieces of their experience and integrate them to construct objects that they never saw and events that never really happened."[11]

The above was written of the individual eyewitness in a judicial setting. Social memory undergoes yet further modification. Some of Halbwachs's major work was on the tortured history of Palestine from Roman times to the nineteenth century. This was a land of multiple claims and clashing narratives fragmentarily preserved in hagiography, archaeology, and religious polemic through two millennia. Deploying an immense erudition, he carefully unpicked the many layers of memory that overlaid the holy sites in Palestine, from Iron Age Jewish kingdoms through successive appropriation by Roman, Romano-Christian, and Islamic communities as each came to control the sites. Halbwachs was born soon after Prussia's defeat of France (1871) transferred the provinces of Alsace and Lorraine from France to the German Reich, where they remained till France retook them in 1919. The region was a target of German *revanchisme* in the 1930s. Teaching at Strasbourg, an old town where the university had only just been remodeled along "French" lines in the 1930s, Halbwachs was well aware of how sites of memory were subject to the accidents of history.

In a sentence from which I have drawn for the title of this book, he wrote: "We can remember the past only on condition of retrieving the position of past events that interest us from the *frameworks of collective memory*."[12]

Social memory, however, provides only the frame that both validates and invalidates the recollection of past events. Halbwachs worked from the social psychology of the 1930s. He was therefore deeply influenced by the sociologist Émile Durkheim (1858–1917). Durkheim was especially concerned with the conditions under which social cohesion was generated in an intrinsically atomized industrial society. As a Durkheimian, Halbwachs frequently and unselfconsciously represented "society" as an active agent that pruned and structured its collective memory. He also, however, recognized that social groups were shaped, or indeed defined, by their distinctive reconstruction of common memory. The examples of such groups he gives are families, religious communities, and social classes. These, he argued, tend to pull "society" apart. But the latter's efforts at integration required it to prune back overdeveloped group memories.[13]

This was a widespread process. Helen Siu et al. described the simultaneous shaping of ethnic narrative and ethnic group in East Asia: "But ethnicity as history cannot be separated from the *evidentiary processes* by which history is understood; it cannot be more real, more important, or more primary than the manifestations by which it is recognized."[14] In other words, recognition of a group identity results from a narrative of the group, and its collective acceptance makes the group. Writing in 1982, the historian of Judaism Yosef Yerushalmi put it sharply. Collective memory, he wrote, is a social reality sustained and transmitted "through the conscious efforts and institutions of the group."[15] That replication is a part of the self-knowledge (or collective memory) that *any* coherent social group must produce. It is the social process by which this happens that I will illustrate and discuss throughout this book. In his important work on Jewish historiography, Yerushalmi points out that when "we say that a people 'remembers' we are really saying that a past has been actively transmitted to the present generation and that this past has been accepted as meaningful." Forgetting is a break in transmission, gradual or sudden. It occurs when human groups fail to transmit what they know "out of rebellion, indifference, or indolence, or as the result of some disruptive historical catastrophe."[16]

Yerushalmi also considered the place of religious communities in Halbwachs's frame of thought. In a separate work on the memories imprinted by rival faiths onto the landscape of Palestine, Halbwachs recognized how religious communities could nurture separate, and mutually contradictory, historical memories.[17] Yerushalmi wished to explain why members of the long and erudite rabbinical tradition were so unconcerned about the history of their *own* time. For them, he argued, the biblical interpretation of history had revealed a pattern that would recur in the future too. In its ensemble, the biblical record seemed capable of illuminating every further historical contingency.[18] In his path-breaking *Time Maps: Collective Memory and the Social Shape of the Past*, Eviatar Zerubavel also pointed out that "not everything that happens is preserved in our memory, as many past events are actually cast into oblivion. Acknowledgedly historical events still form only that small part that we have come to preserve as public memory." Nor is the creation of this mnemonic archive a purely random process. Zerubavel shows also that groups consolidate themselves around memories of a common past and that "acquiring a group's memories and thereby identifying with its collective past is part of the process of acquiring any social identity."

That transfer of collective memory becomes especially important when the bearers of one social identity supplant those of another. Over a half-century ago, Halbwachs analyzed how "Christian collective memory could annex a part of the Jewish collective memory by appropriating part of the latter's local remembrance while at the same time transforming its entire perspective of historical space." Halbwachs was well aware of the role of political authority in the making of the social framework within which legitimate memory, as distinct from an individual dream or fantasy, is shaped.[19] Furthermore, with his focus on the community of memory—a mortal human community—Halbwachs well knew how historical contingency can shape, alter, or extinguish social memory.

We may see this best in Halbwachs's study of how the vicissitudes of political power changed the sites of memory in Palestine, from pre-Roman times to the twentieth century. He carefully teased out how the returning Crusaders (after their capture of Jerusalem in 1099) began implanting their memories by building shrines and churches that physically embodied their "knowledge" of the major episodes in the life of Jesus Christ. Yet the twelfth-century landscape that they conquered was vastly different from that governed by Pontius Pilate in the early first century CE. It had been modified first by the active erasure of memory by the Romans following their suppression of the last Jewish rebellion in 70 CE. They first demolished the Jewish Temple and most of the city. Then they built a legionary garrison fort and temples of non-Christian gods over important Jewish sites. The city and its environs were subsequently rebuilt on Christian lines after 330 CE under the first Christian emperor, Constantine, and his mother Helena. Such political investment in the sacred city made it a special target of destruction by the Persian (Sassanid) kings during their incursions into the later Roman Empire. Then, three centuries after Constantine, the city was incorporated into the great Islamic empire of the caliphs. They adorned it with Muslim sites of memory placed squarely atop older ones. Christians, both local and from the growing stream of Western pilgrims, were accommodated within a peripheral domain.

It was to this setting that the Crusaders came as conquerors in 1099. They sought to impose an expatriate biblical folklore made and transmitted hundreds of miles away. They nonetheless energetically set about "identifying" and building at numerous sites across the sacred landscape (in the process removing many Islamic monuments). The Crusaders were driven out after a century and a half but maintained a threatening presence around the Mediterranean for centuries longer. Muslim rulers still accommodated Christians, and pilgrims were able to visit the sacred city of Jerusalem. The Christian Quarter was reduced to the northern part of the city after the Ottoman conquest in 1517. Thus Halbwachs notes that the city had been drastically remodeled several times through the centuries after its total destruction in 70 CE. The important element in the Christian narrative memory of Jerusalem was not so much the much-modified land but the group of believers and "their commemorative work."[20] Pilgrims still came armed with textual traditions (the four Gospels) and apocryphal tales such as the Stations of the Cross. Jerusalem and its environs were transformed to conform. The process left a landscape studded with Christian sites of memory competing with older Jewish ones, with an Islamic overlay over them both. But as the Ottoman Empire weakened, various Christian denominations began to dispute the control of key buildings and, not incidentally, the goodly incomes arising therefrom. From the mid-nineteenth century, the Russian Empire and (short-lived) second French Empire began extraterritorial defenses of the Greek Orthodox and Roman Catholic Churches, respectively, even though they were under Ottoman suzerainty. A stronger Jewish presence appeared under British administration after 1917.

Interest in the study of memory intensified in the West after the dissolution of the Soviet bloc. Regime fiat in the USSR and its allies had, for decades, enforced a standard public recollection of the past. But after 1989, events and persons unrecorded by the official historians of the Soviet era suddenly bubbled up into historical memory. Halbwachs's works had been translated into English a few years earlier and began to be widely read across the anglophone world. The German Egyptologist Jan Assmann published a series of essays and books that sought to develop ideas of social memory beyond Halbwachs. He endorsed Halbwachs's core idea, terming it a "social-constructivist" one. But he threw aside Halbwachs's important ideas on the erasure and overwriting of historical sites of memory. He also did not adopt Halbwachs's view of historical contingency in the making and erasure of memory. Assmann saw the survival specifically of the Judaic and Hellenic traditions as a result of their own intrinsic virtues.[21] (Biblical and Hellenic roots have long been invoked as the origins of Western civilization.) Assmann wrote: "How did these two particular streams of tradition—unlike Babylon, and unlike Egypt—survive the decline of the Ancient World? This question takes us back to the origins of the semantic formations from which the two cultures emerged. In both Israel and Greece, simultaneously although for the most part independently, two crucial stages in the process fixed these meanings: (1) the production of foundational texts from the 8th to the 5th century [BCE], and (2) the canonization of these texts, together with the development of an interpretive culture in Hellenism."[22]

I would observe on point 1 that a text only becomes foundational *after* the tradition that it founded has been established. The authors of many lost texts may have thought they had produced something more lasting than bronze, and yet no trace of them remains. As to the second point, the maintenance of a "canon" requires the continuous sustenance of those who reproduce it. Yet history—including the history of Egypt—is furnished with many examples of lost canons, of texts made illegible by the disappearance of trained scribes (such as Egyptian, Aztec, and Maya glyphic records) or burial of the canon in the mounds marking long-fallen cities, or both. Other forgotten canons survive, but read only by a precariously supported handful of scholars. This is true of pre-Hispanic Aztec manuscripts, of which a few survived post-Conquest destruction by the new Spanish rulers.[23] Nor were the Spanish the only conquerors to erase much of a literate tradition. The polymath Abu al-Rayhan Albiruni (d. 1048) described the process for Khwarazm (Central Asia): "Ḳutaiba bin Muslim had extinguished and ruined in every possible way all those who knew how to read and write the Khwârizmî [Pahlavi] writing, who knew the history of the country and who studied their sciences. In consequence, these things are involved in so much obscurity that it is impossible to obtain an accurate knowledge of their history since the rise of Islâm (not to speak of pre-Muhammedan times.)"[24]

Assmann occasionally shows some flashes of an awareness of historical accidents of this kind, as when commenting on the differing fates of the northern and southern Jewish peoples. The northern kingdom, he writes, was destroyed by the Assyrians in the late eighth century BCE, and the survivors were deported. These "deported people dispersed in their new environment without a trace." But by his account, the southern kingdom survived Assyrian onslaught, only to face neo-Babylonian conquest and deportation in 587 BCE. Assmann supposes that the southerners then consciously sought to carry away texts in order to preserve their cultural identity. That then "laid the foundations for cultural mnemotechnics and contrapresent memory, dramatizing the dangers of forgetting through a change of circumstances, and teaching them to think beyond the borders of the land they were in."[25] This is pure speculation: there is no ground for Assmann to assume that the difference arose from a conscious response by the southern intelligentsia and did not originate in contrasting policies followed by Babylonian kings and emperors. The first deportation to Babylon came in 597 BCE. It followed a negotiated surrender and involved only the urban elite, including the king. The destruction of the city came a decade later. It was possibly this two-phase, Babylonian-controlled process that allowed the social reproduction of the Jewish clerical classes to continue in exile.[26]

In any case, the Bene Israel of Western India illustrate how a religious identity can survive the decay of a canonical textual tradition and the loss of temples and priests. Around 1900 the Bene Israel were an endogamous Jewish community of some 10,000 people. When exactly the founders of the community arrived has never been firmly established. They may have been the remains of a trading diaspora isolated by the Karimi Arab capture of the Indian Ocean trade around 1200.

When they first do emerge in the historical record in the sixteenth century, they were mainly a caste of oil pressers living by that profession in dozens of coastal villages south of present-day Mumbai. Their observance of the Sabbath led to their being known as the "Saturday" oil pressers (as distinct from the "Friday" oil pressers, who were Muslim). They did not possess any copies of scripture, not even of the Torah. They were largely illiterate speakers of Marathi, the regional language, and in many ways similar to their Muslim and Hindu neighbors. They did, however, orally transmit the first lines of the major Hebrew prayer.[27] They had no memory of ever having had a synagogue; their first one was built in Bombay in 1796. They had also adopted a regional solar-lunar calendar and observed a number of Jewish festivals under Marathi names that usually described some activity or foodstuff emblematic of the festival. These Jews might have been those mentioned in a letter of the Jewish scholar Moses Maimonides written in 1199. He mentioned a copy of his works being taken to Yemen, adding that this helped revive Judaism as far as India. He wrote that Indian Jews "know nothing of the Torah and of the laws, none save the Sabbath and circumcision."[28] The Bene Israel's recognition as a caste within the caste system meant that they could maintain their distinctive domestic practices without friction with the larger population among whom they dwelt.[29] Indeed, this encapsulation may have ensured their survival as a normatively closed marriage pool, even as they lost all of the canonical texts of the Jewish faith.

That brings us to the older and more widespread way in which memory was represented and reproduced across the world: through oral narration and periodic collective performance.[30] These forms of social memory were not confined to scribes and specialists and therefore were more durable than texts, continuing after the decay of the cloister and dispersal of its inmates.

THE FIRST CLOISTERS

I have already introduced Dipesh Chakrabarty's concept of the cloister as a site within which modern historians dwell. His work reconsidered their place in both "history's cloistered and public lives."[31] But historians, or even other accredited custodians of social memory, are not the sole occupants of the cloister, that privileged site of knowledge production. They are, in fact, a minority among the specialists who work there. But the fact of their social acceptance should not be taken as a given. We must ask: how is social sanction—the process that adds a certain narrative to the socially recognized past—achieved? In other words, how were what Halbwachs termed "the social frameworks of memory" constructed in historical time? The many ways that this was, and is, done in different societies will be an important theme in this book. Let me revert to Assmann's observation about the importance of the formation of a "canon," a body of texts that were deemed to embody the standard for cultural memory, as "absolute truth." He identifies the bearers and transmitters of the canon, these new intellectual elites, as (mainly) members of the sacred orders in their societies (rabbis, ulema, maulanas, *shastris*, etc.). But he fails to make the connection between the existence of such elites and the institutions that housed them on the one hand and the resources that sustained them while they focused on their canonical functions on the other. Rather, he falls back into a complacent valorization of whatever has been canonized (as "the Judeo-Christian tradition") in the contemporary West. The next section of this chapter will look more closely at "cloisters" and their creation and dissolution through time.

Chakrabarty describes the professional life of cloistered modern historians as one lived through specialized journals, conferences, professional associations, and so on. There are, he continues, entry requirements by way of specialized training that are needed to participate in internal debates. These debates invoke the protocols of verifying knowledge according to "the judgment of the practitioners of the discipline." This, of course, raises the question of who determines the membership of that body of practitioners? If we go back to the beginnings of civilization, it was members of a religious foundation or temple guild that supported much professional production of social memory the world over.

Thus, the earliest stable institutions for making and transmitting written pasts were bodies such as a temple-centered college of priests. The great temple complexes of Babylonia and Egypt were coeval with the earliest states. Mesopotamian clerics invented the earliest scripts—initially to maintain records of the claims and dues of the deities whose servants they were. That skill carried over into the maintenance of lists of kings together with records of their benefaction or malefaction, gift or confiscation.[32] Additionally, the Babylonians believed that the gods sent messages to humans through astral phenomena. Close observation of these laid the foundations of astronomy and mathematics.[33] The Egyptian hieroglyphic script was invented not long after cuneiform. Temple inscriptions and stelae, as well as papyri, have survived to the present (but were unreadable for many centuries). The pharaohs who ruled Egypt came to consult the deity Amun in his great temple at Karnak and also drew important functionaries from among his college of priests.[34] Such Babylonian and Egyptian temple custodians were thus the world's earliest writers of chronicles. They sustained a tradition of record through near three thousand years. This is a period longer than the Roman script has been used (so far), and much longer than the modern discipline of history has existed. But, in time, their cuneiform and hieroglyphic scripts were forgotten, their gods overthrown and their cloisters became shard-strewn mounds of earth, or ruins buried beneath wind-blown sand.[35]

Egyptian historiographic tradition was anchored around great temples that incoming rulers found it expedient to support. The priests hailed Alexander of Macedon as a god after he conquered the country, and he was quite ready to accept that status. The Hellenic dynasty that followed him continued to patronize temple estates even when they came to cover a third of all arable land. But the Macedonian conquests had, however unwittingly, precipitated social and linguistic processes that ultimately extinguished three millennia of historical writing in the Middle East. The ancient Egyptian historiographic tradition slowly fell into abeyance after the Persian and Hellenic conquests of the region. Augustus Caesar claimed all of Egypt as an imperial domain, but the temples worked out arrangements whereby they continued to receive a sizable share of the agrarian surplus,[36] and devotees still flocked to them with offerings. But decay set in with economic decline in the late empire.

Then in 356 CE Emperor Constantine ordered the closure of all pagan temples throughout his empire, drying up the flow of offerings that might yet replace landed incomes. Emperor Theodosius in 380 CE declared Christianity the state religion, and Christian iconoclasts destroyed sacred statues and other items all across Egypt. Several churches and monasteries sprang up on the same sites. But after the imposition of Arab rule in 642 CE, these parvenu sacred places were also gradually deserted.[37]

As a result, the dynastic lists transmitted by the hellenized Egyptian Manetho were, for a thousand years, Egypt's main historical legacy to the later Hellenic tradition and, indeed, to Western tradition. That was, of course, until the decipherment of hieroglyphic script in the nineteenth century. Similarly the cuneiform script and its records across numerous archaeological sites were only readable again in the later nineteenth century. Prior to this, Europeans only knew that, like the Egyptian Manetho, a Mesopotamian priest named Berossos had left a Greek history of Babylonian civilization that was, however, little noticed by the later Roman and Christian world. As a result, both of these works only survive in fragments found embedded in other texts.

Furthermore, like the Christians of the eighteenth century, the Hellenic Greeks dismissed other civilizations' claims to an antiquity exceeding their own. The historian Elias Bickerman has commented that under "the double impact of Greek power and of Greek science, the barbarians, mostly ignorant of their own primitive history, as soon as they had become a bit hellenized, accepted the Greek schema of *archaiologia*." Even peoples with strong literate traditions bent to political advantage. Inventing kinship with the dominant Greeks "was a trump not to be neglected. The [Jewish] Maccabeans officially acknowledged that their people were relatives of the [Greek] Lacedaemonians."[38]

So the hieroglyphic and cuneiform traditions each lived through more than three thousand years, the period separating modern Greece from Homer. But after that long epoch, texts in Sumerian and eastern Semitic languages became "totally alien to Greek, Parthian, Roman (Byzantine), Sassanid and Islamic empires and were completely forgotten."[39] Greek sciences were, however, valued in the Roman Empire and thus widely transmitted to its successor states. The Roman Catholic Church further winnowed the traditions of the empire. It shaped Europe into the loosely defined world of

Western Christendom and conceived a new, but holy, Roman Empire. It was largely clerics who provided the materials slowly reused by the precursors of history in Renaissance Europe. All these processes were dependent on the presence of a clerical class whose works were preserved by libraries and recopied in scriptoria across Christendom for many centuries. And that clerical intelligentsia was also the nascent bureaucracy that managed the kingdoms of early feudal Europe.

Nor did this fail to affect their output. It is well known that European monks who composed and copied historical narratives often slanted them to encourage pilgrim traffic to their own monastic shrines. They sometimes forged charters to authenticate tenaciously held claims to land or income. Indeed, historians now view twelfth-century forged charters as a genre with distinct traits, such as attempts to reproduce early formulae and simulate archaic charter formats.[40] Such forgeries show that their authors knew that the historical past had been different and that the king's or baron's clerks also would have been aware of this. They therefore aimed for archaism. Such efforts at secular forgery thus betray an emerging understanding of irreversible change through history.

East of the original Roman empire lay the rival empire of Parthian and Sassanid Iran. No complete histories in Pahlavi have survived, but the Iranian tradition, like its Indic contemporary, made no distinction between the factual, the legendary, and the mythical. Intellectually, the religious foundations of the pre-Islamic Iranian world shared many aspects with the Indic. As in India and elsewhere, the Iranian narrative of the past ordered the passage of time through a list of successive rulers, but not by solar or lunar years. Historical epochs were seen as already shaped by cosmic forces, and historical narration was oriented toward edifying and instructing the hearer and reader. This, the historian Ehsan Yarshater wrote, led to the general "absence of critical curiosity in Iranian historiography." Expository features of the oral epic were retained in the written tradition. Yarshater sees historical writing as the work of scribes strongly affiliated with the clergy and the nobles. There was, however, an organized narrative of successive rulers, called the "Book of Lords," which covered history from the beginning of the world to 628 CE and was written under the last Sassanid king, Yazdigird III (ruled 631–651).[41]

Southern Asia certainly had a large scholarly community, although its rulers never aspired to establish a state religion on the Iranian pattern. After 300 BCE, the intelligentsia were supported by growing networks of courts, monasteries, and endowed colleges, as well as village endowments for Brahmans. Immigrant Magians from Iran and their sun worship were integrated into the priestly order as Maga, sometimes called Shakadwipi, Brahmans.[42] Yet the documented practice of history received less scholarly attention in South Asia than in the Eastern Mediterranean world. Almost from the beginning of European writing about Indian intellectual history, the consensus was that even protohistory had not been written there until the coming of the Arabs after 700 CE.

Nonetheless, the Indic tradition possessed a term for history—*itihāsa*, extant in the early classical phase of the tradition itself. The word *itihāsa* itself is usually analyzed as a compound reading "thus indeed, it was" in the singular past tense of the verb "to be," (*iti ha āsa*).[43] We need not be concerned with the accuracy of the etymology: the point is that it was readily accepted by the learned and it therefore tells us the criteria they accepted—at least formally. The fact that the verb "to be" was in the past perfect *singular* would require the existence of a unique past. But history was not intended to be an unstructured body of recollection of past events: it should have purpose and structure. The definition given in a widely known *śloka* (verse) runs: "Narration of past events that provides salutary guidance regarding the attainment of erotic desire, wealth and power, ethical conduct and release from rebirth—that is called *itihāsa*."

The next step would have been to develop and standardize the protocols of authentication for past happenings (*purvāvṛttam*). But, as in Iran, determining the exact facticity of the "common stock" of past events was less important within this tradition. The rules for examining historical evidence were not formalized, even though other rules, such as those of etymology and grammatical derivation, were minutely specified very early in the formation of classical learning in India. Even the rigorously hard-headed *Arthaśāstra* by Kautilya cited mythic events to illustrate, rather than substantiate, its reasoning. The author was focused on future policy, not past detail. The Mahabharata, despite its many impossible and implausible events, was usually labeled *itihāsa*, not least within the text itself, as in the declaration of the benefits of listening (*phalaśruti*): "Hearing this history named 'victory' releases the listener from all sins, just as the moon emerges from eclipse. It should be heard by those desirous of conquest."[44]

V. S. Pathak has argued that the early historic period (c. 500 BCE to 500 CE) had seen an early effort at creating genealogical and historical records—especially, he argues, maintained by the Bhrigu clan. But during the middle centuries of the first millennium CE, this movement toward historicism in Indian learning was diverted by devotion to specific savior gods (especially the forms of Vishnu). Earlier narratives such as the Mahabharata were then rewritten to glorify specific deities.

A further literary turn after the seventh century CE, Pathak continues, was marked by the archetype of the *cakravartin*, meaning universal emperor. This became the template to describe every monarch. The template included two motifs: the winning of a princess and union of the king with the goddess of royal fortune. The biographical narrative of every ruler then had to conform to the standard model. Pathak analyzed this through a scintillating study of five "historical" poems from the Sanskrit tradition. He argued that the poets had winnowed factual elements from royal lives in order to employ a narrative of royal triumph consummated by union with a queen who embodied the glory of the kingdom.[45] Pathak's analysis depended on placing these texts within a standard chronological frame built by the empiricist historical tradition that already existed when he wrote. It was only by cross-reference to contemporary inscriptions and other sources that he could establish how individual poets had rebuilt their narratives to fit a heroic trope. Less romantic dynastic marriages evidenced elsewhere, he commented, were ignored in order to craft such narratives.[46] The consciously chosen archetype meant that the establishment of the authenticity of actual events was less important than the molding of the narrative into a preselected frame. This valorization of the eternal archetype over the contingent event then effectively devalued the historical fact viewed as uniquely located in time. Rigorously conceived then, time had no *unique* moments: every moment would return many times in the course of many cycles.

This brings us to an argument developed in 1989 by Sheldon Pollock, a leading Sanskritist. He began by pointing out the mythic and stereotypical elements in early Greco-Roman historical narrative with the intent of showing that the "ancestors" of the modern West shared traits with early India. But he was constrained to add that "still, the general absence of historical referentiality in traditional Sanskritic culture remains an arresting, problematic, and possibly unparalleled phenomenon." Pollock argued that the centrality of the Vedas to the Indian classical tradition meant that methods developed to study them would go on to dominate intellectual inquiry.

There were initially three approaches: the etymological, which sought to recover past linguistic usage in order to understand the texts; the historical, which sought to explain in terms of real past events; and the analytic (*mīmānsā*), which postulated the Vedic texts as timeless. It was the defeat of the etymological (*nairukta*) and historical (*aitihāsika*) schools of Vedic learning that resulted in the dominance of the *mīmānsā* doctrine in the classical period and after. (As it happens, that also coincides with the domination of the savior cults postulated by Pathak.) Pollock proposed the hypothesis that, when the Vedas were emptied of their "referential intention," other sorts of Brahmanical intellectual practices seeking to legitimate their truth-claims had perforce to conform to this special model of what counts as knowledge, and thus suppress the evidence of their own historical existence—a suppression that took place in the case of *itihāsa*, "history," itself.[47] Thus, Pollock continued, *itihāsa* became the true and eternally repeated, for which therefore the contingent had little or no significance. It was then more easily refitted into the narrative frames that Pathak described.

But outside the arenas of philosophical debate, both the literati and the rest of the people, high and lowly, had a sense of both their past and their future, one that did not need to be confronted with others' pasts. Offerings to the ancestors, for example, clearly recognized and reproduced links between past and future, encompassing seven generations centered on the living performer, who was at once descendant and ancestor.[48] A living sense of the presence of the ancestors was significant enough for oaths to invoke them. Thus village chiefs gathered as witnesses in a complex property dispute were asked to "remember the forty-two"—which was to invoke twenty-one pairs of ancestors—in order to ensure they spoke truthfully.[49]

The molding of social memory is especially evident in texts (often embedded in the Puranas, which were encyclopedic compilations of traditional learning) praising the spiritual power of particular shrines or deities and particular pilgrimage spots. There is little doubt that there was an active oral tradition that interacted with the textual. This extended to texts like the Mahabharata, which were considered histories. The team of scholars engaged in establishing a critical edition of the Mahabharata had to deal with multiple traditions across Indian regions. Texts were perishable, and in India, scripts were unstable. So the more durable and public sites were visually legible monuments, such as rock carvings, hero-stones, and sati stones. The last two are carved pillars—sometimes of wood, though surviving older examples are, naturally, of stone—that commemorate acts of self-sacrifice by men and women. Some were inscribed and dated, but many were not. In a society where few could read, the stones were nonetheless part of local memory as long as the community lasted. They might then be invoked as mute witnesses to past events. For example, when a claimant to a hereditary estate in Western India made his case, he did so armed with several classes of proof. He sought to authenticate his narrative by a genealogy linking him to the original holder, to locally well-known events such as the invasion of the warlord Naroji Ghorpade, and to a still-extant masonry memorial to a widow-immolation in his family.[50]

War, famine, or other calamity might sometimes displace or scatter communities so completely as to erase their understanding of the monuments. New settlers on the land then contrived their own explanations from the carved images that they no longer understood. Thus a number of stones commemorating heroes show the warrior dancing with heavenly nymphs after his death.[51] This is probably the source of the "popular tradition" quoted by Grant Duff (in 1826) that the "Gursee," a caste of musicians, were the original inhabitants of the country. At least one folk tradition was reinventing the dancers in terms of their present. The original import of the stone had worn away as its community of memory scattered. The invented tradition had then been incorporated into a Sanskrit purana, which stated that the land had been given to his musicians by Ravana, the demon king of Lanka.[52] The latter's defeat by Rama would also explain why the musicians no longer owned it. This example of the incorporation of folklore into textual narrative is an example of how Sanskritic as well as vernacular traditions included narratives that clearly percolated up from oral and local traditions. Thus local and familial historical memory multiplied as the Sanskrit "great tradition" made no effort to make *itihāsa* live up to its etymology.

Moving east from India, the institutionalization of history in China had a clear link to imperial power, and that led to considerable integration and continuity. The need to verify and record the predictions of competing soothsayers and diviners in early China had led to the appointment of a court official charged with "interpreting portents in the starry bodies and watching for auspicious signs." Records of events began to be compiled in order to verify past predictions. This laid the foundation of the East Asian tradition of historical writing, long sustained by an imperial court and anxiously aiming at an accurate record.[53] The post of grand historian under the Han dynasty existed for the official purpose of recording and interpreting astral phenomena. But over time, it grew into a large office and a source of patronage to learning. Under the Qing dynasty, more than "nine hundred scholars worked on the *Veritable Records* [official history] of the Ch'ien-lung emperor [ruled 1735–1796] alone."[54]

The historian Benjamin Elman has also shown how deep-rooted the tradition of historical critique had become in the Qing period. However, unlike the Babylonian historical tradition, the Chinese one did not die out two thousand years ago but flourished into the late nineteenth century. Chinese imperial governments, Georg Iggers wrote, maintained greater continuity in historical practice, since an official establishment of historians was sustained through successive regimes. This itself, he pointed out, was due to greater political centralization in China in contrast with decentralization in Europe. The boundaries of empire fluctuated and dynasties changed, but an imperial ideal that laid claim to historical legitimacy persisted. The history office in China, therefore, generally escaped the periodic neglect suffered by historical practice at the hands of the many authorities—church-, royalty-, and city-based—that sponsored or censored historical writing across Europe.[55]

As we have seen, the major tradition of China had in fact long grappled with many of the same issues as the West, but within a divergent, more "secular" frame. That continuity into recent times ensured that China was precociously advanced in debating the question what kind of narrative should be deemed historical. In 1089, the Chinese historian Wu Zheng was already vigorously asserting that historical thought needed an underlying factual foundation, with its didactic and literary features as an essential complement to the impartial factual base. The historian was, however, assumed to be a near-contemporary recording the facts of his time and drawing on the testimony of earlier historians' records. Later historians presumably would work from the histories compiled by earlier contemporaries.[56] In his great comparative study of Eurasia from 800 to 1800, the historian Victor Lieberman suggested that the social framework of history was stable in societies where it was anchored (as in China) by a series of successive imperial states staffed by a class of gentry-literati. He also suggested that the phonetic scripts of India, as well as the separation of Muslim and Hindu literati, made it difficult to sustain an integrated literary tradition, and consequently also historical memory. China's stable nonphonetic script facilitated the creation of a continuous record.[57] I would offer an alternative explanation for the South Asian cases. After all, the multiplicity of historical memories seems to have been the most common condition, as we shall see in the next section.

GREAT TRADITIONS AND LITTLE TRADITIONS

Literate civilizations did not occupy the whole of either the Old or New Worlds. Nor were written texts widely available even within literate civilizations. Finally, even groups that deeply valorized the written canon could, as the Bene Israel case shows, nonetheless maintain a lived practice without texts. In this context, it is still useful to recall Robert Redfield's distinction between the "great tradition" of an overarching civilization and the "little traditions" sustained in encapsulated and subordinated folk communities, which constituted the majority whose tribute and labor enabled the bearers of the high civilization to live and refine their cultural attributes. Outside the early temple-cities and imperial capitals, therefore, local and folk traditions propagated mutually contradictory but noncompetitive narratives of the past. Furthermore, the many peoples that lived beyond the reach of early states also periodically infiltrated or overran settled agrarian societies. Their adaptation to and acculturation in the new territory would add new elements of what was previously their own "little tradition" oral memory to the "great tradition" of the power elite they had displaced. Literate society then had to adapt to the historical memories of its new rulers. The genealogies of the conquest elite would find a place in the writings of their new scribes and secretaries. Local folk deities might grow to permeate the "great tradition," and, on the other hand, a formerly "great tradition," like that of the imperial Inca, might gradually shrink into the life of the little community. There was thus a dialectical relation between the oral and the textual in historical memory. We shall consider examples of all these processes later in this chapter.

The literate elite were, furthermore, never immune to popular religion and culture. Consequently, even in regions with a deep textual tradition such as China, there was a steady infiltration of popular narrative and religious belief into written history. David Johnson has argued persuasively that episodes in the Chinese *Annals*, for example, reflect myths surrounding a popular water deity. He gives this as an example of how it is impossible to separate the orally composed text from the definitely textual in "traditional literatures." This assimilation of genres, he continues, was most complete in works written for a nonelite public.[58] Performative rites such as making offerings to the earth gods that might have originally been transmitted orally as folk religion then became part of elite religious behavior. On the other hand, Indic ideas of Yama, the god of death, entered Chinese literature through translations of Buddhist texts. Yet they came to form part of Chinese peasant consciousness.[59] The porous structure of Asian religious life eased such transmission up and down political hierarchies, as when Hindu rajas in Odisha (Orissa) adopted autochthonous deities as tutelary gods.[60]

Durable social hierarchies have sought to create durable records. Independent of the old world, the three major culture regions of pre-Hispanic Mesoamerica—Maya, Inca, and Aztec—all developed systems of record.[61] The elaborately carved glyphs used by the Classic Maya elites in what is now southern Mexico and adjoining countries had become illegible even before the arrival of the Spanish. The cities were abandoned, and the urban elite that memorialized their achievements in glyph inscriptions faded into the residual farming populations of their area.[62] A century or so later, and quite separately, another new empire grew up in the Andes. The Inca rulers consciously sought to control "all forms of intentional historical messages." Special schools passed on a secret general history to generations of specialists housed and fed at state expense. These specialists and high state functionaries decided the official narrative of the deceased rulers and adjusted the genealogical narrative to reflect changes in relative power.[63]

Quipus (or *khipus*, knotted bundles of dyed cord) were one of the record-keeping systems of the ancient Andean world. Only a few specialists possessed the capacity to create and "read" them. Their form meant that, as Tom Cummins describes, they were not recognized by the early Spanish as "forms of memory" at all and therefore not initially targeted in the campaigns against indigenous religion. Readers of quipus were, in fact, periodically called into court to testify in legal disputes about property and tribute. However, revolts in the 1560s attracted Spanish attention to the danger of indigenous memory persisting in forms illegible to the conquerors. The Third (Church) Council of Lima directed bishops to seize the quipus because they were being used to "preserve memories of their old superstitions and rites and ceremonies and evil customs." But even before active suppression, these skills and memories were already withering away after the Spanish destruction of the state that had fostered them.[64]

Formerly elite memories could be retained as "little traditions," even after the elite was displaced downward. This was true in the Andes. Memories of a time before the Spanish endured, motivating a revolt as late as 1780. But details were lost, so that an early Spanish narrative by the convert Garcilaso de la Vega then became the major source of historical memory less than two centuries later. Image and performance persisted longer in folk memory. As with the customs of the Bene Israel, it was their annual repetition that rehearsed and transmitted them. Thus Catherine Julien writes that the genealogical tradition of the Inca kings had survived long into the colonial period, through both visual representation (a series of portraits of the twelve rulers from Manco Capac to Huascar) and performance (processions showing the same sequence of rulers).[65] It did not live through a textual tradition or an authorized oral memory. One can, however, visualize the very young gathering to watch and re-creating these processions when they reached maturity. Paradoxically, the genealogies were then perhaps disseminated among many more than had ever learned the standard narrative before the Spanish conquest.

But modern schooling, migration, and all the changes associated with modernization could erode memory. In the late twentieth century, anthropologists working among Quechua-speaking peoples in the old Inca territory were still told stories of the time of the Inkarrí or Inca king (Inca Rey). The genealogical line remembered earlier had been lost. The slow erosion of memory—and/or its reshaping—is evident in several of the works reprinted in the volume edited by Ossio.[66] We can clearly recognize the role of sociopolitical frameworks in the perpetuation, erosion, and extinction of memory in the region.

Our consideration of the painted "books" of the Aztecs and the complex patterns of knotted, colored threads used by the Inca empire brings us to a distinct domain of social information: meaningful signs. Parallel and independent practices existed elsewhere too: consider the European coat of arms. Originally motifs displayed on shields and weapons, these had helped illiterate warriors distinguish friend and foe. But with the stabilization of Western European feudal society, this knowledge was taken over by experts, the heralds. By later medieval times, only an adept could decipher heraldic symbols and interpret elements like lions rampant or couchant, colors, keys, or the narrative bar sinister (the latter signifying noble or even royal, but illegitimate, descent). Illiterate warriors and gentry could recognize some familiar symbols, even if Latin liturgies and feudal registers were a closed book to them. Impugning such displays could be "scandalous words provocative of a duel."[67] South Asian hero-stones and donative inscriptions offer another example of a simpler symbolic language. Carved representations functioned as simple "glyphs" or pictographic signs. Thus the representation of the sun and moon indicated the permanence of a grant, and that of an ass and a woman that the mother of anyone who violated the grantee's rights would be penetrated by that animal. Likewise on hero and sati stones, a battle scene remembered a warrior death and a woman's upraised hand with bangles on it represented that she had immolated herself on the death of her husband.[68]

European church monuments of all kinds also functioned as mnemonic prompts. So they had to be reworked in new political contexts. In Britain, the most wrenching change indubitably came with the Reformation and its accompanying confiscation of many wealthy cloisters and expulsion of their residents under King Henry VIII. Nor, indeed, was collective amnesia necessarily a consensual decision. The Protestant Reformation in England demanded a conscious forgetting, and Tudor authorities sought to reinforce it. That reinforcement "could take the form of widespread, bureaucratic, and authorized erasure of the names and images of saints from books and churches." So, for example, the name of Thomas Becket, who had defied an earlier King Henry, was carefully erased from his major "site of memory," Canterbury Cathedral, at the order of Henry VIII.[69] A countermemory was, however, preserved and periodically reintroduced from offshore, by the powerful Roman Catholic Church. This body maintained a marginal existence in the English dominions but enjoyed vast power in counter-Reformation Europe. So royal diktats could not completely override either institutional or folk memory, even if a powerful monarchy controlled the sites of memory themselves.[70] But the Tudor monarchy's effort at erasure illustrates the power of glyphs and monuments in perpetuating historical memory.

ORAL TRADITION AS GREAT TRADITION

The overwhelming power of literacy in recent centuries has obscured the extent to which oral tradition was institutionalized and regulated in the past. This was usually achieved by the training and sustenance of a mnemonic elite, men who learned and transmitted key learning. The memorization of enormous texts, like the Vedas and their adjuncts, by Brahmans in India is a well-documented but not unique example. The use of oral history as the major source for the modern construction of historical narrative was first developed for Africa. It was pioneered by the University of Wisconsin historian Jan Vansina.[71] In an influential work published in 1959, he sought to lay out "the usual rules of history as they apply to oral traditions."[72] Recourse to textual sources was difficult in Africa and other parts of the world. Political changes resulting from decolonization also contributed once more to a critical acceptance of oral history methods. Vansina's ideas were deployed in a major survey of oral traditions across the world also written by a historian of Africa, David Henige. Henige's book includes a review of scholarly use of oral tradition in the West over the past millennium. It had begun with unquestioning acceptance of the *Iliad*, the Norse sagas, and a range of minstrels' tales. A more skeptical attitude came in the mid-eighteenth century, with the critical scrutiny, and ultimately rejection, of the supposed traditions of the Celtic bard Ossian as transmitted by James Macpherson and Thomas Chatterton.[73] (Those findings then contributed to nineteenth-century historians' rejection of apocryphal stories and led to a general search for textual primary sources on stone, bone, papyrus, or parchment.)

Henige also distinguishes between "testimony" about the past, defined as individual or familial beliefs of happenings not widely known, and "oral tradition," defined as something "widely practiced or understood in a society . . . handed down for at least a few generations."[74] The latter would be strongly shaped by what I have termed the social framework of memory. Major oral traditions, or the authorized memory of a society, needed to be sanctioned and transmitted in specific ways. Vansina pointed out that even seemingly nonpolitical oral genres of poesy and narrative were molded into a congruence between tradition and social structure. Rwanda and Burundi, for example, were two culturally similar kingdoms in central Africa. But, he pointed out, it was "easy to show that the additional Rwanda genres are linked to political institutions that [did] not exist in the same form in Burundi." The absence of hereditary kingship in the latter also meant that the "Rundi political system did not favor historical memory." On the other hand, a king ruled through a landowning aristocracy in Rwanda; that generated "a need for legitimacy and an interest in history."[75] Where social structure required long genealogies, remembered time sometimes extended thirty generations before the present. Smaller, less stratified social groups were content with simpler frames of time. Vansina recounts some informants (from the 1960s?) placing a migration story in the time of the grandfather of a chief titled Ngobila, but the same story of Ngobila's grandfather was being told eighty years earlier, and even in the seventeenth century. Vansina reads this as a structural feature of social time and social space for that community. "Time and space become congruent with society."[76] It presented no difficulty for a closed social group that had only oral traditions of itself, and never read what outsiders wrote about it.

But as Vansina shrewdly observed, the depth of genealogical and historical memory was structured by the society in which it was generated and transmitted. Hierarchical societies where genealogy was a contributor to status and where competition between lineages was important supported, for example, specialized chanters of genealogical history. These men also competed for recognition among themselves. As a result, when James Fox in the 1960s collected the traditions of the Rotinese people of Indonesia, he found that most names of rulers and several incidents in the kingdom's history between 1680 and 1965 had been accurately preserved by professional "chanters." He verified this against contemporary Dutch records. Comparing his own work with that in other parts of the world, Fox concluded that the shaping of historical memory varied with the type of society that reproduced it. Status societies preserved longer genealogies; segmentary societies more readily truncated them. But in status societies it was the genealogies of higher-status lineages that were preserved, while ordinary folk had "shallow" genealogies. Fox quotes Edmund Leach on the Kachin of northern Burma in the 1950s: "Commoners are only interested in genealogy as a means of establishing correct relations with their immediate neighbours in the same community; the genealogies of commoners are consequently quite short, four or five remembered generations at the most."[77] Inequalities of power and status structure social memory just as they structure society.

Without imperial or sacerdotal centralization and the associated literati as found in Burundi or Mexico or Peru, the rise of dynastic power and warrior clans built upon genealogical traditions characteristic of lineage societies. I have already noted that such "tribal" peoples took shape along the borders of settled lands and periodically entered them as conquest elites. Their genealogical traditions then hybridized the older literate ones, contributing to the development of new ethnic boundaries. Thus written text moves into oral tradition and oral tradition may deposit as text. Franz Rosenthal's erudite study of Islamic historiography described this among the pre-Islamic and early Islamic Arabs. In the Middle East of late antiquity, living genealogies depended on the presence of active social entities that maintained them. The disappearance of a social group meant the loss of its genealogical tradition. Another distinct source of early Arab historiographic tradition lay in chronologies and in narratives of celebrated "battle-days," often dated. Rosenthal observes that, originally, works in which no dates were found were not classed as histories. But the absence of large-scale political organization in the pre-Islamic period of central and northern Arabia had precluded the "experience of a continuity of great political events." There were only traditions of individual tribes and families. This class of verse-studded stories narrating great deeds was, however, never juxtaposed in "some kind of historical sequence."[78] But when there was no one who retained a genealogical memory, the memory had no social function and could be forgotten. Genealogical literature starts "when genealogical lines become dubious and it is felt that their literary fixation would help to clear up doubts and prevent frauds."[79]

I have already noted that the triumphs of literacy were not permanent either. New nonliterate conquest elites might replace older literate societies. The latter's ruined cloisters were transformed into mounds of earth until found by archaeologists in later times. Successor societies in such areas might later reconnect to different literary traditions of the past. For example, the Swat Valley in today's Pakistan was, until at least the eighth century CE, a major center of literate Buddhist monastic life. We know that the literati would have looked back to the historical Buddha in the central Gangetic Plain over a thousand years earlier. But that past was literally buried by the mid-second millennium. When a regional narrative of the past reemerged after

1500, it was that of the new dominant Yusufzai tribe, a branch of the Pakhtun (also called Pashtun or Pathan) peoples. These constituted a relatively new conquest elite at the beginning of the sixteenth century. These Pakhtuns traced their ancestry to the hero Qais, through Yusuf, the eponymous ancestor of the Yusufzai. The entire Pashto-speaking Afghan people (many millions) also claimed descent from Qais. Exact genealogical memory in the Swat Valley, however, was socially institutionalized only with the sixteenth-century conquest of the valley by the Yusufzai. All claims to landownership and consequent political dominance stemmed from that conquest. According to legend, a holy man, Sheikh Malli, ended internecine disputes after the victory by allotting the valley to all the recognized descendants of Yusuf, the tribal ancestor. These were divided into thirteen branches sorted "in terms of their relations to each other through their closer patrilineal ancestors." The rights of each branch were then shared by their major segments. All landowners (in the 1950s) could still be located within this genealogical structure: each one belonged to a named *khel*, or major tribal segment. On the other hand, actual ramifying descent groups were largely absent among nonlandowners. Their origin stories only went back to the names of culture-heroes who had established their particular craft specialty.

The Yusufzai for some centuries controlled the important route through the Khyber Pass and, until displaced by the Sikhs, also the city and plain of Peshawar. Pakhtun rise to political power had, by the seventeenth century, led their participation in the Persian historical tradition of their times. Barth was told of these works, and it was suggested that he consult them for the upper part of the genealogies found therein. These authors had already "made the effort of collecting the facts, and it would be silly of me to waste time doing it all over again." Thus the part-written, part-oral genealogy claimed to be at once "an actual list of fathers and sons" and also to show "the structural interrelations of different groups of living men." This effort resulted in occasional anomalies, and Barth notes that the presence of an established literate tradition prevented their adjustment through the creation of new fictitious genealogies.

This political use of genealogy across the Afghan lands was astutely observed by Mountstuart Elphinstone on his abortive mission to the court of the Shah in Kabul in 1808–9. He was told that the Afghans were all descended from "Afghaun, son of Irmia or Berkia," a son of the biblical King Saul. They had come eastward from Babylon when the Jews were carried off there. Up to this point, Elphinstone stated cautiously, the legend did not differ significantly from the scriptural tradition with which he was familiar. The Afghans also claimed that they had consistently preserved an Abrahamic monotheism down to the revelation of Islam. At that point, they sent an expedition to Arabia headed by "Kyse," who was later named Abdurrashid, in order to aid the Muslims in their struggles against "false religions" in the Arab world. Thus they were voluntary adherents to Islam who had not (as standard Persian histories claimed) converted after conquest by the armies of the later caliphs.

Elphinstone noted the important place of this genealogy in determining (or reflecting) the social and political structure of Afghanistan. He noted that even if one doubted the very existence of "Kyse Abdooresheed," it was to him "that all the Afghaun genealogies refer, and *on those genealogies the whole of the divisions and interior government of the tribes depend*."[80] They thus provided the framework for the political and social life of the tribes and of the kingdom whose political life they effectively constituted. That in turn ensured their reproduction as the approved form of social memory in the region and beyond. Afghan soldiers across South Asia carried this memory with them into lands where they came as a conquest elite.

THE FORGOTTEN PUBLIC LIFE OF HISTORY IN THE MEDIEVAL WEST

Western Europe is a world region that has often presented itself as the crucible of modern historical practice, as possessor of a continuous tradition from Thucydides and Suetonius to Hume and Mommsen. Select Greek and Latin historians then provided a benchmark against which other historical traditions were measured.[81] François Hartog has observed that Europeans had long hailed Herodotus as the "Father of History." Even those who perceived him as overly credulous merely saw his younger contemporary, Thucydides (who died c. 400 BCE), as the true founder. David Hume, the eighteenth-century British philosopher and author of *The History of England*, declared that "the first page of Thucydides [was] the beginning of real history."[82]

Cultivated men might revel in Thucydides and cultivate Voltairian skepticism, but the socially vital historical investigations were into noble status. Emerging medieval monarchies could often only pay their warriors with honor and status that brought exemption from taxes. Emblems on shields and armor displayed and explained the status of the bearer and, for example, indicated the form of address prescribed for that rank. The display of emblems on houses and funerary monuments provided a lasting record of family status.

So, even while the struggling man of letters David Hume wrote a *History of Great Britain* (published 1754–62),[83] the distilled historical research of a large team over several generations was being expensively printed in Paris under royal patronage: *Armorial général ou registres de la noblesse de France* (in English, *The Register of the Nobility of France*). Generations of inquiries by heralds and pursuivants (investigators) were compiled into the ten volumes printed between 1734 and 1768. The D'Hoziers, who compiled the great *Armorial*, represented the culmination of generations of heralds and genealogists, bearers of socially vital histories in Europe for centuries, who kept records and sent out pursuivants across their jurisdictions to record and verify. As we saw, heralds recognized the symbolic language of coats of arms that formed a parallel set of glyphs in an increasingly literate society. In Europe by the early Middle Ages, armorial glyphs like these had evolved into displays of family affiliation and honor.[84] They gave visible honor and status in a heavily illiterate society. Beginning as genealogists and poets, heralds gradually developed into organized fraternities, ultimately recognized or replaced by centralizing monarchies in England, France, and Spain.[85] Their decisions had major fiscal effects in the latter two.

The first entry in the D'Hoziers' *Armorial* was that of the royal family, a genealogy already carefully curated for eight centuries. Bernard Guenée has analyzed how royal genealogy emerged from the originally neutral king-lists maintained by church authorities in France. Early monastic authors, he observed, were satisfied with listing the succession of one ruler, or indeed pope, by another.

But this would not suffice for the Capetian dynasty. Hugh Capet maneuvered himself into the kingship in 987 CE and swiftly established his line as hereditary kings. For the Capetians to have a clear dynastic claim, the idea of kingship as a lifetime appointment with each succession ratified by the great nobles had to be categorically rejected. Hence Capet claimed a different legitimacy, one founded on genealogical succession from parent to child (or later, father to son). By 1146, clerics realized that everything depended on the favor of the Capets. So the "most remote relatives of the Capets were searched out and proclaimed" as being such, thus obliquely exalting the Capetian line and doubtless pleasing its collateral kindred. Meanwhile, the dynasty itself went through a phase of emphasizing its descent from Charlemagne, even if that required tracing descent through the female line. Clerical patronage-seekers began to establish such a descent but so did great houses such as Hainaut and Champagne. Thus by 1270, great erudition and considerable propaganda had "not only convinced the people that France had an unbroken line of kings after Clovis but that all of them belonged to the same lineage." Inconvenient old prophecies, such as one attributed to St. Valery, that the Capetian line would rule for seven generations and no more, had to be pruned when seven generations in fact elapsed in the early fifteenth century. Royal propagandists were especially vigilant with the emerging vernacular text tradition.[86]

The Capetian dynasty came to the throne of France at the end of the tenth century. Clerical bureaucracy and royal power had increased hand in hand, but both suffered a setback in the fourteenth century. Military disasters and political disruptions led to a breakdown in recording and taxation. The consequent transfer of fiefs into the hands of wealthy commoners (*roturiers*) during the troubled late medieval centuries resulted in the revived and fiscally needy monarchy seeking to tax such holdings, or simply exact payoffs by the threat of such general inquiries. Nobles holding such lands were, in principle, exempt. As a consequence, there was considerable effort to establish the historic status of nobles and the exemptions of lands they held. In ancien régime France, noble status thus brought tax privileges and career advantages, especially in the army.[87] But authentic tradition now needed to show historical documentation.

The Gigots had carefully preserved their papers and claimed connection to an ancient family (variously spelled), first mentioned at the end of the eleventh century. The *Armorial* could, however, state definitely that at the end of the fourteenth century a cadet branch was established by the noble Mathieu de Gigord in the Vivarais area: "With him commenced the authenticated lineage." Mathieu made a will on November 9, 1426, and left his possessions to three infant sons. He is listed therefore as ancestor in the first degree.[88] One could fill up several pages with the history of the family and its lands. The Gigot family can thus be traced back to at least the thirteenth century.

Nonetheless, in 1657, Raymond de Gigot had to suffer the indignity of having to start a lawsuit against the tax-farmer who demanded the tax called *franc fief* from one of their domains. Seigneur Raymond then produced deeds and documents that proved that he was "indeed noble, issue of a Noble race," one descended from centuries of distinguished ancestors who had never damaged their nobility (presumably by acts of treason or resort to low employments). The verdict confirming the Gigots' status came at the end of 1658, and the tax assessor was warned not to molest the said noble's lands in any way under penalty of a heavy fine.

Nor is this the only example of the careful historical research carried out by the office of the Judge of Arms: it is manifest through the many volumes of the D'Hoziers' compilation. Narratives were not simply based on documents provided by the family; there was also a scrutiny of the lists of witnesses to monastic charters, again cross-checked with lists of priors and prominent clergy, and with records of grants conferred by the kings of France. As in England, genealogies were to be verified against earlier contemporary materials, such as church records, inscriptions, and monuments. The development of historical records and methods may easily be identified here.

As the French monarchs strove for absolute control of their nobles, recognition of noble status was gradually centralized in the hands of a royal officer, the *héraut*, or herald. The *Armorial*'s dedicatory preface to King Louis XV recollected that "the illustrious body [the nobility of the realm], anxious to transmit to posterity the full record of the dignities, honors and rewards that they held the justice and grace of the monarch, had petitioned his great-grandfather, Louis XIII, following ancient usage, to establish exact public registers that would contain the names and surnames of the nobles, their coats of arms, and their memorable deeds." Louis XIII, anxious to check the course of usurpation of titles that had begun in the disordered times of Henry III, created the office of Councillor Judge of (coats of) Arms, whose role was the regulation of the display of armorial symbols. There was to be no appeal of his decisions save to the Tribunal of the Marshals of France. The Crown affirmed this effort in several judgments in the reign of Louis XIV.[89]

The text then elaborates on how Kings of Arms had long held jurisdiction over symbols of nobility. This had been exercised in the provinces by heralds and pursuivants, who moved around their charges, regularly updating their registers with the titles and arms of noble families. In order to maintain good order, Charles VIII had in 1487 created the office of Marshal of Arms for the whole kingdom of France. But disorders and usurpations nonetheless increased during civil wars beginning under Henry III. Henry IV, who succeeded him, had first to reconquer the realm before he could organize it. He paid little attention to disputes of status. In 1614 the nobility, then gathered for the meeting of the Estates-General of France, petitioned the monarch to regulate the use of arms by the creation of a complete register. No one was to display arms not recorded in the register. This, they petitioned, would check the very common usurpations of the insignia of honor by *roturiers*, or commoners.[90]

Across the Channel in England, gentry status had relatively few privileges and was less politically fraught. Nor was its adjudication a major source of revenue to the Crown as it was in France.[91] The Crown left it largely to the College of Arms, just as benefit of clergy (that is, leniency for criminal offenses) was often awarded at the whim of the magistracy. Popular traditions often took their own, different routes to establish a general history. Beneath the great dynasties and fabulous stories of Trojan descent, however, truly fierce contests occurred over the truth of family history and consequent honorable status. In sixteenth-century England, the "kings" of the College of Arms had allotted territorial jurisdictions and went out periodically to verify if those of "low degree" were unauthorizedly displaying armorial bearings on their houses, clothes, or sepulchres. Sir William Dugdale, Garter King of Arms at the end of the seventeenth century, instructed another king as to how a "visitation," or inspection of claimed status, was to be conducted. He also laid out the inevitable fees due to all the officers concerned. The instruction enjoined historical inquiry. If someone claimed the right to display arms by prescription or immemorial descent, he needed to "make out his pedigree, by any Authentique evidence for more descents than the memory of any man Living can reach: it will be proper to register the same with a Voucher of those Authorities, vizt auntient writings, notes from publique records, Registers of Churches, Monumentall Inscriptions, or what else may be relyed upon, as of Creditt."[92] The methods of the historian are clearly present in these instructions. The herald was a historian, even if the history was one of emblems and monuments, casques and coronets.

These were issues over which men of even modest rank and means contended with great bitterness and no little expenditure. Verbal derogation could lead to bloodshed. So Edward Spencer of Huntingdon County was charged with uttering "scandalous words provocative of a duel" when he told the plaintiff that he was "noe gentleman."[93] Family history and local tradition played a major part in these disputes. Thus in one case where the plaintiff's right to display certain arms was challenged, a witness was asked to respond to the following assertion: "Have not the arms described in the libel been set up in a house in Morton upon Lug, co. Hereford, ever since it was built?" Clearly the case turned on invoking a living local history marked by notable houses and their emblems. Beyond running the risk of duels, those who impugned another's honor might also face significant monetary costs. "The Defendant [Willett] had said that Henry Sandys was base gentleman, and that he (the Defendant) was a gentleman and a soldier and as good a gentleman as Richard Sandys; was descended of the house of Warwick by the mother's side, and by the father's side from the house of Mortimer, Earl of March; and that his arms were three wolves' heads, three moor-hens, and a lion rampant." The verdict delivered on December 5, 1639, awarded 100 marks' damages (£66.66) and £20 for costs, so the litigation cost Willett nearly £100 in an era when a soldier might be paid £1 a month.[94]

The third unified monarchy in Western Europe, that of Spain, emerged last and from a more recent period of frontier warfare and political expansion than did France or England. For several centuries, all that impecunious kings could assuredly offer local warriors was the opportunity to plunder and recognition as "caballeros" and "hidalgos." The military and political condition of medieval Spain during the anti-Moorish war of reconquest (c. 1000–1200) meant that fighting men had to be recognized as noble warriors without too much scrutiny. They were initially often recruited from wealthier peasants who procured a horse and weapons and formed part of the small garrisons of the frontier castles of, for example, Catalonia. But those dubbed *cavallers* soon assimilated to their lords and claimed privileged exemption from taxes and from the seizure of their properties for debt.[95]

Several Spanish kingdoms grew out of the slow reconquest of the lands ruled by the heirs of Arab conquerors. The reconquest began in the mid-eleventh, paused around 1250 and ended in the late fifteenth century. This formative period of monarchies in Aragon, Navarre, and Castile (among others) gradually deposited an established stratum of nobles of various social origins across the country. By the late thirteenth century, this status became hereditary, though the king could still ennoble his subjects. Noble status was signaled (among other things), by a "known territorial estate" (*solar conocido*) and, importantly, by having enjoyed for three generations the privileges of nobility (*hidalguía*), especially exemption from most direct taxes. In the northern plains, the ownership of a fortified homestead or castle bearing a coat of arms was a well-recognized marker of nobility. A pedigree was secondary and local recognition was important. The late thirteenth-century legal compilation, *Las Siete Partidas*, recommended three generations of noble descent for recognition as an *hijosdalgo* (hidalgo). It argued that "the ancients" had considered that to be the limit of dependable memory.[96]

Gradually, however, even this relatively open military class sought to close its ranks and define its membership. Ambitious commoners and impoverished warriors became difficult to distinguish from each other. The tax exemptions available to the hidalgos now began to be keenly watched, since the burden shed by a recognized noble fell on the rest of the community.

Judges with special jurisdiction over the lesser nobility (*alcaldes de los hijosdalgo*) existed starting in the fourteenth century. They began to inquire into the claims of poorer men, claims that, as García Hernán points out, essentially depended on local reputation, as documents were often lacking. The *Pragmática de Córdoba*, for example, specified that anyone who claimed exemption by status needed to prove that the exemption had been enjoyed by his father and grandfather. He also had to show that he himself possessed the reputation of being a hidalgo in the place where he had lived for at least twenty years and that the council of the place where he lived had exempted him solely by reason of his status. It was therefore based on a largely oral history that existed in the township or community.[97] Nor should this be reduced to a matter purely of tax exemptions: family honor and status and personal reputation were keenly guarded and ferociously contested. (The right to fight duels of honor, for example, was a cherished privilege of all nobles.)

In 1391, a fanatical prelate incited an especially ferocious pogrom against the Jewish population of Seville. All were robbed and thousands brutally massacred. Similar episodes occurred elsewhere. About a hundred thousand Jews converted to Christianity in order to save their lives. The already educated and affluent among these "New Christians" soon became prominent in the emerging royal administrations in the area. This included tax assessment and collection.

The stigma attached to Jewish identity now transferred to the converts prominent in taxation and finance: it became racialized. Less than sixty years after the great pogrom, a protest by the city of Toledo against the king's demand for a war tax boiled over into an uprising that was diverted into an assault on the persons and property of the New Christians. In 1449, the governor of the city passed the first legislation stigmatizing New Christians. Pamphleteers defending the equality of New Christians then proceeded to invoke historically authenticated genealogical information to point out that many of the extant great families of the nobility had, in fact, married into lineages of known "converso" ancestry. Attacking New Christians was thus to impugn the pure descent of great nobles.

But it was of no avail: popular riots against converted Jews broke out repeatedly across Spain. The religious orders began efforts to expel and exclude men of "suspicious" descent from their fraternities. Since the church was a useful way of warehousing the redundant sons and daughters of influential families in comfortable surroundings, one can see how established cliquish interests would profit from excluding educated conversos. Cathedral chapters began to add the criterion of purity of blood, of not having any *known* converted ancestors. The most rigorous ones demanded of witnesses supporting a candidate that they swear that he did not descend from any lineage of Jews or Muslims (*moros*), and that they had never heard even a rumor to the contrary.[98] José Antonio Guillén Berrendero indicates the growing influence of a literate bureaucracy in these processes: a treatise of 1567 specified that the petitioner was supposed to promptly submit a *written* genealogy identifying his mother, father, and maternal and paternal grandparents. Guillén adds that the energization of parish records and registers after the Roman Catholic Church's Council of Trent (which concluded in 1563) provided fresh resources for this process. It consequently became more rigorous in later centuries, especially as the enlightened monarchy in Spain sought to shrink the number of impoverished gentlemen, now seen as an obstacle to economic growth.[99]

As in France, important powers and privileges depended upon the proof of noble status, and a microhistorical inquiry was an essential part of it. The sharp restriction on the creation of new nobles imposed after Charles V came to the Spanish throne in 1517 enhanced the value of the established noble status. Nobles were most numerous in Castile, but overall the status was enjoyed by only about 8 percent of the population in peninsular Spain.[100] The "symbolic capital of genealogies" gained value, and their scrutiny became a source of contention—and profit.[101] The diversity of the Spanish empire in the Americas added another level of complexity. In Spain's overseas possessions in the Americas, miscegenation led to official efforts to rank society into *castas* shaped by ancestry more complex than simply "purity of blood." Endangered by English and French military operations in the 1620s, the local government relaxed restrictions for militarily adept lower castes. In the early eighteenth century, an elite of mixed descent could document generations of military service to the crown. They thus had the "credentials to secure some of the privileges of 'whiteness.'" Individuals now sought royal certificates declaring them to be "white," a status that provided important access to office and honor.[102]

But if familial history and genealogy were closely scrutinized, larger claims of what we would now think of a historical descent were more capriciously accepted (or rejected). Julia Crick studied medieval "histories" so as to open a way to an understanding of the "historical culture" of their readers. She has written that the popularity of narrative histories in that period "seems almost inversely proportional to the quantity of reliable information which they impart."[103] Thus the English cloister contained the sober chronicler William of Malmesbury, but also the inventive and vastly more popular Geoffrey of Monmouth (died 1154/55). The latter's *History* and also the associated poem "Prophecies of Merlin" proved hugely popular. The "Prophecies" enlarged the legends of King Arthur and Merlin, and invented that of King Lear. Geoffrey's *Historia* claimed to be a translation of an old British text, though centuries of research have not recovered any such root source. A third work was his verse biography of the same wizard Merlin. An extant ninth-century Latin history of the Britons already contained the idea that the kingdom of Britain was founded by Brutus, a descendant of Aeneas, the son of Priam, who fled from the sack of Troy. This was a popular origin myth: it bypassed Roman conquest by affiliating the British with the ancestors of the Romans themselves. This soon became fashionable. Even known descendants of Scandinavian conquerors in Normandy later began claiming Trojan descent, surrendering the historically valid cachet of being conquerors for status as vanquished refugees from the fallen Troy.[104]

Geoffrey was soon translated from Latin into Anglo-Norman, French, English, Welsh, and Norse. His work also circulated in Latin manuscripts found across Europe. It placed third in popularity after first-century Valerius Maximus (fl. 14–31 CE) and the church father Orosius (died c. 430 CE) if judged by the number of surviving manuscripts. It also saw numerous verse translations into medieval vernacular languages, and elements of its narrative were copied into other histories, both vernacular and Latin, all across Christendom. Geoffrey's work was enthusiastically incorporated into historical memory, emerging even into statecraft and high politics. Within less than a century, it was being cited to justify Edward I's claims to rule Scotland and also in a clause of the Magna Carta.[105] Vernacular historical tales, Guenée argues in another essay, also served as banquet hall entertainment. So singers had to deal with rapidly changing fashions among their publics. Thus the Second Crusade left many lesser nobles interested in stories of the "romans" (the original romances). But themes changed from time to time. The "matter of Britain"—King Arthur, Merlin, and all—became the most popular story from the time of the great poet Christian of Troyes. From the beginning of the thirteenth century, it was supplemented by song that told legends of Alexander, Charlemagne, Pepin, and the Crusades. Diverse narratives thus pleased a changeable public. The resulting deposit of legend and fable constituted the historical culture of the Western European nobility.[106]

Thus, well into the seventeenth century, European historical tradition was content to accept the historicity of the English Brutus, of Merlin, and of King Arthur (none of whom have ever been satisfactorily identified). Alfred

Nutt, a leading scholar of Western folklore, wrote of the historical tradition of early modern Europe:

> Now we know that the Troy Saga, the legend which places a fugitive from Ilium at the outset of some of the chief nations of modern Europe, is destitute of any and every kind of basis, historical, racial, archaeological, or linguistic. . . . Yet for centuries it was regarded as gospel truth; it was embodied in every national chronicle, in every princely genealogy; it was relied upon by statesmen and monarchs; it was accepted by the learned cleric and by the wandering minstrel.[107]

Such heroes who founded entire communities were exemplary ancestors.[108] But in some cases—as in Norman England—their lines had been extinguished by new conquerors. It was to these new potentates that older monastic establishments now had to justify their privileges and possessions and refute the conjecture that they had been usurped in the confused interregnum. Thus older legends had to be rehearsed by the learned as (literally) what anthropologists call "charter myths," assertions of title and claims of status, backed quite often by a "historical" hagiography.[109]

A small band of secular European historians only began to emerge from the ranks of the humanists during the sixteenth century. They nonetheless had to conform to the political and ecclesiastical climate in which they found themselves. Anthony Grafton has described how "Baudouin, Bodin and the rest convinced the erudite patricians who managed universities and learned gymnasia to see history, as they did, as a formal discipline, one comparable to law in utility and status."[110] But the genealogical basis of monarchy and nobility in many parts of Eurasia made a certain kind of historical inquiry both necessary and perilous.[111] If power changed hands, the same inquiry might be construed as subversive of the ruling authority.[112]

Just as early modern science overlapped with astrology and alchemy, so too did heraldic study help shape the matrix of history. The Elizabethan antiquary and historian, William Camden (1551–1623) was, after many impecunious years, appointed Clarenceux King of Arms, or senior member of the College of Arms. Wyman Herendeen wrote that Camden's work, added to his appointment to the College, "brought together groups and areas of activity and intellectual enquiry that had previously been separate, and helped to precipitate changes in historical, antiquarian, and heraldic research and writing."[113] Camden's earnings enabled him to endow the first "readership" (professorship) in history at Oxford, perhaps the first such post in England.

That endowment was a step toward the glacially slow shift of formal control over the official discipline into the hands of members of a newly created and secular learned profession: historians. Degory Wheare (d. 1647) was the first holder of the Readership. He delivered and later printed his inaugural lectures in Latin, the language of the learned across Europe. The third Latin edition appeared in 1636. It was but slowly that such learning filtered into the language of the common people, who continued to struggle over more concrete historical claims to status of the type adjudicated by the relevant Herald. The first English translation I could trace appeared in 1710.[114] Nonetheless, Camden's endowment represented the first bridgehead for the modern discipline in the cloisters of an old and conservative university. The cloistered life of the discipline had begun, at least in England.

Even then, history had to be firmly set in the unchallengeable frame of revealed religion. Wheare published a long conspectus of histories that students should read, including a wide range of "pagan" authors. But it was firmly set in the cosmic frame of the Four Monarchies, established by the church from at least the fifth century CE. Its prophetic myth was then appropriated by the Protestant enemies of the Roman Catholic Church. For them, that church was but a continuation of the Roman Empire and hence constituted the Fourth Monarchy. That the Protestant Reformation portended the coming of the fifth and final monarchy was the burden of one of many learned tracts offered to the new monarch and Parliament upon the ouster of the Stuart monarchy in 1688.[115]

But when appropriating the scholarly legacy of Rome, Christian tradition then had to wrestle with an epistemological break. This came between the cyclical view of history widely shared among ancient civilizations (including the Greco-Roman), as against a Christian one in which history flowed linearly to a time when divine intervention would bring all history to an end. Well before the apocalypse, there was the difficulty of reconciling direct divine intervention in history, as exemplified by the birth of Jesus Christ, with the otherwise secular history of the Roman Empire. This presented the Christianized Western historians with a major dilemma. Ernst Breisach describes how this problem was variously resolved—but never wholly to their own satisfaction—by various members of the church intelligentsia.[116]

In the kingdom of France, where royal control of printing and clerical oversight of scholarship were stronger, François Furet argues that the discipline of history emerged out of relatively safe antiquarian studies of the vestiges of the Greco-Roman past. Such studies slowly undermined the church narrative of universal history and gradually encroached into biblical antiquity. At the end of the seventeenth century, "modern historical research was born of the application of the procedures of critical reasoning to the exploration of Christian antiquity."[117] But I would argue that the genealogists and heralds had already developed the tools that antiquarians could employ. The fear of their inquiries also encouraged those with a pretension to nobility to develop defensible narratives and preserve their supporting records.

THE DISCIPLINES NEXT DOOR AND FOLK TRADITION TODAY

Heralds and genealogists of the old type have little space in modern historical writing. But the historians' cloistered niche is circumscribed by the quarters occupied by many other branches of learning relevant to the reconstruction of the past. These adjoin, and periodically infiltrate or invade, history. At all times, however, they constrain the methods historians may use and assumptions they may make. In Europe, for example, all early scholarship functioned within some church institution, and all scholars therefore started from the received historical frame of Western Christianity. Nor do the historians of today work without an external cosmological frame and a singular universal time.

Neighboring disciplines may do more than delimit the bounds of historical inquiry. They may also ask the questions that historians then seek to answer, or supply the concepts they employ. The sociology of Halbwachs is an obvious example, with the social thought of Max Weber being another. Every historian who invokes "legitimization" to explain a text or policy is drawing from Weber. The wider role of social theorists in stimulating historical inquiry has been recently surveyed by Peter Burke. He points to how Lucien Febvre and Marc Bloch, founders of the famous French journal *Annales*, championed such learning from neighboring disciplines. The duo sought, for example, to apply analytic ideas from psychology and linguistics to the study of history.[118] Occasionally, of course, intermediaries working as culture-brokers led historians on unsuccessful adventures, for example, Eric Erikson into psychohistory, or Robert Fogel and Stanley Engerman into cliometrics: both were (in my view) futile efforts to fit sources on to a procrustean bed shaped by their own transiently fashionable practices of knowledge.

On the other hand, some important neighboring disciplines have been virtually ignored by historians. That includes contemporary psychologists' many careful, experimentally tested studies of the working of memory.

Others are recognized, though not always employed, even by leading historians. Philology, for example: Leopold von Ranke's greatest claim to be deemed father of modern historical scholarship was that he applied "to modern history those documentary and philological methods which had been developed for the study of antiquity."[119] This was assisted by the extant medieval practices developed for the scrutiny of deeds and charters. The centuries-old practice of studying the provenance, age, and handwriting of supposedly original documents still sometimes bursts into popular consciousness. This was the case when "the Hitler diaries," too hastily authenticated by the famous Oxford historian Hugh Trevor-Roper, were revealed to be forgeries.[120]

Accepted "common knowledge" thus provides frames of explanation and unquestioned assumptions that inform the discipline. But these must change as the world of learning changes. The increasing strength of causal, empirical models in the natural sciences from the early nineteenth century slowly created a whole domain of the "supernatural" (and consequently incredible) to which earlier accepted forms of proof are now consigned. We may cite the ordeal as an example. This was a rite in which divine powers were invoked through tests, such as making a barehanded disputant pick up a heated metal object. Such practices were widespread across Eurasia. Divine intervention was supposed to ensure that the rightful claimant would not be harmed and that the false one would be exposed. Such tests would be deemed laughable today. Yet the ordeal was a recognized form of proof in many societies for centuries. Miracles are by definition supernatural. The Roman Catholic Church still requires authenticated miracles in order to recognize a pious individual as a saint—but a historian who seriously invoked the miraculous in historical explanation would be thought mentally unbalanced. Surrounding disciplines have thus removed earlier acceptable forms of explanation. Neither judges nor historians can now accept ordeal or miracle or divine revelation as a form of proof.

Adjoining disciplines have not only curtailed but also expanded the tools available for historical practitioners. It took Western historians centuries to break free from, for example, the biblical idea that the world was only seven thousand years old.[121] This breakthrough was achieved not by historical inquiry but by advances in geology that gradually permeated the reading public and the academic world. In 1863, John Hunt, president of the Anthropological Society, declared that "geology has within a few years become a great science, and the most ignorant or superstitious dare not assail her conclusions."[122] Modern geology in the West emerged following Alfred Lyell's adoption of "uniformitarianism" to explain observable traces of past change in the earth's crust. This doctrine meant that the biblical chronology (that the earth was only seven thousand years old) could not be salvaged by postulating intense cataclysms such as no longer occurred. That granted, the magnitude of visible changes meant that millions of years would have been needed to effect them. That in turn required a tacit—and soon explicit—rejection of the Genesis creation story and destroyed the short chronology of terrestrial existence that the Christian church had long imposed on European historians.[123]

Contemporary to, but unconnected with, the new geology came modern comparative and historical linguistics. One can scarcely ignore the enormous impact of the science of language on the other human sciences. The historical profession was profoundly influenced by the discovery of the Indo-European language family.[124] That discovery depended solely on etymological, grammatical, and phonetic analysis. But it implied a process of historic and prehistoric changes in related speech communities that had dispersed across vast distances. All discussions of prehistoric and historic migration were revolutionized as a consequence.[125] The study of African history has been even more substantially shaped by the discoveries of modern historical linguistics, which allowed the tracing of otherwise unrecorded migrations.[126]

Historians must therefore realize how much they depend on fellow residents in the cloister and consciously draw upon them, rather than allowing an unconscious osmosis along favored boundaries and rejecting others. Psychology, forensic science, and archaeology have done much—and can do more—for historians practicing today. Radiocarbon dating only became possible after twentieth-century physics discovered that allotropes of the same element vary in their rates of spontaneous atomic decay. It took many decades for the resulting laboratory techniques to become available to archaeologists. Consequently, the C-12-to-C-14 ratio began to be used as a dating technique for organic material. That discovery and later applications of nuclear physics have dramatically changed our knowledge of the past. It has, to give one prominent example, conclusively overthrown the long-held tradition that the Shroud of Turin was the original winding-sheet that wrapped the body of Jesus Christ when he was entombed. Likewise, forensic methods developed in the context of contemporary criminal law have been applied to human remains from far earlier periods.[127] Furthermore, these protocols have the immense social authority of science and mathematics behind them. As a result many new protocols of proof have been accepted and earlier widely accepted methods of legal proof, such as the ordeal by fire or water, have been abandoned.[128]

It is well known that Thomas Jefferson, founding father and leading intellectual of the American republic was, also a slave owner. That he had children by at least one of his slaves was long suspected but also vehemently denied.[129] The long dominance of the American historical profession by white Southerners obviously influenced the debate.[130] But meanwhile, advances in the discipline of genetics suddenly revolutionized the study of biological descent and provided a new technique for tracing it. Y-chromosome DNA matches showed that either Thomas Jefferson, or a man in his paternal line, was the biological father of at least one of Sally Hemings's sons. Given that Hemings was, from her youth, an intimate member of Jefferson's personal entourage and that he made her accompany him on his major travels, the evidence is as conclusive as it can be.[131]

The Hemings case is one where DNA reinforced a case already supported by documentary and circumstantial evidence. But modern forensic genetics has gone further and overturned the apparently most robust evidence: that of eyewitness narration and circumstantial record. The Innocence Project in the United States has used genetic testing to refute hundreds of apparently ironclad narratives of past crimes. As of September 12, 2016, this project had voided convictions in 344 cases.[132] Each of these convictions, I must emphasize, had required the prosecution to prove its narrative of how the accused perpetrated a specific crime "beyond all reasonable doubt." The evidence quite often included both eyewitness and material evidence. Each verdict was a miniature history built out of rigorously verified information. Each such narrative had therefore met a standard of proof significantly higher than academic historians are generally required to achieve. But each microhistory was sufficiently undermined for the reluctant custodians of the judicial process to reverse their verdicts.

And so on. . . . It is practically certain that yet newer methods will emerge and further modify the body of recoverable evidence for historical inquiry, even as they eliminate some earlier ones. Thus, the space available to historians has grown in some directions and shrunk in others. In both cases, the source of change lies in the larger social frame within which all practices of knowledge work.

Sometimes scientists too succumb to folk understandings of descent and unwittingly insert what are effectively racial categories into the models that process their data.[133] Scientific research in genetics has also generated a new, lucrative, commercial DNA industry. Sites such as ancestry.com and 23andMe began to market to individuals in search of themselves. These had to slacken scientific standards significantly so as to achieve a spurious exactness, keyed to modern political boundaries and "folk" ideas of race.[134] A team of three scholars who studied these commercial tests wrote that they "tend to employ samples from limited sub-groups and generalize findings to extended populations (like in the case of West Africans for all African population)." They studied the discussion pages of the white nationalist Stormfront and found discussions of "whiteness" and subjective evaluations of genetic tests, such as the following: "When you do 23andme, the results directly from 23andme are bull****, if 23 says you are 100 European that is not enough and you have to look at GEDMATCH *for the real answer*." Another thread contained the following: "Once uploaded, you can run your data through a number of calculators, and find DNA matches. (. . .) I find it is best to use multiple estimations and explore via services like Gedmatch. For me, in the past 500 years, I'm pretty sure I'm 99.7%+ European."[135]

A few centuries ago this writer might have been equally firmly convinced of his noble descent—perhaps from King Arthur, perhaps from Aeneas of Troy, and may have sought eagerly for authority in Virgil or Geoffrey of Monmouth. New, alternative microhistories are thus eroding the remaining authority of the professional historians who painfully ousted heralds from the field a few centuries ago.

2 The Many Pasts of the Indian Subcontinent

INDO-PERSIAN HISTORIOGRAPHY HAS HAD A PROFOUND EFFECT ON historical memory in South Asia. It gained subcontinental influence during the Mughal effort to unify imperial memory and went on to provide the narrative spine for much early British writing,[1] which in turn percolated into school textbooks and print magazines and thus into the emerging public sphere in colonial India. But a consideration of this school requires an excursus into the history of West Asia.

The rise of Islam and accompanying Arab conquests across the Middle East resulted in the establishment of a great empire stretching from Spain to the lower Indus valley by about 750 CE. Beyond sacred history, the new Islamicate imperial formation also synthesized and spread other forms of historical writing. One source lay in oral pre-Islamic Arab practices. Among the Arabs, as in many parts of the world, rival and parallel histories and chronologies existed side by side. The Arab conquests changed that. Muslim Arabs united into a political community that achieved great successes, conquering one great empire and seizing the most productive lands of another. These events obviously provided a great store of glorious historical memory for the new power elite. The Qur'an added a unified chronological frame of reference to the memory of heroic feats. Franz Rosenthal observes that this gave historiography exceptional significance in the culture of the Islamic world. Perusal of historical literature "helped to inspire loyalty to and enthusiasm for the religious and cultural heritage of Islam" among youthful readers.[2] Polemic around claims to authentic orthodoxy led to the accumulation of evidence around the first century of Islam. R. Stephen Humphreys has argued that the emergence of historiography by the early 700s was rooted in the need to explain "the triumph and trauma of Islam's first century."[3]

Following that triumph, Arabic was soon the prestige language of scholarship and so became the exclusive language of historical writing for early Muslims and even many Christians.[4] The latter already had some tradition of universal history—something that a monotheistic theology would need to develop, since the single God would rule everywhere and his design would therefore unroll through a single universal time. All classical Islamic chronography, Chase F. Robinson writes, was animated by the effort to chart and learn from "God's final experiment in organizing mankind along theocratic lines."[5] That was the origin of the strong chronological frame in Islamicate narrative histories. This was the assumption that allowed Albiruni to work out the incompatibility of Persian and pre-Islamic Arab chronologies.[6] Thus the resources for historical writing were gathered in the centers of the new empire of Islam, and efforts at universal history, such al-Tabari's began to appear there. The Arabic word *ta'riẖ* (*tārīkh* in Persianate form) was adopted widely across the Islamic world.

This new Islamic world developed continuous traditions of historical study.[7] These were then implanted in the Iranian world and brought from there to South Asia. The universalism of the new faith encouraged efforts at universal history, that of al-Tabari (838–923), being one of the earliest.[8] The study of successive generations (*ṭabaqāt*), developed originally as an auxiliary to study of the traditions of the Prophet (hadiths), was also adopted into Indo-Persian historical writing.[9] Among the important contemporary sources for the history of the early sultanate in North India is work by Baihaqi and Minhaj al-Siraj Juzjani. The latter exemplifies the application of both the study of successive generations and the application of a universal time. Juzjani traces the generations from Adam to his own times.[10]

In the eastern part of the caliphate, the Arabs had conquered a functioning empire. The Sassanid bureaucracy had to bend to the needs of the Arab conquerors, and so while Pahlavi or Middle Persian continued to be used in eastern Iran for a century after the Arab conquest, it was ultimately replaced by an Arabized "New Persian." The Samanids and the Ghaznavids who ruled eastern Iran depended on scribes and accountants using this "New Persian."[11] The new sultanates provided the institutional frame for the growth of a new Islamic learning among court intelligentsia. One of its earliest examples came in the early eleventh century, when the learned scholar Albiruni (962–1048) was brought back from Khwarazm by the conqueror Mahmud of Ghazni (ruled 998–1030). Albiruni then studied Sanskrit, secured a range of texts, and wrote a careful and often sympathetic account of Indian learning at the time. While providing extensive and detailed accounts of mathematics and astronomy, he was not able to construct a chronologically grounded history from the works available to him.[12]

Albiruni was drawing from the new Arab science of reconstructing authentic prophetic tradition as applied to history. That was something novel to the

Indo-Iranian world of the time. The new method originated in study of the traditions of the doings and sayings of the Prophet and his immediate associates, matters vital to the shaping of standards for the new Islamic community. Disputes soon arose about the authenticity of some of these. The new community had absorbed various scholarly traditions from across the Middle East. In response to rationalist critics who questioned the authenticity of their narratives, the scholars of the hadith developed increasingly rigorous forms of authentication. Two principles began to be deployed to verify traditions. The first was the axiom that the chain of transmission should be traced back unbroken to a contemporary of the Prophet. The second was that each reporter in that chain should be known for piety, trustworthiness, and ability to memorize. That second criterion demanded knowledge of the personal lives and careers of the witnesses through whom this knowledge came. No witness could be attributed prophetic insight: all were fallible and mortal humans. The study of hadith thus stimulated auxiliary scholarship describing the lives and reputations of successive generations of the early Islamic community.[13] Thus the new faith began with a strong commitment to rigorous historical inquiry in (at least) its own sacred history. Furthermore, the rigorous monotheism of Islam and the older biblical sense that divine providence worked through human history both required a common, universal time throughout the created universe. These standards began to influence other historical inquiry too.

Meanwhile, the prestige that the older Iranian dynasty had possessed among pre-Islamic Arabs also began to revive. The historian C. E. Bosworth commented on how this prestige was claimed as early as 744 CE, by the Umayyad caliph Yazid. He was leader of the Muslim community worldwide and patrilineally a pure Qureshi Arab, but born of a slave mother. He nonetheless felt the need to claim: "I am the descendant of the Persian Emperor, my forefather was Marwan, and both the Emperor of Byzantium and the Khaqan of the Turks were my ancestors."[14]

Thomas Trautmann observes that the new Turkic power elite centered in Lahore and Delhi from the late twelfth century solidified their rule by introducing an immigrant Persian clerical elite into South Asia. Thus the new centers of power—at Lahore, Delhi, and many regional capitals, east to Lakhnauti and south to Gulbarga—came to provide patronage for Persianate literati.[15] A section of these composed historical works in the "New Persian" manner. Much of our knowledge of the political and military history of the period derives from these works, supplemented by coins and inscriptions.[16] The new Persianate dynasties of eastern Iran and then North India, Julie

Meisami argues, were even more in need of glorious royal ancestry. Most were known to be of recent origin, usually from Turkic slave-soldiers. They sought to legitimize themselves by claiming genealogical connection to the pre-Islamic kings of Iran. She adds: "what extent these claims were actually believed is difficult to ascertain, but the propagation of Iranian historical traditions must have played an important role in making them both vivid and respectable."[17] Thus New Persian histories began to emerge in the eastern Iranian lands under the patronage of ever-newer rulers, like the Samanids and Ghaznavids, as well as that of the founders of the Sultanate of Delhi who were, by origin, elite slaves of the sultans of Ghur.[18] But given the recent birth of these lineages, court historians had to contort themselves to provide suitably ancient genealogies for these parvenu monarchs. Even the rigorously scholarly Albiruni, who wrote scathingly about the many patently false genealogies current in his time, still judged it prudent to insert a disclaimer. The genealogies of his patrons and of the Prophet Muhammad were indubitably true.[19]

Writing under Ghurid and Delhi patronage, Fakhr-i Mudabbir (1157–1236) would still only go so far as to trace the Ghurids back to the mythic Iranian anti-hero Zahak, who had ruled for a thousand years. The more pliable Juzjani, writing under the Delhi sultans in 1260, was prepared to have a Ghurid ancestor present at the court of Caliph Ali, who conferred a patent of investiture and a banner on him. These were both supposedly preserved by his descendants.[20] He (and his successors) sought to move the prophetic narrative forward to "substantiate the authority of contemporary Muslim rulers."[21] Such historical work thus formed a new and distinct tradition of its own. Rosenthal asserts that while history was not much prized among classically learned men in the Islamic Middle East, it came to occupy the foremost place in the education of princes, especially among Turkish- and Persian-speaking Islamic peoples.[22] It was these Islamicate Persian traditions, more open to the adoption of legend and hearsay, rather than the austere and rigorous tradition of Arabic scriptural inquiry, that were transmitted to India. But the theology within which they worked meant they retained the tight chronological frame of early Islamic *tārīkh*, even as they dropped the "chain of informants" requirement mandated for the study of the traditions of the Prophet and his companions.

The use of a universal chronology caused early British historians to judge Indo-Persian histories as being authentically historic, because their "frequent citation of names and dates resembled European notions of proper history-writing."[23] British and Persianate historians of the early period were both rooted in the biblical narrative from Adam to Jesus and beyond.[24] They recognized elements of biblical story in Indo-Persian texts, and that reinforced their own sense of the latter's validity. The scholarly missionary John Marshman wrote in 1836 that, barring "the exception of the history of the Jews, in the Sacred Records, the authentic annals of no ancient nation extend more than two thousand eight hundred years beyond the present date." As a devout Baptist, however, he accepted the Noachian flood myth and sought confirmation of it in Indian and other texts while denying their chronology.[25]

Of all the major Persian histories, Fereshte's *Gulshan* was probably the earliest widely available to colonial historians. It was loosely translated and published by Alexander Dow in 1768, and a second enlarged edition appeared in 1772. Dow's text was later superseded by a three-volume translation by John Briggs in 1829 under the title *Rise of the Mahomedan Power*.[26] Briggs's translation was amply used by Marshman and many successors. Briggs also published a lithographed Persian text in 1831, and Avril Powell believes that this edition was widely used by many subsequent Indian textbook writers.[27]

The Perso-Indian historian Astarabadi (usually known as Fereshte or Firishta), had, like many of his peers, also framed his narrative of South Asian history as having an obscure pre-Islamic period that ended with the conquests of Mahmud of Ghazni. His introduction is titled "On the beliefs of the people of Hind and the rise of Islam in these lands." It cited the translation of the Mahabharata by Abul Fazl in the time of Emperor Akbar. Fereshte commenced by reporting that according to the people of Hind, there had been four epochs. (This was of course, the four-yuga cycle of Indic cosmology.) He then moved through an account of Indian beliefs, of prominent kings, and then of the division of the earth among the sons of Nuh (biblical Noah) after the great flood. After dealing briefly with the early period, he provided a much more closely dated and largely dynastic history beginning with the "rise of Islam in these lands."[28] This chronological frame was soon adopted by early British historians. It later provided the basis for a division of South Asian history into "Hindu," "Muslim," and "British." Transposed as ancient, medieval, and modern, the three-epoch sequence provided a frame of reference used well into the twentieth century in schools and colleges across the subcontinent.

Arab interest in chronology and historiography thus brought in a new historical vision across the world of eastern Iran and its penumbra as far as Lahore in the Panjab. It was this new synthesis that spread with the establishment of Ghorid rule, first in Delhi (c. 1200) and then eastward as far as central Bengal before 1220. A new class of Persianized bureaucrats and soldiers established conquest states across the Gangetic Plain, dominating an often rebellious countryside through periodic military expeditions. As we have seen in the previous chapter, there was no tradition of writing tightly dated chronicles in India at the time.[29] But until Mughal times, the Persian historical tradition was nurtured by immigrant literati, often first- or second-generation immigrants from Iran. These men wrote largely for royal courts and for their own Persianate peers: in other words, for a few elite readers. Thus the new courtly scholars wrote for only a small if powerful population, the readers and hearers of Persian. Other narratives of a historical past existed at a popular level outside the larger cities and even in the women's quarters and servants' hovels within and around the great mansions.

OTHER HISTORICAL MEMORIES UNDER THE SULTANS OF DELHI

The struggles for power that marked the rise of the sultanate likely had a disruptive effect on other intellectual elites. Life in the towns, temples, and monasteries where the older literati lived could not have remained unaffected by the Turkish conquests. Great Buddhist monastic libraries were destroyed during the thirteenth-century conquests of the Gangetic Plain.[30] The extinction of any major royal house also meant the loss of, for example, genealogical information. So Nayachandra Suri in the fourteenth century lacked the Chahamana genealogical information available to Jayanaka two centuries earlier.[31] Regionally dominant clan lordships had a deep and enduring presence in greater Rajasthan (termed Rajputana in British-era records). This area was never as thoroughly subjugated by the sultans of Delhi as the more fertile lands of the Gangetic Plain. The major kingdoms of the area were, however, repeatedly shattered by attacks after 1200, but the fragments also repeatedly knit together into structurally similar clan territories. Still, as V. S. Pathak has demonstrated, key genealogical links might be lost along with records. At the same time, the irruption of Timur in 1398 definitely smashed the Delhi Sultanate into several regional kingdoms.

We have little evidence about the patterns of social life beneath the level of major towns, garrisons, and religious centers from the thirteenth to the fifteenth century. In fully conquered areas, the pattern might be that observed by the Arab visitor who came to the court of Muhammad bin Tughlaq. Ibn Battuta in the 1330s reported that even in the vicinity of the capital, direct state authority did not reach below the group of a hundred villages. Each of these had a fixed tax assessment. Ibn Battuta himself was given the revenue of two and half villages, which were assessed at 5,000 dinars.[32] Other historians describe the imposition of crop-sharing in kind upon villages east of Delhi during the reign of Alauddin Khalji (ruled 1296–1316), but it does not seem to have been an enduring practice. It would, in any case, only have been useful or necessary near large garrison towns. Elsewhere, it seems likely that a broadly tributary structure, supplemented and reinforced by tribute-collecting expeditions, funneled the rural surplus up to the royal coffers. Significant parts would be consumed or intercepted by intermediaries of various kinds.[33]

Meanwhile, around the courts and mercantile centers, Jain monastic organizations and their dedicated communities of monks also maintained both a religious and literary tradition within the lands of the sultanate and at the courts of other South Asian rulers.[34] We know that Jain bankers and jewelers remained important functionaries in all kingdoms. The mintmaster and keeper of the royal jewels under Alauddin Khalji was the Jain Thakkura Pheru. This, given the vast amount of bullion from many sources that came into Sultan Alauddin's treasury, was an important function. The mintmaster wrote a text on assaying, bullion types, and coinage titled *Dravyaparīkṣā*. His and other Jains' political influence was reputed to have secured various concessions for Jain pilgrims and sites from both Khalji and Tughlaq sultans.[35] Here we can see how institutionalized memory and specialized literati who sustained it maintained an unbroken continuity by virtue of a business elite's place in the structures of medieval states.

Away from the major cities and across subordinate parganas, or village clusters, the social and military structure retained clan hierarchy and political obligation as its binding characteristics. Genealogy was central to this. The Rajputs, whether Hindu or Muslim, of North and Northwest India patronized bardic genealogists organized by caste and lineage.[36] These men were the bearers of socially authenticated memory and were supported as such. Bards in turn built upon their role as oral bearers of historical memory to memorialize their own claims to land or income. These grants could be very substantial—in 1614, for example, the kingdom of Bikaner contained 2,742 villages. Of these, 175 were held tax-free: sixty-four were held by royal priests, but many more (111) had been given to bards (*charan*).[37] In the kingdom of Marwar, around 1880, bards still possessed over 350 tax-free villages, whose total assessment would have been over 400,000 rupees.[38]

This was, however, only one shard of historical memory. A humbler one included the bards, who continued to practice the arts of memory in village society. As genealogists they would always find a place as long as family lineages were important in matters of status and marriage. Emulation led middle peasant castes to also support such men. Even in the 1880s, landholding peasants in North India too patronized panegyrists and genealogists drawn from the performing castes of Ḍom-mīrāsī. Conversion to Islam did not significantly reduce the power of these men, though many began using only the name *mīrāsī* (Arabic; literally, "hereditary"). Denzil Ibbetson's ethnographic account of the Panjab in 1880 stated that the "Mírási is to the inferior agricultural castes what the Bhát is to Rájpúts."[39] The experienced colonial official John Nesfield analyzed occupations in the census of 1881 in today's Uttar Pradesh. He commented that most great "Chattri" (meaning Rajput, or Thakur) families still supported a genealogist, but the practice "is becoming less common every year, and the Bhat has been falling lower and lower with the declining power of the Chattris, for whose sake they came into existence."[40]

Further south, in today's Vidarbha region of Maharashtra, genealogies were maintained by the hereditary heads of county gentry. When Harry Rivett-Carnac sought to introduce new strains of cotton in Central India in 1867, he persuaded several hereditary officials from Nagpur to accompany him to Berar (Varhad). One of them was a hereditary *deshmukh* who brought "an elaborate genealogical tree (in which all deshmookhs glory)" with him and traced a link between his family and that of his hosts.[41] In Central India, Radhakrishna, deputed to collect folk lore for the gazetteer being prepared by C. E. Luard, the colonial supervisor of the region, recorded (among other performances) songs of past feats of mighty Bhil warriors. These were sung by hereditary bards who came annually to the postharvest bounty of their Bhil patrons.[42] In each case, however, the reach of these little histories would be limited by the social power of the community to which they catered. Recitations in a wealthy peasant's courtyard or in the village square would not need to agree with what was being sung in the next village, let alone with the Persian history written at a faraway court.

The veneration of burial shrines and sacred sites has deep roots in Asia, especially in the Buddhist tradition. Narratives of past wonders performed at the site were part of the memories associated with such shrines. Alongside the Persian histories, therefore, another memory, that of largely—but not exclusively—Muslim holy men and their shrines also began to be implanted across the religious landscape of South Asia. We do know that their publics and patrons included many nobles and officers, as well as multitudes of humbler devotees. Successful sites then attracted more gifts. Priests and attendants spread narratives of their shrines and encouraged more offerings and larger congregations. Returning pilgrims may also have served as recruiters.

In many cases the histories told here ran contrary to the official Persian narrative. Indeed, one might almost say that any holy man (or sometimes, woman) worth his (or her) salt would have defeated some remembered tyrant by using wonderful powers conferred by divine grace. Several of them also raised men to kingship as a reward for devotion. David Lorenzen has remarked that tales of such feats would serve as vicarious wish-fulfillment fantasies for many powerless and oppressed plebeians.[43] Particular shrines and pilgrimages also had their own body of myths and memories associated with them. Texts in various languages extolling the virtues of particular shrines continued to be written into recent times.[44]

Each of these would have an active interest in promoting the story of their own sacred site and increasing traffic to it. The many disputes and lawsuits around shrines of every denomination over control of their lands and their offerings attest to the all too secular motives of many custodians of the sacred.[45] Simply the occupation of a sacred site conferred some numinous power. So, for example, at some point in the 1760s, a fakir tended to a *takiya*, or shrine, near a quarry on the outskirts of Pune. The son of Punjaji, a (Hindu) messenger, began cutting firewood close to the site. The holy man told him to desist: when ignored, he hurled a stone that struck the boy, who died a few days later. The fakir promptly fled. Deprived of other compensation, the boy's father did not cremate the child, but rather buried him in the *takiya*. He seated himself there and began collecting offerings as customary. This might have become a permanent arrangement and, given a miracle or two, have established a lineage of affluent custodians of this well-located shrine. That was not to be: Rewa, a courtesan of the city, petitioned the peshwa against Punjaji. She was then permitted to install a fakir of "her own kind" at the shrine and manage the dues and collections accruing there. Punjaji was sternly warned not to interfere.[46] From other historical examples, one can easily imagine the growth of a narrative tradition at such a site too.

One of the most important grew up at Muin al-Din Chishti's shrine at Ajmer, the former capital of Prithviraj Chahamana. It grew into one of the great shrines of South Asia, and its fame has drawn pilgrims for centuries. P. M. Currie studied the shrine in the 1980s and observed that the recognized historians of the Delhi Sultanate never mentioned Muin al-Din Chishti or his Ajmer mausoleum. But this did not prevent a body of memory growing up around the shrine by at least as early as 1324, under Sultan Ghiyasuddin Tughlaq (ruled 1320–1325). Mughal imperial patronage from the 1560s especially spread the fame of the Ajmer shrine.[47] Interestingly, the Tughlaq period (1320–1398) was also when the tomb of Salar Masud Ghazi—who had supposedly died in battle three centuries earlier—had also become famous enough to be noted by the Arab traveler Ibn Battuta.[48]

This was the shrine of Ghazi Miyan, the completely apocryphal nephew of the historical Sultan Mahmud of Ghazni (ruled 998–1030). Shahid Amin recently combined intensive fieldwork and a careful consideration of a variety of archives to study this widely popular heroic (Ghazi) figure. Amin perceptively shows how recurrent patterns of pastoral life and seasonal celebration were linked into a common narrative that created a livable history of past conflict for the diverse peoples of the sub-Himalayan plains. In the legend, Ghazi Miyan was a heroic warrior for Islam, supposedly killed in battle and buried close to an older religious site. But, according to the narrative, he died on his wedding day and in the act of rescuing cows that were being stolen by a tyrannical Hindu king. Amin links this narrative to communities for whom cattle-herding was central to their livelihood, such as the North Indian Ahir caste. Sontheimer has also recorded legends of deified defenders of the herds current among the Dhangar and Gavli pastoralists of the Sahyadri Mountains.[49]

Seasonal migration from the scorched southern Gangetic Plain toward the moist submontane forest across the Ghagra River would be an old pastoral strategy, one with deep roots across the Indian subcontinent. Seasonal pilgrimage is also an old custom and would often coincide with the dry-season movements of grazing animals. The woodlands of their ultimate destination would also periodically serve as a refuge zone, especially from cavalry attack. The first Mughal emperor, Babur, observed at the beginning of the sixteenth century that dense thickets were the refuge of those evading "tax-collectors."[50] The occupation of an older sacred site by Muslim custodians would not disrupt the ecologically necessary pattern of migration, and the sanctity of the site could be maintained by a new narrative. Refugees and travelers would be introduced to this herdsmen's sacred site, and they would popularize it when they returned to their home regions.

Acceptance of its occupation by new custodians would also be eased if the holy man buried there also acquired the role of a martyred protector of the herds. Once stabler kingdoms were reestablished across the Gangetic Plain, returning peasants might carry back traditions of worship at the shrine in Bahraich. The wardens of the shrine and their emissaries would develop a strong financial interest in maintaining and enlarging the pilgrimage. Thus, even before the emergence of a written tradition, the story of the Bahraich shrine was socially and politically anchored in its community of devotees. By the time the pilgrimage was noticed by literati, these devotees were being drawn heavily from the lower classes, Hindu and Muslim, of town and country. This is a classic example of the process described by Halbwachs for Palestine. Sacred places, he wrote, "commemorate not facts certified by contemporary witnesses but rather beliefs born perhaps not far from these places and strengthened by taking root in this environment."[51]

Thus reconstituted, the social memory of Ghazi Miyan was annually reinforced, when crowds of plebeian folk across North India reunited and gathered for the pilgrimage. Parties then traveled hundreds of miles to meet at the shrine. Its custodians, as well as local and regional patrons, were invested in the maintenance and propagation of a narrative whose essential structure they could not change.[52] The shrine has also, down to the present, attracted the devotion of large numbers of plebeian Hindus and Muslims from far across North India.[53] Different texts could tell the same story through the centuries, but as Amin shows, also vary its emphasis.

Amin, however, misses the opportunity to set the shrine is sociopolitical context. The cultural and economic interests dependent on the popularity of the pilgrimage provided a stable basis for the reproduction of the legend. The legend itself was deeply embedded in social practice and the annual cycle of fairs and feasts. The more orthodox might condemn aspects of the practice, but the validity of the core narrative was not controversial. Amin also accurately notes that there was, until the nineteenth century, no "popular countermemory" to the hagiography of the saint of Bahraich. Rival claimants or bearers of an alternative narrative had been completely replaced, leaving no social frame around which a different memory might entwine and stabilize. External efforts at replacing the folk tradition with a purist Hindu one began only in the late nineteenth and twentieth century. But it had not been notably successful at the time of Amin's research.[54] The slow effort implanting of a new "memory" had begun only with "developments in the fields of language, script, and pedagogy in the second half of the nineteenth century."[55]

Parallel and coexisting memories can, however, be found in cases where shrines were shared, or as J. J. Roy-Burman calls them, "syncretic."[56] Such memories survived at some sacred places, such the famous shrine of Khandoba at Jejuri, east of Pune. This, according to G. H. Khare, is one of the four most popular shrines in Maharashtra. Khandoba is the most common family deity, across all castes. In the twentieth century, the worship of Khandoba, or Mallari, was found in Telangana, Karnataka, and parts of Tamil Nadu. He was worshipped at eleven major shrines and at hundreds of small shrines dedicated to him across the Indian peninsula. He also had Muslim followers who worshipped him under the name Mallu Shah.[57] Thus worshippers from different traditions worshipped at the same shrine.

Even if the Bahraich shrine was not explicitly shared, worshippers from there joined collective worship at other shrines. So in 1667, it was reported that Hindus traveled to a Kalika temple (today's Kalkaji shrine in Delhi) and had their heads ritually tonsured there. The followers of Khwaja Muin al-Din, Shah Madar, and Salar Masud Ghazi joined in a common procession and came there and tonsured their heads too. This, the informant told Emperor Aurangzeb, was *bid'at* (heretical innovation).[58] Yet it had clearly persisted close to the imperial capital for a considerable time. The historian Cynthia Talbot has remarked how a narrative of Prithviraj and the city of Ajmer that contradicted the Mughal and Rajput royal version was sustained into the twentieth century by devotees of Khwaja Muin al-Din.[59] Contradictions with court history do not seem to have bothered devotees, even though several came from court circles. It is thus evident that many forms of collective memory coexisted, with the new Persian political and military histories as simply an additional branch of memory. North Indian vernacular historical traditions continued to be propagated, narrated, and performed alongside the court-centered Persian histories. Before colonial education became the major route to state employment, lineage and district traditions could remain oblivious to the emerging imperial Persian narrative of Indian history. It is to that Persian narrative that we now turn.

THE MUGHAL INTEGRATION IN CULTURE AND NARRATIVE

After an initial conquest of North India by the Mughal emperors Babur and Humayun (who ruled 1526–30 and 1530-40, respectively), the empire had to be effectively reestablished by Akbar (ruled 1556–1605). The great plains stretching east from the Indus to the Ghagra and Son Rivers came to form the heartland of the Mughal empire by 1560; Bengal was added by 1590, and Odisha (Orissa) by 1592. Powerful Rajput kingdoms had revived the more rugged and arid territories south and southeast of the Indo-Gangetic Plain, but most were gradually reduced to tributary status by the end of Akbar's reign.

The new empire had a wider and deeper understanding of rule, one informed by the synoptic outlook that James Scott has called "seeing like a state." This may have been a trend in Asian statecraft already, perhaps informed by the Mongol practice of organizing tribal soldiery in decimal units, with ten thousand warriors, families, and herds forming a *tuman.* At any rate, soon after Babur overthrew the Lodi sultans of Delhi in 1526, he was presented with a money estimate of the lands that those sultans had claimed to rule. He commented that land yielding a thousand *tankas* would maintain a horseman and so the Lodis could have raised 500,000. Elsewhere, he copied down an estimate of the tax revenue of those parts of Hindustan that he had conquered. The numbers—down to fractions of a *tanka*—are too exact to be accurate.[60] They do, however, illustrate a drive to "make a society legible, to arrange the population in ways that simplified classic state functions of taxation, conscription and prevention of rebellion."[61] The mature Mughal Empire intensified these efforts. This was never entirely achieved, but it was an aspect of a great epistemological exercise: to measure, to know, and to control.[62]

But the imperial enterprise was not confined to political economy. Conscious efforts at cross-cultural meetings and the writing of a universal history of their domain were also part of the Mughal imperial enterprise. Several translation projects were undertaken from Sanskrit, with the central one being the Mahabharata. Carl Ernst, a pioneer in the field, observes that the "political context for the Mughal interest in Sanskrit lies in the imperial program devised by Akbar and followed in varying degrees by his successors." A translation of the Mahabharata perceived as, at least in part, a history was an important part of the new empire-building effort. Considerable resources were devoted to it at the direct command of Emperor Akbar himself. Ernst perceptively remarks that while earlier translations had addressed practical sciences like mathematics, alchemy, and divination, it was Akbar who inaugurated the study of the Sanskrit epics as history.[63]

In addition to Sanskrit, Hindi poets enjoyed patronage and support at the imperial court. The Mughals from Akbar onward took an active interest in indigenous traditions and, as many scholars have noted, consciously incorporated them into the greater imperial histories they compiled. The great descriptive compendium of the empire, the *Ain-i Akbari*, which formed part of the *Akbarnāma*, also included histories of pre-Islamic kings of India and accounts of extant dynasties. That effort, as Audrey Truschke has convincingly argued, redefined both Islamicate knowledge and Akbar's sovereignty.[64] Persian, however, remained the court and administrative language, but the cross-cultural approach of the empire encouraged the import of both regional vernacular and Sanskrit traditions as sources. For our study, the most important feature was that the new scholars the Mughals patronized enabled the Persianate world to gain wider access to Indic tradition via Persian translation of the Sanskrit epics.[65]

The reign of Akbar was also the beginning of a century when the greater resources afforded to court historiographers allowed a stronger effort at the collection of historical and contemporary documents. Akbar's ecumenical views and political strategy also enhanced the collection of Rajput and other chronicles and oral traditions.[66] Beyond works composed around the imperial court, many regional rulers were also moved by imperial request or example to collect and record their own histories.[67] Various accounts of the twelve provinces included in the *Ain* clearly drew on such oral and written sources.[68] In less than two decades, the gist of the translations from Sanskrit that Akbar commissioned began to inform the larger Persian-speaking sphere. That work fed into the synthesis of Mughal histories of their new domain. Truschke delicately unravels the tensions in the dynamic relationship between the emperors, Persianate literati, and theologians on the one hand and the Brahman and Jain worthies who both adorned the court on the other. The latter supplied the core texts that traveled into the larger Persianate world. Truschke's idea of tracing these in Fereshte to illustrate how quickly the Persian translations were integrated as historical sources is a subtle and powerful one.[69]

The frame of Abul Fazl's historical writing, however, remained that of the new Persophone tradition of the Genghisid and Timurid houses.[70] Persian histories were widely current and (as we saw) still being read and translated in the colonial period. Knowledge from Persian historical records was, however, patchily distributed.[71] There was, nonetheless, no effort at narrative standardization. At most, there might be emulation of imperial practices, as shown by the spread of Mughal aristocratic dress around the Indian subcontinent. Nor were any mechanisms created by which discordant narratives were marginalized, unless they bore on the doings of the emperors themselves. In that event, it was evidently prudent for men about court to write secret histories, as with Badauni, a court official who was strongly critical of Akbar.

The reemerging Mughal Empire incorporated many of the Rajput elite into the imperial system. Their status was recognized and reinforced, and they began to share in the wealth of the empire as generals and governors far from their home territories. They were also encouraged to supply dynastic traditions for imperial historical compendia, notably the great work of Abul Fazl c. 1595. Greater political stability, in turn, led to the creation of a more consistent narrative tradition. Historian Norman Ziegler, an early student of these records, has commented on the greater stability and accuracy of Marwari and other Rajasthani chronicles from the end of the fifteenth century. That was a period of political consolidation under independent rulers in Rajasthan, all of whom were ultimately drawn into the framework the Mughal Empire by the early seventeenth century. But, as Ziegler points out, the Mughals also had an unprecedented interest in the history of these ruling families. The sixteenth and seventeenth centuries were periods of considerable internal conflict and change in Rajasthan, encompassing both the rise of particular Rajput clan segments and ruling houses to positions of great local authority and centralized rule, and the imposition of Mughal dominance throughout the area. Significantly, the rise of historical literature coincides with the increasing authority and prestige of Rajput ruling houses. This indicates a greater effort on the part of local rulers to collect and preserve their traditions and histories. Many of the genealogies, such as those of the Rathors of Marwar, which trace Rathor ancestry back to the illustrious Gahadavala dynasty of Kanauj and further back to mythical Puranic beginnings, also appear in the early part of this period. Mughal alliance and recognition—as well as the wealth injected into Rajput lands via far-flung service to the Mughal emperors—further solidified authority in the Rajput world.

Talbot has shown how this more solid political frame contributed to the stabilization of Rajput oral traditions into written text. She dates the first manuscripts of the *Prithvirajraso*, a long poem celebrating the legendary King Prithviraj, to this period.[72] The work focused on the great Chahamana house of Delhi and Ajmer and gained the support of Mughal-era kings of the region. It was then canonized by its inclusion in James Tod's *Annals*.

Political stability through the 150 years of high Mughal rule also permitted the production and survival of a large body of textual material in several languages. Stable clan kingdoms linked their own political integration to mechanisms of control and verification that focused on bardic genealogies. Ziegler describes how social pressure might be directly or indirectly applied to the bards, through ridicule or the withholding of largess. "In addition, disputed testimony could be checked with other specialists or argued in pulic debate, allowing for the correction of fact or the supplying of necessary detail." Hence a certain historicity is "not altogether surprising, given the rising prestige and authority of Rajput ruling houses, and indicates an increasing vested interest in both the content and accuracy of the traditions. In this period, the traditions cease to be the private concerns of small families and lineages, but become public concerns as well."[73]

But the might of regional kings and chiefs across the North Indian plain was based on the readiness of the peasant militiamen to die for their cause. The recognition and glorification of this ethos also propagated bardic traditions that celebrated the valor of lower-ranking men, such as the heroes Alha and Udal. Govind Rajnish, a historian of Hindi literature, recently found that the Alha-Udal ballad was still sung by troupes of musicians across the North Indian plain in the 1980s. But the poem was protean. He notes that over many effortful years, he could not find a bard who could recite the fifty-two episodes of the entire epic. Each performed parts and depended on others to complete them.[74] Versions also varied considerably. This, Rajnish rightly says, marks it as a folk-oral epic even if inexpensive print copies were now widely sold.[75] The folk epic tradition was strong enough for a late seventeenth-century version of the *Prithvirajraso* to add a long chapter that used the Alha-Udal story to reinforce that of their main hero.[76] There were many strands of social memory. We shall explore others in the next section.

PARGANAS AND CLAN HISTORIES IN NORTH INDIA

The long-famous shrine of Bahraich had been anchored by folklore and folk practice, its story told by troops of pilgrims converging at the shrine each year. But it was provided with a Persian historical narrative in 1627, during the high Mughal era, perhaps marking its adoption into the transregional Persian canon.[77] That text then became a prime historical source for colonial depictions of the early Islamic conquests. Thus a "folk" tradition gradually won recognition from the high intelligentsia in the centers of imperial power. Shahid Amin perceptively notes the integrative elements in the Persian history. He remarks on its "professed reliance on 'Hindi histories,' its imbrication in Gangetic popular culture, its narration of the life of a historically recalcitrant personage."[78]

But the legend and pilgrimage of Ghazi Miyan was not the only historical tradition anchored by everyday practice in North and Northwest Indian society. Beneath the superstructure of imperial authority, much of the Gangetic Plain was held by small kings and aristocratic clan lords whom the imperial records generically labeled zamindars, meaning landholders. These lords usually held one or more parganas, lived in fortified centers, and were supported by local warrior followings. The lordship of considerable tracts might change hands, with newcomers seizing control of large clusters of villages while still nominally subordinate to the empire or its successor states.[79] Some incoming dominant brotherhoods (*barādarī* or *qaum*) were Muslims, often claiming Afghan identity or, alternatively, the sacred status of *sayyid*, descendant of the Prophet. Descent and lordship served to anchor stable narratives: lordship and its genealogical narrative was directly tied to land title and local dominance. At the end of the eighteenth century, Jonathan Duncan, longtime governor of the Banaras region (ruled 1787–1795), commented on how kinship ties and a strong sense of honor united communities of dominant landholders who could therefore defy the tax-collector's agents.[80]

As late as the 1950s, Thakurs ("lords"—another name for Rajputs) of a village cluster studied by the anthropologist Bernard Cohn narrated two "pasts." One (which Cohn terms mythic) connected them to the divine king Rama, as well as to warrior heroes of the past, such as the historical Prithviraj of twelfth-century Ajmer. The second, which Cohn termed the "historical" past, genealogically connected all the Thakurs to Ganesh Rai, a Raghubansi Rajput, who along with his two sons reportedly conquered the territory named Dobhi, then containing a hundred villages. As with the Swat Yusufzai, that sixteenth-century conquest was the baseline for all claims to land. Cohn wrote:

> The seemingly simple question of "Whose land is this?," is almost invariably met with the reply "Ganesh Rai had two sons," and then the land is traced through fifteen or sixteen generations. All the lands in the village and the land throughout the taluka follow the descent line from Ganesh Rai. Every adult male Thakur can trace his descent from this ancestor. Two Dobhi Thakurs meeting for the first time will sit down and compare their formal relationship and appropriate behavior to each other. Not only is the formal kin history of the Thakurs discussed, but events in the lives of ancestors are talked about.

Tales of past insult followed by violent revenge were also part of the "historical" past of Thakur villagers. While Cohn did not explore this aspect of memory in his account, it is evident that challenges to the genealogical narrative would have been perceived as threats to both family honor and property and met a strong response. Thus local Muslims had a variant upon the Thakurs' history in which four Muslim lords had conquered the village from the aboriginal (and likely mythic) Soeris but had then been displaced by the Thakurs. But they were careful not to claim descent from these Muslim lords—that would have been an imprudent challenge to the ownership rights of the Thakurs. On the other hand, in Cohn's time, lower-caste dependents largely repeated the historical narrative of their employers; any other course would be to challenge their title to land control and dominance. But distinct lower-caste "mythic" narratives had an explanation of their unfairly stigmatized origins.[81]

Traditions originating in such structures of power would be the firm historical memory of such regions as fell in the domain of powerful warrior fraternities. They would not necessarily agree with each other. But aristocratic marriage patterns required mutual recognition of genealogy, and that needed an accepted common narrative. Across the North Indian plain, the caste-cluster termed Rajput or Thakur developed and maintained a pattern by which lower-ranked families sought to marry daughters into higher-ranked ones (hypergamy). These wider networks provided military and political support essential to preserve land control. Military and political alliances were predicated on these marriages and on the mutual recognition of kin and clan ties. As Malavika Kasturi summed it up, official degrees of kinship were found in the genealogies, but practical relationships were determined by "the agency of the actors involved."[82] Equally, villages and parganas were held by identifiable families or clans. Kinship relations between these, as well as their larger affiliation, were publicly known and periodically demonstrated, in both ceremonial and military settings. John Malcolm's political role in stabilizing the early colonial order across Central and Western India required a deep understanding of local patterns of allegiance and alliance. In his view, the bardic castes of Charans and Bhats derived their importance from their place as "conservators of the purity of different Rajput classes." Furthermore, their evidence was always taken as the best proof of such claims to land, as that depended on the descent of the disputants. Malcolm also observed that extended kin ties were often vital for the preservation of petty kingdoms. When the inept ruler of Ratlam was threatened by a Maratha army, his kindred rallied from across the region, even though the majority were subjects of other states.[83]

Charles A. Elliott, however, tried to reconcile too many of these geographically distinct narratives with each other, the result being a chronological "stretching," as different stories could not all refer to the same time. Elliott was aware of Berthold Georg Niebuhr's exposure of the fictions to be found in the Roman annals transmitted by Livy, and argued that this had excessively prejudiced historians against legend as history. He asserted that, unlike Livy, he had available a number of living traditions to compare with each other. It was "after testing and trying them in every way by comparison with each other and with external land marks" that close enquiry would yield a “precipitate of historical fact.”[84] Elliott’s official duties in settling land titles, adjudicating claims to tax-free land and fixing taxes indeed gave him an intimate knowledge of these “facts on the ground.” His study frequently refers to them. But he also demanded grants and title deeds.

Superior powers had sought to manipulate kin alliance and kin enmity to maintain their own authority. The resulting official documents either conferring or legitimizing claims to local office or lordship were also part of the lineage memory for any important family. Narratives originating within such a structure of authority would be focused on claims to genealogical seniority, to marital connection, and to *zamindari* and other rights recognized by kingly authority. But there was agreement on these matters of strong local significance. Elliott was, for example, able to find reliable lists of marriages contracted by the Dikhit clan. He commented that “marriages from the time of Puthemul clearly shews the decadence of the house. The Rajahs have formed connections only with the clans which inhabit the neighbourhood of Diktheana [Dikhit home territory].” This meant that they were not recognized important allies by dominant clans at any distance. Equally, then, genealogists on either side of the divide would not face the need to reconcile family histories. Family tradition might also be sustained with authentic documents, as in his example of the Gehlotes, who claimed to have conquered their cluster of twelve villages from an apocryphal “tribe of Kories” in the time of Alamgir (Aurangzeb) (ruled 1658–1707). Their connection to that emperor was substantiated by several “firmans addressed to Sena Singh and Alum Singh [which were] still preserved by their descendants.”[85]

W. C. Benett’s study of an adjacent district also observed that genealogies (like the legend of Ghazi Miyan), tended to be hazy in their early stages. Thus a regionally celebrated Raja Manikchand could simply not be dated within the genealogical frames offered by different clans. He was described as having been involved in episodes from the time of Mahmud of Ghazni (died 1030) to Timur (died 1406). Similarly, the Sayyids of Manikpur associated their landed estate with one Qutbuddin, who was a lieutenant of the fifteenth-century Sharqi kings of Jaunpur—but then also claimed it as a grant from a Delhi sultan (Qutbuddin Aybeg or Aibak) who had lived two hundred years *before* the Sharqis. Benett observed that “like all the Muhammadan families of Roy Bareilly and Pertabgarh, they have no satisfactory pedigree.”[86] This may have been because too much information might prejudice their narrative and consequently their sacred status and associated landholdings. Like Brahmans, the Sayyids only needed local recognition to enjoy their lands. Then, as now, possession was nine-tenths of the law. The Islamic acceptance of parallel cousin marriage among paternal kin meant that the wider connection cultivated by Rajputs, who were required to marry outside their circle of kin, was unnecessary for the Sayyids. Cousin marriage, in fact, would preserve estates undivided better than out-marriage would.

On the other hand, we can also find an admixture of the fabulous and miraculous, but the social logic and consequences of narration underpinned these traditions. So the stories of glorious and practically independent Rajput kingdoms within a day's ride of Turko-Afghan regional centers were clearly exaggerated. Peter Jackson has firmly established how Alauddin Khalji was able to tighten his control over the whole Gangetic Plain east of Delhi. His Tughlaq successors intensified the building of garrison towns that became the later *qasba* settlements in the region. The Sharqi sultans ruled from Jaunpur from 1394 to 1478, when the area came under the Delhi sultan Bahlul Lodi. Benett sought to accommodate the legendary Raja Tilokchand in this setting by having him conquer the eastern Gangetic Plain after the fall of the Sharqi sultans and establish a kingdom that ruled until the time of Humayun, the second Mughal king (ruled 1530–40). In fact it is clear that there was no such revanche in the fifteenth century in the Jaunpur area, as even casual reference to Babur's accounts of his campaigns in the region immediately shows that overlordship was held by Indo-Afghan barons.[87]

The only powerful Hindu rulers Babur identified were in today's North Bihar and Rajasthan. However, when Benett sought to compile genealogies, he found considerable consistency between the accounts of the three major Rajput clans of the Rai Bareli district. This is not, as Benett thought, evidence of their "truth." I would ascribe this to the sustained dominance of the district by these groups, with the consequent standardization of genealogical information.[88] Genealogists could not fabricate with impunity: each tradition needed a powerful patron to sustain it. John Malcolm, who governed Central India when the kin-based system was still powerful, commented that the importance of hereditary bards depended on their conservation and authentication of genealogies.[89] Therefore, continuity of political authority would result in continuity of historical narrative. Its instability or collapse might leave an incoherent set of traditions, as happened in early colonial Bengal. But by contrast, local Rajput power across the central Gangetic Plain survived strongly into colonial times. The participation of many local lords and gentry in the revolt of 1857 frightened the government of India into creating a special protected class of *taluqdar*s, great landlords, out of the bigger chieftaincies in the former kingdom of Awadh. It was the existing regional power of this class that generated the coherence of local histories found by Benett and Elliott, and indeed a century later by Bernard Cohn.

Tod's effort to write a coherent history from bardic and priestly records is the subject of an outstanding chapter in Cynthia Talbot's recent book, *The Last Hindu Emperor*. She shows how his book was deeply influenced by the traditional history of the kings of Udaipur, transmitted via the Jain cleric Gyanchandra. Cushioned by these grants and by the competition for honor and status among Rajput kingly lineages, bardic families maintained an autonomy that made potentates anxious not to offend them.[90] At the same time, public competition among bards in mastering the common body of genealogical knowledge meant the formation of a relatively homogenous narrative. The resulting history was deeply satisfying to the sense of self of its heroes, the Rajput houses of Western India, even if occasionally critical of particular rulers. Major narrative strains from this integrated structure of memory were then supplied to Tod and other officials. Tod's narrative of the Rajputs generally—and of Prithviraj in particular—were inducted into the emerging public memory of Hindi-speaking North India in the nineteenth century.[91]

With British rule, some narratives of the Gangetic Plain began to be compiled and analyzed alongside the findings of the nascent paleographic tradition and the findings of students of Buddhism, now energized by Samuel Beal's translations of Chinese pilgrim accounts (into English, in 1884). But Buddhist memory had disappeared from the landscape. In 1890, the archaeologist Adolf Führer produced a compendium of inscriptions and sites identified across the Gangetic Plain, in what is modern Uttar Pradesh. The story that Cohn was told about Muslims or Rajputs conquering the district from some aboriginal or lower-caste population was echoed all over the region. Führer recounts many such stories told of old, large habitation mounds in Uttar Pradesh. Several were identifiably Buddhist sites, some indeed mentioned by the seventh-century pilgrim Xuan Zang. This was found, for example, in the Pratapgarh district at the site known as Tusaran-Bihar. In another example of erasure and overlay at the ancient Gangetic site of Dālmāū, Führer reported that the town was

> said to have been founded by the Râthor Dâla Deva, brother of Raja Bâla Deva of Kanauj, a contemporary of king Bahrâm Ghor of Persia. Though there are remains of more ancient buildings, tradition asserts that the Bhârs of the great tribe of Ahirs took possession of Dâlmâu after the death of Raja

> Pratâpa Chandra of Kanauj in A.D. 530. In A.H. 423 [1031–32 CE] Sâlâr Sâhu invaded the place and granted it to Malik Ábdulla. The existence of the tombs of Maliks Ghâlib, Mubarâq, Ali, and Wali, and of other shahids, are proofs that the Musalmâns had possessions here in the time of Sa'id Salâr Masa'ûd. The town prospered during the reign of Sultan Iltitmish of Dehli, by whom the tomb of Makhdûm Badr-ad-dîn Badr Alam in mahallâh Makkhanpûr was erected, which was repaired in A.H. 1023, as stated in a Persian *inscription*. An *inscribed* slab, dated A.H. 716, records the appointment of a mu'azzin to a Jami Masjid by Mubâraq Shâh I, and another slab, dated A.H. 759, mentions the erection of a masjid by Firuz Shâh Taghlaq.[92]

We thus find a total loss of Buddhist memory, the embedding of the same sites in an apocryphal Ghazi martyr narrative, additional elements drawn from the Persian epic the *Shahnama* and histories of past kings inferred from modern place-names such as Dâla Deva from Dālmāū. Finally, still legible Persian inscriptions from the fourteenth century CE onward all were combined by local literati into a conjectural history of Dālmāū. A continuity of urban life did not by itself produce a continuity of historical memory.

EASTERN INDIA: TWO PATTERNS OF HISTORICAL MEMORY

The maintenance of kingly narrative traditions sustained by associated bardic families that we have discussed for the Rajput lands of northern and western India did not occur in the deltas of the Mahanadi (in Odisha) and Ganga (in Bengal). In 1230 CE, around the same time as governors under the Delhi sultans were tightening their grip across Ganges Valley, Anaṅgabhīma of the imperial Gaṅga dynasty of Odisha ritually dedicated his kingdom to the deity Jagannatha of Puri, whose monumental temple had been built in the previous century. The shrine and associated body of priests, custodians, and scribes lasted into the twentieth century. Odisha, on the other hand, only remained independent under the rule of the Gajapati dynasty until its overthrow by Afghans from Bengal in 1568. The interregnum was short, and the Afghans were conquered by the Mughals by 1592. The temple was restored.

As a result, the Odisha region preserved an epigraphic record and a hereditary priesthood centered on the great temple of Jagannatha in Puri. Hermann Kulke spent decades studying the great temple. His research included a close reading of the different texts produced by the shrine. Its first great chronicle was written around 1600, soon after the Mughal defeat of the

Afghans of East India enabled the reestablishment of the worship of Jagannatha in Khurda and Puri. A Mughal ally was installed as raja with power to oversee the temple. Kulke is able to show how "all-India" genealogies such as those in the Sanskrit epics and puranas were joined with epigraphs of earlier dynasties, lists of land donations, and the traditions of priestly families to produce a new chronicle of Jagannatha. This history was needed, he argues, to renew the "broken continuance" of the Jagannatha worship. This grew into the "continuous history of Orissa [that] is in fact the projection of the history of the Jagannatha Temple, and of those events which took place in connection with the god Jagannatha and his 'Great Temple' at Puri."[93] The temple history supplied narratives collected under early colonial rule. These were embodied in Andrew Stirling's 1818 *History of Orissa* and thus carried a written historical tradition into the colonial era. Thus institutional stability created a stable historical memory of the temple. This social memory was propagated across the region and Mughal India by seasonal pilgrimages to the shrine. Thus the enduring worship of Jagannatha provided the frame for a regionally unified historical memory in Odisha.[94]

North of Odisha, in Bengal and eastern Bihar, the Sena kings were the last major regional dynasty whose existence is attested by inscriptions, ruined buildings, and the Sanskrit works they patronized. After their fall in the early thirteenth century, a number of powerful governors ruled under the suzerainty of the sultans of Delhi. Then several dynasties ruled as sultans of Bengal. Bengal was gradually conquered by the Mughal Empire in the 1580s. Major riverine areas were also subjected to slave-raiding by the Portuguese and their Arakanese allies. Bengal therefore did not attain an institutional stability comparable to Odisha or Rajasthan, even in Mughal times. But a king-list of some kind existed in the vernacular tradition as evidenced by Abul Fazl listing sixty-one kings who had ruled over the province prior to 1203–4.[95]

Nor did a Persianate historical tradition develop here. A number of Arabic and Persian inscriptions recording the construction of mosques survive from the Sultanate period (c. 1200–1585), but no Persian chronicle appears to have been written in Bengal. The region figured in Persian histories that mentioned it as a peripheral part of the larger sultanate or empire. The first Persian history devoted to Bengal itself was *Riyažu-s-Salātin* by Ghulam Husain Salim, completed in 1788. It was written at the behest of the East India Company official George Udney by a Persianate clerk from Awadh. It was translated into English by Maulavi Abdus Salam in 1902. It drew heavily on Fereshte and the *Akbarnāma* for its history and statistics.[96]

It is in fact striking that no secular narratives seem to have been composed by Muslims domiciled in Bengal even though a large fraction of the population had converted to Islam by the eighteenth century.[97] Internecine warfare, slave-raiding, and the frequent displacement of local lords may have prevented the development of stable lordships. Members of the ruling elite under Mughal rule were Rajput or Irani or Central Asian (Turani), and they were transferred in and out of the province. Elite Bengali Muslims followed the lead of those in North India and sought to develop a narrative of their expatriate origins in the pure lands of the Middle East. Most of their effective functionaries were local Hindus, often of scribal caste origins. *Kayath* (scribe) often appears where the *Ain* lists the communities or castes (the original would be *aqwām*) of landholders in Bengal. These gentry of the pen grew into a regional aristocracy under the governor Alivardi Khan in the eighteenth century. The only stable Muslim elite seems to have been custodians of religious sites, several of which existed as early as the mid-fourteenth century, when Ibn Battuta visited the famous shrine of Shah Jalal in Sylhet. Even then, the major scholar of medieval Bengal, Abdul Karim, is constrained to say that very few collections of sayings or letters of Sufis who lived in Bengal before 1538 have ever come to light.

Still, folkloric tradition intended to glorify particular shrines grew up around any major one. The shrine of Shah Jalal in Sylhet had one version of the fall of Lakshmana Sena in which that event was predicted by the saint. But the Sanskrit text depicting the holy man Shah Jalal of Sylhet predicting the Bengal king Lakshmana Sena's defeat by the Turkish general Bakhtiyar Khalji was a sixteenth-century forgery. Karim argues that it was forged to strengthen the shrine's claim to certain lands covering 22,000 bighas.[98]

The shrine of Bu Adam in Bikrampur had a more dramatic foundation myth. Bu Adam supposedly came from Arabia with 7,000 warriors to protect a poor Muslim being oppressed by another legendary king, Ballala Sena. These warriors all died in the holy war, and so the land was liberally provided with their miracle-working tombs. Ballala Sena ultimately defeated Bu Adam and cut him in two. But misfortune struck the king: he and his whole line perished. Bu Adam's head was buried in Chatgaon (colonial Chittagong) and the rest of the body near Bikrampur, in the Dhaka district. Thus two shrines with two sets of custodians were accommodated in one story, each provided with the legitimacy of a martyr slain in a foundational moment.[99] As political centers rose and fell, these shrines, local and regional, were probably the major repositories of social memory.

Meanwhile, the new Vaishnava devotionalism of Chaitanya (1486–1533 was founded in central Bengal after 1500 and spread to the Mathura region during Mughal times. Its traditions were anchored around *shripats*, temples supported by land endowments. The most recent historian of this religious tradition remarked on their importance in underpinning the networks sustaining the faith and its gurus. In conformity with other hagiographic narratives across South Asia, it featured stories of successful contests with a Muslim ruler, likely intended to be Ala al-Din (or Husain Shah), who ruled from 1489 to 1520.[100]

Many parallel narratives of the past thus coexisted. One of these served as the "frame narrative" of the marriage brokers and genealogists of the Hindu upper castes, and was current among them by the sixteenth or seventeenth century. This harked back to a mythic Ādiśūra, who was supposed to have instituted the system of ranks and on to the last Sena rulers of Bengal—Lakshmana Sena and Ballala Sena. It continued that after their displacement by the sultans of Delhi, the maintenance of caste purity had become the duty of the genealogists. This legend was sufficiently well known for it to be incorporated into the two earliest histories of India written in Bengali.

These earliest recognizable histories in Bengali prose appeared a few years after the first Persian history, but also under colonial sponsorship. These are the works of Ram Ram Basu and Mrityuñjaya Vidyalankar, printed in 1801/1802 and 1808, respectively. The authors were both teachers at the colonial College of Fort William in Calcutta and wrote at the suggestion of their English patrons. William Carey encouraged Basu, a teacher at the new College of Fort William to try his hand at history. Nikhilnath Ray, the later editor of Basu's history, consulted Carey's unpublished papers in Serampore. He reported that Basu was already "a perfect master" of Arabic and Persian at the age of sixteen, and these skills brought him to the notice of Rammohan Ray. Basu read the latter's unpublished Bengali work on monotheism, and his editor reported that Basu modeled his own Bengali prose style on that text. In 1800, soon after the College of Fort William was established, Basu was appointed "additional *paṇḍit*" there. He taught Bengali. Carey described him as of "a peculiar turn of mind. Though amiable in manners and honest in dealings, he was a rude and unkind Hindoo if anybody did him wrong."[101]

Basu wrote and Carey printed a Bengali-language history of a legendary zamindar of Jessore in central Bengal. This was the first Bengali-language printed history. It begins by stating that Bengal (*Baṁgabhūmi*) had seen many rulers from Raja Chandraketu onward, but only their names had survived. Nothing was now known of how either their rise or their undoing had come about. Basu wrote that the first historical tradition came from the late sixteenth century: "At present, the first king of whom anything is known was Raja Pratāpāditya, who is mentioned in Persian texts, but there is no complete, integrated narrative about him. I myself belong to the caste segment of that Raja and *have heard of him from elders of my father and grandfather's time . . . [this account] is being written in conformity with what has been heard [by me]*."[102]

Basu's work has been much studied and reprinted as the earliest example of historical prose in Bengali. The author, however, was reputedly proficient in Arabic and Persian as well, and mentions consulting a Persian history of Pratapaditya, the subject of Basu's history. No such separate history has been found to date; it may never have existed. But as the quote above makes clear, Basu's main, if not only, source was the legend of this king, as preserved by his still prominent descendants.

Basu wrote his history of Pratapaditya, the legendary ruler of Jessore (modern Bangladesh) who was ousted by the Mughals in the early seventeenth century, in a plain, rhetorically "factual" fashion. He described Pratapaditya's family as professional scribes and accountants under various rulers in Bengal. Their rise to greatness began in the time of Sultan Suleiman Karrani, who ruled from Gaur in central Bengal from 1564 to 1573. The founder was of the family fortunes was one Ramachandra, who came to Gaur, the capital of the Sultanate of Bengal. After living there some time, he secured clerical appointments for his sons in the records department of the sultan. Shibananda, the middle son, rose swiftly in the sultan's esteem, and the latter's two nephews were enrolled in Persian studies alongside Suleiman's sons, Wajid and Daud. Then Daud made the mistake of defying Emperor Akbar. The clerical family then selected an abandoned estate in Chandkhan or Jashahor in South Bengal and founded a prosperous settlement there as a future refuge. When the Mughals invaded Bengal, Shibananda and his kinsmen offered to supply all the records, provided they were confirmed in their extensive lordship. This was done, and so they were established in the new government too. But Vikramaditya's rash successor Pratapaditya overreached, defied the Mughal emperor, and was destroyed by an army sent by Emperor Jahangir (ruled 1605–1628).

At this point, Basu moved to highlight the role that this incipient dynasty had played in creating an aristocracy of descent, the *kulin* system of the three Bengali upper castes. Maharaja Vikramaditya and Raja Vasanta Ray, he wrote, proceeded to identify the "best" families of Brahmans, Kayasthas, and Vaidyas and settle them in their new estate with grants appropriate to their status. This was the case of the lineage of Syamsundar Ray in the Jessore district. Himself a Kayastha of the Baṁgaja section, Basu ended his history by mentioning these descendants: "These select few are distinguished descendants of Raja Vasanta Ray [Pratapaditya's uncle]. Among them, descendants of Raja Syamsundar Ray are now the most eminent. They are the heads of Yaśahara [modern Jessore] society (*goṣṭhīpati*). They are the custodians of the rest of *Baṁgaja kāyastha* society and the chief among all their caste fellows."[103]

Basu exaggerates considerably and freely draws on folk-literary motifs and tropes. His book is, however, fundamentally a history of enterprising men of the scribal class who rise in the king's service, accumulate property, and grow into local potentates before the greatest of them overreaches and is crushed. But one branch, he notes, survived as big landholders into British times and parlayed their landholding status into a caste headship among their own scribal caste. Most importantly, though, Basu did not invoke the lineage histories harking back to legendary kings that were also current in upper-caste Bengali society.

Basu's stance was adopted by Nikhilnath Ray (1865–1932), who edited, enlarged, and republished the text in the early twentieth century. His family claimed descent from the famous Pratapaditya lineage. Ray, a historian, lawyer, and sometime manager (dewan) of Cossimbazar zamindari in Central Bengal, wrote an extensive set of notes to the original narrative. Commenting on Basu's text regarding the leadership of the Kayasthas of Jessore, Ray noted that after Pratapaditya's death, the estate was managed by Vasantaray, who maintained his grip on Jessore society.

> [But] as Vasantarāy's descendants fell into poverty, many irregularities emerged in Jaśor society. Nūrullah Khān was appointed faujdār [garrison commandant] of Jaśor at the end of the seventeenth century. His dewān [chief fiscal officer] was the celebrated Rāmbhadra Rāy . . . [who] by virtue of being the faujdār's dewān became very powerful. . . . Having accumulated much wealth, he turned to shaping a new subcaste [*nūtan śamāj*]. For this purpose he began to bring many aristocratic *kāyastha* families to settle in Pūṁḍa. But at the request of the descendants of Nīlakanṭha Rāy . . . he desisted from this enterprise.

Instead, the editor claims, Rāmbhadra agreed to install the original line of Nīlakanṭha as *goṣṭhīpati* but created the post of "deputy *goṣṭhīpati*" for his own lineage. In the next generation, the Chodhurīs of Ṭakī became wealthy and powerful and strove to acquire the headship themselves. Failing at that, they installed an older lineage in the position and assumed the role of "deputy *gosṭhīpati*" themselves. The Kayasthas of Jessore were thus divided into two sections. Then Krishnakanta Sen from Murshidabad rose in power and wealth as a result of being the East India Company's salt tax collector—and he too created another separate section under his own control.[104] Like Basu, Ray also explained lineage dominance by invoking social and political power.

Basu's colleague, Mrityuñjaya Vidyalankar, on the other hand, published a larger history of the universe, beginning with a brief description of its long cycles of millions of years. It then described Jambudvipa as one of seven continents in the salt sea, finally coming to the land occupied by people who observe the system of four castes (*varṇa*). The usual Puranika succession of dynasties is then described, with the epoch of Hindu emperors ending with the Muslim conquest of Delhi.

Thus from Yudhishthira (of the Mahabharata) down to Prithu Raja (Prithivraj), Hindus ruled in Delhi for 4,267 years in the first part of the Kaliyuga (Dark Age). (The *Ain* puts the period of pre-Islamic rule in Bengal at 4,544 years.) After Prithu Ray (Prithviraj), the throne of Delhi was occupied by Yavanas (meaning Muslims). A list of kings follows, including even the regnal (*julusi*) eras of the successive Mughal emperors. Interestingly, Vidyalankar dates Mughal sovereignty to the conquest of Delhi by Amir Timur in 1398, though he recognizes that other rulers occupied it until Timur's descendant Babur reconquered it in 1526.[105]

At some point during the four thousand years of "Hindu" rule, a Bengali king, Dhīśena, a Vaidya by caste, found that the throne of Delhi had been vacated by its spiritually minded occupant. He then installed himself with the consent of the ministers. His son and successor was Ballala Sena. He introduced the system lineage ranking (kulinism) among the five Brahman lineages of Rarha (Western Bengal). Vidyalankar then describes the origins of the five Brahmans as going back to the time of Adishura, a king of Bengal who wished to conduct a sacrifice in order to save his people from a severe drought. So he used his friendship with the king of Kanyakubja (Kanauj) to bring five Brahmans from five *gotras* (lineages) from there to perform the rituals; all Brahmans of these *gotras* are descended from these five. They were accompanied by five Kayastha servants; Kayasthas bearing those family names are their descendants. He then adds that the Brahmans already in the country were separated and formed the group known as the "Seven Hundred." Descendants of the five Brahmans were ordered not to intermarry with them.

At that time, during Ballala Sena's rule, his son Lakshmana Sena was king of Gauḍa (in Bengal). Ballala Sena became infatuated with a low-caste girl, and the matter became a scandal. He and his son exchanged sarcastic letters on the matter. (These are reproduced in the book.) Then Ballala Sena died, and Lakshmana Sena became emperor. He examined the qualities of the descendants of the original five Brahman immigrants and established a ranking system among all Brahmans. But the system was evidently lost after the fall of the Sena kingdom. The *Rajabali* therefore tells us that it was only later on that Debibar, a Brahman marriage broker (*ghaṭak*), by long meditation attained some insight into the past. But he then wrote just "as he desired. Those he described as aristocratic became aristocrats; those he labeled base (*akulīna*) were deemed base." The ordering that Debibar created, the book adds, is that which stands to the author's own times. The subtext obviously is that the classification was arbitrary and undependable. As far as Kayasthas were concerned, the *Rajabali* is unclear but seems to imply that their lineage rankings were supposedly set some time after Debibar. They were then readjusted by Purandar Basu, known as Purandar Khan, a Kayastha minister of the Bengal sultan Husain Shah in the fifteenth century.

Thus Vidyalankar was evidently skeptical of Debibar's authority, of the perceived stability of the tradition, and consequently of current social standings supposedly decreed in times long past.[106] But like Basu, he too frankly recognized that social ordering was founded on the effective power of local lords and powerful officials, not the manuscripts of secretive genealogists. It is hard to ascertain how many others shared Vidyalankar's ideas in eighteenth-century Bengal. As Partha Chatterjee has remarked, the *Rajabali* reflected the historical understanding of educated metropolitan Bengalis at the end of the eighteenth century. He reads it as an example of the historical memory of elite Bengali society at the time (1808). He classes it as a "Puranika" narrative. Its comfort with predictions of the future certainly derived from *Bhaviṣya purāṇa* traditions, but English influence should not be ruled out either. We have, for instance, an account of the Muslim rulers of Delhi that is likely from sources printed or translated under British sponsorship. The Prithviraj legend had also reached the Calcutta intelligentsia by 1800, and he finds mention under the name of Prithu Ray, the last Hindu king of Delhi. Chatterjee is certainly correct in observing that the *Rajabali* was not a national history but a hybrid narrative loosely ordered on dynastic lines.[107]

Both books, however, clearly drew upon another kind of social memory, one widespread among and important for upper-caste Bengali Hindus. This was the body of legends, verses, and anecdotes that served as charters for social rank. The main object was to establish or deny the status of individual lineages as *kulin*, or aristocratic. This was subject of keen interest among upper-caste Bengali Hindus and had very real social effects.[108]

Well into the nineteenth century, *kulin* status made men of these lineages desirable marriage partners, with correspondingly large dowries. At the very end of the nineteenth century, the institution of "kulinism" was decaying but still powerful. Jogendra Nath Bhattacharya, writing in 1896, described the possibilities of *kulin* status. Men of these lineages were highly sought after as grooms and could simply live off dowries and gifts: "A Kulin of a high class might then marry more than a hundred wives without any difficulty, and there are still some who have such large numbers of wives as to necessitate their keeping regular registers for refreshing their memory, about the names and residences of their spouses."

But, Bhattacharya continued, repeated marriages with inferior lineages had sometimes caused the status to decline through the generations.[109] It must then be evident that pronouncing on status claims would require the maintenance of records of descent and marriage through successive generations. That was, in fact, supposedly the responsibility of genealogists-cum-marriage-brokers (*ghaṭak* or *kulajña*). Their pronouncements were supposedly founded on traditions they had preserved from the times of the last Hindu sovereigns. Lineage lore was probably the most widely known Bengali "history" well into the late nineteenth century, reaching far beyond the works of Vidyalankar or Basu. It was tenaciously defended both by professional genealogists and many among the emerging class of professional, Western-style historians. Bankim Chandra wrote an endorsement of the first edition (1896) of a massive work on genealogical rank and appropriate marriage, titled *Sambandhanirṇaya*. It was also endorsed by a widely read newspaper, the *Ananda Bazar Patrika*.[110] It seems likely that the majority of upper-caste Bengali Hindus, both the literate minority and illiterate majority, were more deeply versed in the historical lore concerning family status than in any other history.

But the pedigree system was based on a history that has many marks of a foundation myth. Vidyalankar had drawn on the legend of a Bengali king, Adishura (likely a mythic founder, a king who has never been satisfactorily identified or dated). The system was then supposedly reformed under Lakshmana Sena, who ruled from 1179 to 1207. He was driven out of his capital by a Turkish army in the last years of his reign. There are strong grounds for believing that the various versions of the legend were only written down in the fifteenth or sixteenth century at the earliest. But few accounts agreed with each other.[111] Genealogical accounts of particular sections of the Brahmans definitely began to be written at the end of the fifteenth century. Two early genealogies of the Vaidya (or Baidya) physician caste can only be dated 1653 and 1675; those referring to the scribal caste of Kayasthas came later than that. Vaidya genealogical texts claimed that Ballala Sena, who was supposed to have founded the ranking system among select Hindu castes, was a member of their caste. Some Brahman and all Kayastha genealogical texts deny it.[112]

In any case, much research has established that not only did the different texts disagree with each other on many details, they also conflicted sharply with the contemporary epigraphic and literary record from the Pala and Sena dynasties. From time to time a powerful landed magnate might exert his power to head a council that adjudicated and enforced ranks, as we see in Nikhilnath Ray's narrative of the Bamgaja Kayasthas. But eighteenth- and early nineteenth-century Bengal saw the swift rise and fall of many such family estates. The early period of the Permanent Settlement (1793–1850) also witnessed many magnates replaced by "new men" with connections to the British regime. Tracts of hundreds or even thousands of villages found new owners, often absentees with few roots in local society. Calcutta society was even more mobile and factional, and wealthy men could set up as "bosses" (*dalapati*) and dominate the social lives of their clients, as S. N. Mukherjee has described.[113] The rapid turnover among elites in the eighteenth century as a consequence of the semi-independence of the Bengal Nawabs (c. 1700–1765) and the chaos of early British rule, however, would have severely disrupted barely crystallized patterns of social knowledge. The rise of the colonial port of Calcutta as focus of power and prestige would have forced a confluence on the nouveaux riche of that city. Then adroit image management, malicious rumor, and the expenditure of money worked to raise or lower particular lineages in this fluid and unstable social milieu.

The well-known Tagore (Thakur) family offer an example. Their lineage was degraded by other Brahmans, probably as a result of enjoying the patronage of Muslim officials, and formed the subcaste of "Pirālī" Brahmans. Panchanana Tagore came and settled in the early English colony of Calcutta. He and his descendants prospered under early East India Company rule. However, that attracted the envy of a local Brahman magnate Durga Charan Mukherjee of Bag Bazar, who formed a faction to degrade them. But they continued to prosper and sustained their efforts to remove their original stigma. British recognition and education helped that effort. A Tagore scion became the first Indian to successfully pass the entrance examination for the "Heaven-born"

Indian Civil Service and that set the seal on their status. By the end of the nineteenth century, Bhattacharya wrote, they were "fast rising in the scale of caste."[114]

The fragmentation of social and political power in Bengal had also splintered historical authority and social memory. Even the district caste assemblies cited as authorities by Ram Ram Basu in 1800 appear to have lost their coherence. By the later nineteenth century, we find only genealogies privately maintained by professional genealogists who were also marriage brokers. They circulated in the public domain through Bengali doggerel rhymes. In the 1930s, the historian R. C. Majumdar sought to study these texts. He found that the original manuscripts were kept—often inaccessibly—in the genealogists' homes, and sayings supposedly derived from them circulated by word of mouth. In some cases, the originals of manuscripts that had supposedly been printed could not be found at all. The genealogists' effort at self-promotion is evidenced by some of the self-glorifying tales to be found in published quotes from the manuscripts. Indeed, the bits of simple rhyming verse cited as originating in these texts strongly suggest a folk-oral origin rather than a literary one.

For example, in the mid-nineteenth century, a well-informed Bengali police officer, belonging to the Kayastha scribal caste heard that the head of the Mustaufi family had humiliated a genealogist named Madhab Basu by shaving his head and ejecting him from the Mustaufi mansion. The latter then wrote a bit of doggerel into his record book. That little verse supposedly sufficed to degrade the lineage from the aristocratic marriage circle of the Dakhinrarhi segment of Kayasthas. (We should note, however, that the wealthy landlord had not hesitated to humiliate the bard, so the latter were clearly not viewed as all-powerful even if they represented themselves as such.) Despite being a Kayastha himself, the author of this narrative could not tell what the Mustaufi's status really was.[115] Another such self-glorifying story appears in an extract from a manuscript called *Paṭivyākhyā*. It narrates how the genealogists went to seek an audience with Srikrsna Bhāduri, who was getting married. But he did not greet them in person. They said to each other, "An aristocrat behaves so arrogantly with genealogists?! Come, let us see if we can find a defect in his line." According to this minatory tale, such a defect was in fact found and publicized. The aristocratic lineage was subsequently humiliated in its matrimonial ventures.[116]

However, such private management of information failed once the genealogical works began to be printed and thus generally available. Close examination of the texts and their comparison with newly uncovered coins, seals, and inscriptions also revealed them to be unreliable and sometimes even recently falsified.[117] The genealogists and marriage brokers clearly felt that authority was slipping away from them into the hands of professional, Western-style historians. Nagendranath Basu, one of the community, collected and published a large number of genealogical texts and associated legends in the early twentieth century. But by now the new Western-style historiography was well established, and its practitioners began verifying texts against each other, and with newly discovered inscriptions and records. It soon became evident that multiple contradictory stories had existed. Clearly, the regional institutional stability needed for the creation of a standard narrative had not existed across Bengal.

Consequently, genealogical traditions were not maintained with any integrity, nor is there evidence of caste councils actually deciding on relative ranks. Unlike the public declarations of Rajput bards—eulogic histories that had to be recited at wedding feasts and other celebrations—genealogical manuscripts were privately maintained and jealously guarded. Their possessors used them to promote or obstruct marriages among upper-caste Hindus. These were events at which large dowries changed hands. There was, furthermore, no incentive to preserve accurate traditions of long-vanished royal houses, and it was simpler to render current folktales into Sanskrit or Bengali as a framing device for the actual, vendible hard-core genealogy. But it was precisely the marketability of genealogical fable that caused it to be modified until social status had become difficult to determine. A unified narrative was only to appear under colonial auspices in the later nineteenth century.

More recently, the late Kumkum Chatterjee represented the *kulagrantha* texts as being authentic folk tradition, oriented to the life of the community rather than the cold factuality of scientific history.[118] These characterizations, however, ignored the limited communities these texts addressed, as well as their narrow social agenda. We should remember that the manuscripts sought to authenticate the status claims of favored lineages among the three upper castes of the Hindu minority of the Bengali population. Indeed, they were casteist to literally the *n*th degree, since even numerically small castes such as Barendra Brahmans or Baṅgaja Kayasthas were defined as split into numerous ranked fractions.

3 Social Structure and Historical Narration in Western India

SOCIAL MEMORY IS SHAPED AND SUSTAINED BY ITS SOCIOPOLITICAL frame. The Marathi-speaking cultural zone of Western India generated an exceptional body of historical memory. It was recorded in a class of works known as *bakhar*, which was recognized as history from early colonial times. The British began visibly to overshadow the Maratha Empire by 1805, and in 1817–18, Pune and Nagpur—the two major cities of Maharashtra—came under British military occupation. The early British regime eagerly sought *bakhar*s, and a manuscript found in the fort of Rairi (in 1803?) was translated and found its way into the diplomatic and military records of the Bombay government secretariat.[1] *Bakhar*s were certainly used by early British historians, such as Edward Scott Waring, who in 1810 wrote in the preface to his *History of the Mahrattas* of the Marathi *bakhar*s that he had consulted: "Their historians (some will deny them the name) write in a plain, simple and unaffected style, content to relate passing events in opposite terms without turgid imagery or inflated phraseology. . . . They do not endeavour to bias or mislead the judgment, but are certainly greatly deficient in chronology and in historical reflections."[2]

The term *bakhar* was certainly well established in official usage by the 1670s, when the Maratha sovereign Shivaji ordered the preparation of a thematic Sanskrit thesaurus that would reduce the excessive use of "Yavani" (Islamic) terms of statecraft. *Bakhair* is listed in a chapter (*lekhanvarga*) dealing with specialized terms used by recordkeepers and accountants; it is given the Sanskrit equivalent *ākhyāyikā*,[3] which itself is given the synonym *uplabdhārtha* in a classical Sanskrit thesaurus, signifying obtained or received knowledge; in meaning, therefore, it was much the same as the Hindustani word *khabar* (news, report).[4] This placement in the section that offers equivalents for standard tax-office terms suggests that the *bakhar* itself was something that the *diwan*—finance minister—often had to address.

It is, however, necessary to address the possibility that the genre was essentially borrowed from the Persianate literati who staffed the uppermost levels of the administration under the sultans of southern India and (later) the Mughal emperors.[5] It is almost certain that some writers of *bakhar*s would have known of or read Persian histories, but this knowledge would not by itself generate Marathi historical narratives—unless the regional setting was such as to prompt such writing. We should otherwise expect this genre to be found all over the subcontinent in various languages, which is not the case. What impulses and settings led Marathi-speaking literati to generate these texts within certain identifiable conventions and in a specific regional language?

One of these settings was the court of law, a forum where people have long had the incentive to produce credible narratives of contested pasts. Officials of the fisc often presided over the judicial gatherings that decided important property claims.[6] Long disputes over patrimonies were the stuff of everyday life in Maharashtra, and, as the historical origins of the claim had to be explained, *bakhar*s were also written as a consequence. We have an early case, from 1610, where the term *bakhar* is used in the proceedings to mean simply a statement of fact (in this case, the location of the boundary).[7] Two hundred years later, a century-long dispute over the hereditary astrologer's office of twelve villages was settled in favor of the Pavaskar family; one of the latter's friends then composed a congratulatory Marathi poem. The poem tells us that at one stage Sridhar Joshi took his plaint to the judge at the provincial governor's court. The local landlord sent his testimony in the form of a *bakhar*, which, however, was scrutinized and rejected by the judge. This did not deter the false claimant from again raising his claim, this time by bribing an important person at the court of King Sambhaji (ruled 1680–1689) and presenting another slanted *bakhar*.[8] A *bakhar* was clearly seen as something that was (or should be) factual.

I would suggest that the resort to softening and omission of truth, to ornamented narrative and rhetorical device has never been entirely absent from history. It is also characteristic of argument in the judicial process, and these qualities may be seen as an important source of many features of the *bakhar* genre itself. These traits would not, nonetheless, detract from the effort at verisimilitude made in the text, nor turn it into a pure work of the imagination. The narrative was as "factual" as the author could make it. It is by looking at how this factuality was achieved that we decipher the understandings of the past embedded in the common sense of the time. Documents and narratives would ultimately be tested in an assembly of regional or village notables. Literally thousands of such gatherings are mentioned in the records of medieval Western India. It is important to note that people of diverse communities and persuasions would be present. Contestants could not, therefore, appeal to esoteric or sectarian knowledge but rather turned to the "common knowledge" or "common sense" of a diverse local community, narrated in a language that everyone could understand.

The local assembly that met in 1610 to resolve the boundary dispute between two villages of Pune district exemplifies this. It was headed by the hereditary Islamic judge Kazi Abdulla and his deputy, Kazi Ismail. Also present were Mir Isiph, deputy commandant of the fort of Kondana; and Nur Miya Vali, custodian of an important Sufi shrine. But the gathering also included two Brahman officials, the heads of the merchants of three market towns, and a long list of village headmen and notables from the nearby villages.[9] Thus Islamic scholars and officials, Brahman bureaucrats, merchants, local gentry of various faiths, and substantial peasants were all present. All these would have to be convinced; they would then authenticate the award with their seals, signatures, or marks. Most proceedings were held in the open or in public places. People of many classes would thus periodically gather to hear, debate, and renew local knowledge and common sense. Some of them might have to stand forth as witnesses, plaintiffs, or respondents. In a largely nonliterate society, such meetings would be important in shaping and transmitting local and regional history. It is therefore not surprising that the English surgeon Thomas Coats observed of Maharashtrian peasants in the early nineteenth century: "They are fond of conversation, discuss the merits of agriculture, the characters of their neighbours and every thing that relates to the concerns of the community, and many of them are not without a tolerable knowledge of the leading events of the history of their country."[10]

Prachi Deshpande would exclude "prose hagiographies" from the *bakhar* genre, but the distinction of sacred and secular was not made in the texts themselves—after all, the *Sabhasad bakhar* credits dreams, omens, and prophecies.[11] Supernatural intervention was accepted and invoked in the prosaic world of the law court: if written and oral evidence failed, disputants could offer to undergo an ordeal. Religious foundations could also get involved in property disputes that required secular adjudication. This even led to a change in the tone of some hagiographies themselves. A full-length hagiographic *bakhar*—the life of the seventeenth-century holy man Samartha Ramdas written in 1793 by his follower Hanumantsvami—opens with a narration of sources and an admission of their incompleteness: "I had [earlier] written a life of the Svami. You asked me to communicate it to you. It has been expanded on the basis of books, and on what the company of his contemporary disciples wrote down and preserved, and also certain stories that I have myself heard. This is communicated to you. Who indeed can tell you everything about the Svami? His deeds are infinite, his qualities infinite and so too his devotion. What is knowable I have written."[12]

WHAT WAS THE SOCIAL FRAME OF THE *BAKHAR* GENRE?

The larger setting for these discourses was the interaction of expanding royal power and resilient local society in the early modern era. I have shown elsewhere that kingdoms and empires in west peninsular India were overlaid upon tenacious patterns of local territorial authority. The ancient clan or tribal territories were transformed into the subordinate but still vital pargana or *naḍu* territories. Beneath these were powerful village communities. A concrete manifestation of their strength was the part they played in adjudicating all sorts of property disputes.[13] Each of these played an important role in adjudicating property rights in their own domains, albeit with the participation and sanction of superior authorities. The establishment of the sultanates only led to the Arabization of some names but did not alter the social power of the gatherings. A full-scale pargana (county) assembly would be called a *got-sabha*; with addition of the *qazi*, the Islamic judge, it became the *hazir majalis* (the assembly of those present). The position of *qazi* soon became hereditary. The document of title or award that it issued would be the *mahzar*, or collective attestation.

Below these great councils where great men and royal functionaries who dominated dozens of villages might gather were lesser sites where claims were argued and village memories debated and formed. They might gather in an official's courtyard, before a royal judge, or at a village temple, depending on the importance of the dispute. I thus ground a genre of memory (the Marathi *bakhar*) in the social and political history of Western India. Later in this chapter, I will show how the effort to generate a "Maratha identity" itself impacted the genre. This will historicize both genre and community and thus explain the creation of the hundreds of Marathi histories that are the subject of this chapter.

Like royal orders, grants, and other documents, the decrees resulting from such assemblies were firmly located in dated time, often with the Shalivahana Shaka alongside the solar Islamic (*suhur*) year; sometimes, a regnal year would be added as well. That all these dating systems referred to the same neutral, commonplace linear time went without saying. Furthermore, implicit in such cross-dating is the idea that time has a single flow, and that different markers or dating systems are arbitrarily placed within it. There was no single eschatological event that changed time, nor did it move to some eventual end of days.

But the law court was not the only time and place where local and family history was rehearsed, contested, and remade.[14] Many *bakhar*s also present themselves as responses from knowledgeable subordinates to a question from a superior authority. This rhetorical device gives us another clue to the origins of this hybrid genre of writing: it stems from an increasingly bureaucratic regime. Successive rulers needed to know their domains, and began by demanding testimony from local officials. Such inquests would be common wherever royal authority had weakened powerful intermediary lords and penetrated to the localities. This is suggested in one of the very earliest, if not earliest, *bakhar*s extant, the *Mahikāvatīcī bakhar*.[15] It records that after the kingdom was conquered by Nagarsya, "Samvat 1228 that is Salivahana Saka 1163 the 7th day of the bright half of the month Magha, Tuesday then the people of the land gathered. The district gentry, their assistants, the village elders, the cleverer village headmen, tax officers, merchants, Brahmans—all communities brought their records, papers and charters and all came into the royal presence."[16] It is most unlikely this happened at either of the dates given (which differ from each other by over 40 years). But such inquiries were common some centuries later.

It is also doubtful if the Raja Nagarsya existed and ordered such an inquest, but later records of such inquiries survive—as, for example, when the Maratha king Shivaji conquered the districts of Cheul and Rairi in the early 1650s. He summoned the hereditary gentry-administrators and chiefs of the merchants and ordered them to provide a complete account of the tax collections under the preceding regime. "Thereupon Appaji Tavji, hereditary district accountant (*deśkulkarṇī*) said that under the Nizamshahs and Adilshahs we would make a lump-sum assessment and did not keep accounts of the [actual] payments made by the peasants." He was punished for this dereliction, and arrangements were made for local accounts to be kept in the future.[17] Historical narratives were important in bargaining over tax rates; thus on the reestablishment of Maratha power in the Satara district after 1708, local hereditary officials were able to produce a detailed memorandum of the tax rates fixed at the coronation of Chatrapati Shivaji in 1674, as well as the changes made under his successor Sambhaji.[18]

Thus the discussion of tax arrangements under different regimes would also involve a historical narrative about political events affecting the pargana.

But it is only in the 1650s that the historical notes gain a degree of accuracy. I believe that this reflects the new demands of the dynamic Chatrapati Shivaji's administration. This, I argue, led officials quickly to collect then-current oral traditions to lend authority to their description of previous tax regimes, and to keep regular notes thereafter.

The history of the Marathi *bakhar*s offers an illustration of an array of institutional domains where historical memory may be shaped and rehearsed. Such narratives emerged in settings where the historian did not stand forth as a judge; rather, he (rarely, she) spoke as a plaintiff, a defendant, or a witness. Narratives were often produced in judicial disputes over heritable property. So they contested alternative stories and sought to ground themselves in witness testimony, documentary evidence, and the "common knowledge" of the local community. That community itself was usually religiously, culturally, and linguistically diverse. The assembly of worthies that acted for it often included rich and poor, high and low caste, Hindu and Muslim alike. The members of the judicial assembly scrutinized documents and interrogated witnesses. Sometimes, lack of evidence forced them to leave an issue unresolved. The award in one such case stated that the matter could be resolved only if a specific original document mentioned by several witnesses was found, but not otherwise. The complete award includes a critical summary of the pleas and a scrutiny of documents produced on both sides, dating from 1773–74. Those attesting the award include Muslims, Brahmans, local artisans, tradesmen, and hereditary village servants.[19]

Matters of caste rights and customs often arose and were adjudicated in the same way. For example, in the 1740s, a quarrel between the castes working in metals (Pancāḷas) and the trader castes (Vāṇi Bakāl) raged in several places and was taken up to the royal court in Satara in 1747–48. This dispute was whether Pancāḷa bridegrooms had traditionally been allowed in procession through the main roads of the entire market-town or not. The traders denied that such a right existed. The king's order sought reports from the hereditary officers of twenty-seven districts, ranging along the west coast and reaching inland into central Maharashtra; eleven local potentates were also consulted. But it is the nature of the information sought that is most relevant here. The addressees were told that the artisan castes had claimed that the matter had been settled in their favor earlier, with documents going back to the time of the regent of the Ahmadnagar sultanate, Malik Ambar (d. 1626). The officials were asked to inform the court of current practice and search their records for any mentions of such a dispute. They were asked to be true to their ancestors and send a detailed and truthful report on the matter.[20] It is clear that the litigants had not resorted to sacred text or ancestral myth. Instead, they argued historically, on the basis of practice confirmed from documentary evidence—in this case, supposedly extant in government archives. This historical awareness also caused families to maintain chronicles of notable events in their family and locality.

This was connected to the protracted legal disputes that were dragged from forum to forum and were reopened with each change of regime. Literati in Maharashtra had frequently to prepare testimonies in such cases.[21] The relation between the maintenance of family chronicles and the defense of patrimonial claims is elegantly illustrated in a book by the late A. R. Kulkarni, doyen of Maratha historians. The volume contains both the chronicle or memorandum book (1627–28 to 1696–97) of the Jedhe family and a separate narrative that explains the history of their patrimony. The chronicle itself is a list of dates together with brief notes of important events: battles, coronations, the births and deaths of important people, and so on. This information was then drawn on to write a *karina*, an explanatory history of how they acquired and held their patrimony.[22]

But gentlefolk like the Jedhes and courtly literati were not the only authors of historical narratives. Not just great nobles but even small-town literati maintained memorandum books listing noteworthy events. So a Brahman resident of Cheul listed sacrifices, ceremonies, the names of Brahmans who attended and officiated, the installation of statues, gifts and fees given, and major political events in chronological order. As the rights to officiate and receive fees were often hotly contested between Brahman lineages, this information was of more than passing significance. Similarly, as many tax-free assignments were held by Brahmans, suspensions of and inquiries into them were important. But other information could also be swept into his memorandum book. Two extracts demonstrate this:

> Śake 1714 *Paridhāvī samvatsara* Bhādrapad dark half [of the lunar month], 14th day, [tax-free] land-grants in the territory of Janjira Kulābā were taken over by the government . . .
>
> Śake 1723 Jyeshta dark half 12th day, a huge fish floated up near the shore of Nāgāṁva harbor. It was thirty or thirty-one cubits long and as thick as the full height of an adult man. All the Prabhus and other folk went to look at it.[23]

Another memorandum book from the hereditary Adhikari family of the same region has been printed in full. It covers over a hundred years and contains a vast amount of local information, as well as major news from other places such as Pune. Memoranda in it include a list of temples, their patrons, and the families possessing rights to officiate in them. It also contained noteworthy events—good and bad—and also lists of fort commandants and governors who had charge of the area, for example, a list of seven fort commandants under the Sīdī dynasty of Janjira, beginning with Sīdī Surul and ending with Abdul Rahīm. It also listed all the administrators appointed under the Angre dynasty that partly displaced the Sīdīs from the area. This would be useful to verify documents and orders, to compile narratives of local history and administration, and as evidence in litigation.[24]

Appeals to common social memory and local landmarks were also used as evidence. One example comes from a suit that began in the early eighteenth century and was resolved in 1785. The plaintiff was a poor goldsmith whose grandfather had been a village lord (*khot*). A summary of the plaintiff's evidence prepared by a clerk sent by the chief justice reads:

> You [the plaintiff] wrote out a plea the substance of which, as supplemented by additional evidence, is [as follows]—that the *khoti* [lordship] of the aforementioned village is anciently ours, but we cannot tell which of our forefathers secured this patrimony. During the Bijapur reign Krishnaseṭ son of Yesaseṭ held the lordship. Krishnaseṭ's brother was Sonaseṭ; upon his death his wife became a *sati*. The immolation site in the village still has a masonry marker. After this Bhagseṭ son of Krishnaseṭ held the office, as did Dadseṭ son of Bhagseṭ. After them it was held by Krishnaseṭ and Lamseṭ, sons of Dadseṭ. Lamseṭ died, leaving a son Sonseṭ, my father. Krishnaseṭ fled the village due to the turmoil caused by the invasion of Naroji Ghorpade, and went to Rangana, lived there five or six years and died. His son Dadseṭ lived at Satara and worked as a goldsmith to support himself, and my father Sonseṭ came back to our village. Fifty or sixty years have gone by since then; owing to poverty he could not fulfill the functions of the landlord's office.[25]

We may notice how the narrative is sought to be authenticated by a genealogy linking the claimant to the original holder, to locally well-known events such as the invasion of Naroji Ghorpade, and to a still-extant masonry memorial to a widow-immolation. Family memory was here built on the landmarks of community memory, as described by Maurice Halbwachs in a far different setting.[26] The hereditary office (the plaint continues) was then usurped for many years.

When challenged, the new occupant also claimed legitimate possession, and the court scrutinized documents on both sides. The displaced claimant had to explain the adverse possession of the incumbent. The judge sought sworn testimony from various villagers, and each of them declared what he had himself seen, as well as what he had learned from his father or other older persons. Documents were also challenged on occasion. So, for example, eleven villagers testified that they had heard that one Keso Tanadeva had forcibly taken the former landlord and important villagers to the temple and extorted deeds transferring ownership to him. However, three others stated that they only knew that the deeds had been written and attested, but they did not know the process involved.[27] The obvious effect of the story was to question the value of the documents produced as evidence and enhance that of local testimony. Plaintiffs appealing to a gathering of worthies and fellow villagers understood the need to involve local sites of memory, artifacts familiar to all from childhood on.

In another case, when Balaji Krishna Pendse claimed to be hereditary mahajan of Murdi, he had to begin by proving that it was a distinct village and not part of the nearby settlement of Anjarle. He appealed not only to paper records but to the evidence that extant lineages were holding other village offices and to visible landmarks. The village's distinct identity was known by the presence of a hereditary offices held by three named lineages, each of which could bear witness. It had its own temples too, notably those of Sri Vimaleshvara and Ganapati, and of Sri Lakshminarayana. It had known boundaries: to the northeast, Sukoṇḍī: to the south sea and salt marsh; and to the west, the river that ran through the fields.[28]

The effort to supply credible evidence could go to considerable lengths, as illustrated with evidence from two different cases. The first has been exhaustively studied by Gajanan Mehendale, a major historian of Maharashtra, and the following draws on his work. The hereditary office of district registrar (variously termed *qanungo*, *deshpande*, and *nadkarni*) was a prestigious and powerful one across South Asia. Two lineages contended for the two posts in two small districts in the mountains east of the Pune. It appears that during the time of troubles that began with the Mughal invasion of the area in the 1680s, a local Brahman family, titled "Saciv" (minister) persuaded the Maratha king Rajaram (ruled 1689–1700), who was then besieged in Senji (Jinji) in South India, that the post of registrar of the Rohidkhora district was vacant. They then secured a grant of it for themselves. The Guptes, a local Prabhu Kayastha family, had older claims to the office and returned to assert their rights. The Sacivs then arrested the claimants and forcibly took many relevant papers from them. The Guptes, however, were undaunted and continued to assert their claim through four generations, right into early colonial rule (1818).

Balaji Pant Natu was an influential courtier at the Satara kingdom that the colonial administration briefly revived under Bhosle rule from 1818 to 1848. Natu was also in high favor with the incoming British government. Crucially, Natu was a collateral descendant of the Gupte line. He may therefore have been involved, if not instrumental, in the fabrication of records that supported their claims. At any rate, at some point in the late eighteenth or early nineteenth century, the Gupte family forged a number of documents, perhaps to replace the ones lost to the Sacivs. These new ones purported to show that their ancestor, Dadaji Naras Prabhu was already in office when the teenage Shivaji Raje Bhosle began to resist the Adilshahi sultans in the 1640s, and that the family were therefore the earliest allies of the rising Bhosle dynasty. This would obviously forestall any claim made on the basis of grants made in the 1690s or later. In one case, the forger actually got hold of an authentic judicial award (*mahzar*), separated a section bearing official seals, and wrote in an award showing that the Guptes' ancestor Dadaji Naras Prabhu was legitimate holder of the post of hereditary registrar.

The forgers also realized that documents would be checked for inconsistency, such as the anachronistic mention of persons or lineages known not to have been present in the 1640s. They therefore used their own surviving papers to prepare a list of contemporary gentry who could actually have attended, and inserted their names as attesting the verdict. Mehendale astutely observes that this meant that the document could not have been refuted by verifying whether the signatories were all alive at the time or not. Clearly, the Guptes had a keen sense of how historical papers were verified and were thus prepared for that scrutiny. Mehendale adds that authenticated papers from a separate archive in the town of Kari show that the Guptes' claims on Rohidkhora were genuine, but that in the course of the feud, they forged many papers so as to also assert claims on the pargana of Velwandkhora, that of their rivals, the Sacivs.[29] The documents artfully created by the Guptes have been widely accepted by many historians, including such stalwarts as Setu Madhavrao Pagdi.[30] (Some were, however, skeptical.)

In addition to providing positive evidence in favor of specific claims, many also knew the significance of refuting contrary evidence. So, in preparation for a lawsuit, the Sitole family compiled a memorandum showing what old documents they possessed from the time of Malik Ambar (early 1600s) to the late eighteenth century. Interestingly, it also included lines of rebuttal for documents held by the other side: "When the Nizamshahi [dynasty] fell, the Idilshahs took over and the district came under Bijapur. At that time the two brothers did not go to greet the new ruler, whereupon he was angered and conferred the *deśmukhī* [hereditary registrarship] on the Ghāṭge family [who might therefore have records too]. Then Viṭhojī Nāik [Sitole] went to Bijapur, got the Ghāṭges removed and secured a royal order in his favor. We have the *farmān* [edict, which would supersede other documents held by their rivals] on (special) green paper."[31] Similarly, when the Jagdales and Yadavas feuded over an estate, the former took pains to compile a set of testimonials from many neighboring landholders. These stated that the estate had been awarded by the then king without an assembly of local worthies attesting to its true ownership. The Yadavas, on the other hand, sought to explain this away by reference to various incidents in the strenuous campaign against the Mughal Empire having prevented this assembly being held.[32] Historical narratives came to be constructed as the outcome of contests over rights and patrimonies. That credible narratives depended on evidence was an idea widely diffused across Maharashtrian society, as our next section illustrates.

UMAJI NAIK KHOMNE AND HIS HISTORY

The idea that documents were important was not confined to the elite. Umaji Naik Khomne was an "organic intellectual" (in Gramsci's sense of the term). He was an exceptional Ramoshi tribal leader who, while in prison, learned to read and write. He also corresponded with British officers regarding his patrimonial claims. After his release, Umaji obtained police charge of part of the hill country near Pune in the early years of colonial rule. He then gradually enlarged it into an independent legal jurisdiction. He rebelled twice: he was initially conciliated by a baffled colonial government but rose again. This second uprising was suppressed with great difficulty, and Umaji was captured and executed.

Plebeian (or subaltern) leaders understood the strategies of appropriation of both archives *and* memories. These methods were deployed in a protracted struggle between the lineages of the Chivhe Kolis and Khomne Ramoshis over the wardenship of the territories subordinate to the great hill fort of Purandar, near the important city of Pune. Claims to hereditary positions already had a long history there.

Subaltern communities participated in these processes, and it is documents generated by them or at their behest that provide the material analyzed here. The writers of such documents would seek to create a "genuine" document by incorporating what they believed to be authentic about the past. The analysis of such documents will then enable us to deduce the historical understanding of the past in the minds of the producers of these texts.

At the outset of his career, however, Umaji was only an impoverished teenaged boy from the Ramoshi tribe. His forefathers had been part of the fort garrison at Purandar. They took the wrong side in a political feud and were ultimately expelled from the fort in 1803.[33] But Umaji never forgot his lineage's claims. The idea that copper plates recorded ancient rights rendered immutable also persisted among the Ramoshis. Such history is laid out in what purports to be a transcript of a copper plate issued by the "Padshah of Bidar."[34] Since copper plates were known to have been used to record land grants under the Hindu dynasties that preceded the Turkish conquest of the Dakhan, it is likely that many village worthies would preserve them, and possible that they might periodically turn up amidst ruined or abandoned dwellings. The idea that antique documents would be on copper plates seems to have been firmly established in the popular mind.

Similar documents were produced in the struggles to establish claims to lands and fees in the strategic fastnesses of the Sahyadri Mountains during the eighteenth and early nineteenth centuries. One such text is among those found in the Pune Archives and printed in the early twentieth century. The text is marked by several anachronisms. It mentions several historical figures, such as "Beerbul" a famous wit and official at the court of the Mughal emperor Akbar (who ruled 1556–1605 but never governed the Pune region). But it also alludes to the wholly legendary Damaji Pant, who was said to have been an official of the Padshah of Bidar during a great famine in the fourteenth century. Moved by the plight of the starving, he permitted the people of the pilgrimage town Pandharpur to plunder the royal grain store. Summoned to account for it, he was saved from a brutal death by the gracious intervention of the god Viṭṭhala, who took the shape of a Mahar courier and arrived at the court in the nick of time with the cash value of the lost grain.[35]

The supposed transcript of a copper plate was among those produced by the famous Ramoshi chief Umaji Naik Khomne in support of his claims to large hereditary estates inherited from his ancestors. The papers were scrutinized by the English official George Giberne, and Alexander Mackintosh mentions that Giberne was struck by the "affection and reverence these people look upon these old, torn papers, which they consider to confer a right withheld, and that they are fully impressed with the idea of their being unjustly deprived of their wuttuns [patrimonies]." He felt "by hints that they have vaguely thrown out, that they mean to claim the *bukshish* [gift] granted by the Padshaw." By "mean to claim" Giberne implied that they would exact tribute from the villages if the British government did not concede the demand. Mackintosh was the commander of the Ahmadnagar Police Corps, which ultimately pursued and captured Umaji Naik during his second rebellion. He also had several long conversations with Umaji. He reports that some copper plates actually existed:

> A Brahmun to whom I have shewn [the copy] expressed great surprise, and immediately observed, that it could merely be the traditionary tale of what was supposed to be engraved on the copper-plates, and not a copy of the original deed. This Brahmun, who is an intelligent man, further told me, that Captain H. D. Robertson, the collector of Poona, put the copper-plates in his hands, and directed him to endeavour to discover the nature of the grant; but that although he kept it for three months, all he could discover was that, it purported that he [the author] had shaken off his allegiance to the Emperor, and established an independent kingdom in the Dekhan, making Kulburga his capital, and after the dismemberment of this extensive state, his descendants, about A. D. 1528, established themselves at Beder, retaining possession of the surrounding districts.

It would thus appear that the copper plate originated in the sixteenth century at the earliest and had no evident connection with either the Chivhe Koli or the Khomne Ramoshi lineages. The incomplete Marathi text in the Pune Archives does indeed mention Haibatji Naik Khomne but only as an addressee. Even that mention is missing from the text translated by Mackintosh. The latter was possibly a different version prepared in the Chivhe interest but seized by the Ramoshi Umaji Naik as part of the evidence for his patrimony, despite the explicit message that the grant should "belong only to the tribe of Kolie."[36]

Umaji himself saw these papers as historically authentic title deeds to a large patrimony granted by the nameless Padshah. Mackintosh once mentioned to him "that the report was that he had treasure concealed in the Poorundur hill. His answer was, that there might be treasure concealed in the hill, but that his wealth consisted in the copper-plate deeds; for that being the owner of these he was master of lacks of rupees; adding that they (the Ramoossies) were the masters of twenty-six forts, repeating the names of several."[37]

But there was yet another document that most likely originated in an effort by the Nizam of Hyderabad to subvert Maratha authority by winning over the Koli garrison of Purandar. Mackintosh continues: "The document on which Oomiah pretended to found his claims to the Mookassa [military prebend] rights of the Kheirbary [region] . . . was granted by one Dewan Ally to the Koley Naiks of Poorundur, and no mention whatever is made of the Ramoossies in the paper. The grant was written about one hundred and four years ago [1726 CE?]."

Mackintosh's narrative is confirmed by a memorandum from the court of the Pant Saciv, the hereditary ruler of the little state of Bhor in the Sahyadri Mountains, dispatched on October 16, 1829. The memorandum stated that Umaji Naik had sent his brother Krishnaji Naik to Bhor, where the latter had demanded the payment of certain hereditary claims in seven specified villages of the Khedebare subdivision. The claims were maintained despite the Saciv's response that the records of previous seventy-five or eighty years had been searched, and no trace of such payments was found.[38] Umaji himself was firmly convinced of strength of his claim as is shown by his letter dated August 3, 1830, to George Giberne, Collector of Pune:

> Command no. 270 from the Presence has been received. It states: "You laid claim to hereditary estates (*watandārī*) but the papers do not refer to *watandārī*, merely to (removable) appointments (*tainatī*). Therefore if you have *watandarī* documents, then produce them, or give up the claims." But the papers I showed the Sarkar in the camp at Jejuri contain references to *watandarī*. I have sent copies of those papers to the government, and if these are read all will become known to the master. The Patsah's gifts are mine and I also have the Padsah's edict (*sanad*). In the past my ancestor received grants because (he arranged the) burial under the fort [a human sacrifice] and because of his valor in battle. . . . If I did not have a rightful claim to hereditary estates, I would never have petitioned. I have a *watan*. I have a *watan*! [repetition in the original] That is why I have repeatedly petitioned the government. Let the master personally examine the papers that I have given the government. Everything will then become clear to the master.[39]

These original documents substantially corroborate Mackintosh's account of the collective memory that had developed among the Ramoshis of Umaji's entourage. But the Purandar documents also reveal themselves to be a remnant of a previous lineage of plebeian claimants, in this case the Chivhe clan of Kolis, prominent in the late seventeenth century but then marginalized by other Kolis of the Purandar fort area. They had clearly been struggling to reestablish their eminence, and in Western India that required them to generate a documentary history of the claim. The documents show the Chivhes busily engaged in writing up a "historical" charter of their claims.[40]

All claimants clearly shared in the popular (and historically valid) belief that truly ancient documents were engraved on copper plates. It is also worth looking at the logic of entitlement embedded in these claims. The first is the date itself: the Arabic year 587. That Hijri year corresponds to 1191–92 CE. This was the year when Delhi was conquered by Qutbuddin Aibak from the Tomaras and the foundation of the great congregational mosque laid within the walls of the captured fort. Clearly the foundation of Islamic rule in the south of India is seen as having occurred simultaneously at the fortress town of Bidar. Thus the implication is that the grant occurred at the foundational moment for Islamic sovereignty in India and thus acquired an especially sacred character.[41] The Gupte family, whom we considered earlier, harked back to another founder, the first Chatrapati Shivaji. Thus we can see that the Ramoshis and their rivals shared in the larger historical understanding of the region. They also knew that claims to land and office had to be supported with documents—and again, like many others, they sometimes created records to support their tenaciously held beliefs.

DID THE SUBALTERN SPEAK?

In India, as in many traditional societies, literacy was long a mark of elite status. This has heavily skewed the historical record against the utterances of the subaltern classes. The transfer from speech to durable document was most frequent in Western India, where, as we have seen, rights to patrimonial property extended down to the humblest. Furthermore, the important role of local communities in substantiating rights and traditions meant that members of the lower classes were often called on to record evidence. That process, in turn, gave rise to historical narratives.

Rural and small-town life was organized around the structure of village and pargana entitlement and honor. These entitlements extended to the Dalit and tribal communities of the region too. Dalit castes were routinely included in the ranks of village officeholders. Before the imposition of colonial systems of survey, measurement and mapping at the end of the nineteenth century, the Dalit caste of Mahars were required to have a current knowledge of both external village and internal field boundaries, as agricultural land was the major asset in a peasant community. Boundaries, both of the village and of individual fields, were sometimes contested. In such cases, the testimony of the hereditary village servants, the Mahars, was crucial to proving or rejecting claims.[42] Thus Thomas Coats wrote in 1819 that the village *watandar* (office-holding) Mahars were supposed to have an accurate knowledge of boundaries "handed down to them by tradition. In boundary disputes, their evidence is generally considered conclusive; which they are called on to give by walking round the boundary in dispute, under an oath."[43] Dalit village servants would therefore have to continually update their knowledge of the latter as the processes of inheritance, partition, sale, etc. changed the rights of specific farming families. Accumulation of such knowledge, the long-serving official T. N. Atre remarked in 1915, had required constant patrolling of village lands and had been one of the most laborious of their tasks.[44] They were thus living bearers of local historical memory in these matters.

The Mahar community was and is an extremely important segment of the Dalits of Maharashtra. They made vital contributions to Ambedkarite politics from the late nineteenth century to the present.[45] They were traditionally village servants (*balutedār*) and ubiquitously present in rural Maharashtra.[46] They also functioned as living embodiments of the territorial memory, and often referred to as "sons of the earth." Thus the invocation of historical research in a Maharashtrian setting led village servants, peasant proprietors, and great nobles alike to develop coherent narratives of local pasts, narratives that would be rehearsed in formal gatherings as well as, in all likelihood, village discussions.

The subaltern was therefore expected to speak and learned to do so in official settings. Colonial officials were disconcerted by the directness with which even ordinary plebeians asserted their claims. An experienced official, Richard Jenkins, wrote in 1827: "The most remarkable feature perhaps, of the character of the Marhattas, of all descriptions, is the little regard they pay to show or ceremony in the common intercourse of life. *A peasant or mechanic, of the lowest order, appearing before his superiors, will sit down of his own accord, tell his story without ceremony, and converse more like an equal than an inferior; and if he has a petition to present, talks in a loud and boisterous tone, and fearlessly sets forth his claims.*"[47]

Such subaltern self-representation is generally hard to find in the South Asian record. This feature of local political and judicial life in Maharashtra allows me to address the historical self-conceptions and traditions of tribal and Dalit (both subaltern) communities in seventeenth-and eighteenth-century Western India just as I have addressed those of other classes. What follows is, therefore, an effort to answer Gayatri Spivak's famous question "Can the subaltern speak?" She answered: that "subaltern cannot speak.

There is no virtue in global laundry lists with 'woman' as a pious item. Representation has not withered away."[48]

I argue that, on the contrary, they *could* speak and were sometimes unique sources of evidence. The particular circumstances of the regimes of power in Western India have left us with more subaltern utterances than were generated or have survived elsewhere in the subcontinent. The documents show many subalterns representing their hereditary office, lineage, and status over time. The role of lineage representative and village co-sharer is obviously a socially constructed one. They spoke as subalterns but still as recognized members of a community and hereditary heads of their section. Their membership extended down to workers who unquestionably belonged to the subaltern classes, such as potters, carpenters, barbers, and village Mahars. The state not only had an infrastructure to hear their voices, it actually elicited them. I will thus recover the actual historical narratives that tribal and laboring groups constructed and transmitted in past centuries. It may seem that the logical place to start would be modern ethnography or oral history. Such an approach, however, assumes that the historical ideas of subaltern groups are immutable and ageless—a subalternized version of the "unchanging Orient" trope now discarded by contemporary scholarship. The mutability and fallibility of tradition is not a novel finding; many villagers were aware of it.

Subaltern women sometimes spoke loudly enough for even the king to hear them out. Such was the case with the barber-woman of Pargaon. The boys of Ghargaon and Pargaon had gone up to the hills with the cattle of both villages. While there, they amused themselves by forming two teams, Mughals and Marathas, and playing at soldiers. The game went on for five days and turned serious. The "Marathas" beat the "Mughals" and began pursuing them. The barber boy fell face down while running away, burst open his forehead, and died of the wound two weeks later. His mother, the *hajāmīn* (woman barber), complained of the wrongful death to the *qazi* of Ahmadnagar. The latter wrote out a verdict that boys had been fighting and therefore no blood-guilt resulted. But she was unsatisfied. She went to other authorities, complaining of the death. Each complaint then required the headman of Ghargaon and perhaps other villagers to respond to an official summons. The headman finally went to the court of the Chatrapati Shahu to settle the case. The king confirmed the *qazi*'s verdict and instructed the barber-woman and villagers of Pargaon not to agitate the matter further.[49]

Ordinary villagers might often be called to testify. Thus when a dispute arose over the hereditary post of blacksmith and carpenter in Sasvad, the peasant landholders, together with office-holding craftsmen, the gardener, the astrologer, the temple attendant, the Dalit village servants, and the Muslim maulana (priest), were all assembled in the village temple and asked to testify on the matter. The reported age of each witness was recorded: the youngest was forty and the oldest eighty.[50] Every village in Maharashtra had at some time required the holders of these offices to give testimony on contested matters. Older men had probably done so many times. Most such testimonies have perished, but many survive and a quite a few have been printed. One example illustrates that individual memories differed. When the hereditary post of headman of Vadgaon (near Pune) was being litigated, the king asked both sides if they would abide by the verdict of the other hereditary officeholders. Then all of the latter were summoned to court. Five village officeholders (*watandars*)—Būd the gardener; Śivji, son of Koṇḍji the barber; Bajāji, son of Vaḍjoji the washerman; and Rāynāk, son of Sāynāk, and Hansā son of Cāndnāk, both Mahārs—gave depositions of what they knew from their fathers and grandfathers. A less detailed statement was given by Nimbāji son of Janoji, the carpenter and Vaḍjā son of Bahirā, the leather-worker. Older witnesses were found in a second round of depositions: so the narrative of Sukhmāli, son of Santmāli, a man of seventy-five, went back to the time of Sayad Burhan, the earliest village headman, who had vanished during the famine of 1629–30.

The above-mentioned five deposed (literally, "gave in writing") that the headmanship originally belonged to Sayad Burhan; he disappeared during the great famine of 1630. Then Dāvji Dāngaṭ, a landholder in the village managed the position for seven years under the orders of the county officials. Then Hasāji Paṭhārā, a grazier managed it for two years. Then Śivji Dāngaṭ came from another village and, declaring that the post belonged to the Dāngaṭs, took control. He was followed by his son Sūryāji who had six sons. The eldest Sambhāji followed him and the current holder Śankrāji was of that family. "This is what we definitely know." Despite widespread illiteracy, ordinary villagers had thus passed on key elements of a local history from generation to generation. But they also understood the limits to their own knowledge. So Nimbāji, son of Jānoji the carpenter and Vaḍjā, son of Bahirā the leather-worker did not have such a detailed history to offer. They affirmed in writing "our forefathers told us that the post had been held by the Dāngaṭs for three generations. We affirm that at present Śankrāji and Harji Dāngaṭ have the position. We do not know for certain if Devji Dāngaṭ's ancestors ever owned the office, or whether he himself has held it."[51]

Presenting evidence of heroic feats and great sacrifices was also a truly foundational charter in medieval Dakhan, and that evidence too was sometimes supplemented with copper plates. Ancient copper plates might become sacred objects long after their scripts were illegible,[52] but they were still clearly perceived as having some talismanic power. Another set of plates was found by Rajwade in the early twentieth century from the headman of Narvad, a village close to the ancient city of Miraj. The headman believed that it described some great feat of arms performed by one of his ancestors. The copper plate bore no date, and the inscription was (according Rajwade, its editor and publisher) carelessly written, without any of the nasal signs. But the script was Modi and the language archaic Marathi, similar (according to Rajwade) to that used in by the poet Bhanudasa:

> Shamannā Metrī [headman of the] Cabār [caste], Narsoji Metrī, and Ashat Khān Loharī Divān Gājī. Dabad Cabār was walking in the pastureland around the fort. Asat Khān had come to Miraj to build the fort sky-high, but whatever was built in the day collapsed in the night, and the towers began to crumble to ground level. Then Dabad Cabār was buried alive in the foundation and killed with a sharp sword. Then he [*sic*] was given [180 bighas, a large area] of land for consolation to the relatives of the dead man, a building in his name together with collections from the headmen of the different caste sections, a silk woman's dress, and the seven rupees due to the headman in the month of Aśvin. From the town office received [. . . incomprehensible terms], a ceremonial dress and eleven rupees; due from zamindars eleven [rupees?]. To feed the gathering, one large measure of grain. Dated 25 month Zilkad Year 2.[53]

The plate was probably not prepared by a Brahman, as it lacked the usual benediction at the top of the document. It had three square seals imprinted on the top and two more after the last line on the obverse of the document. According to Rajwade, several of these suggest a Virashaiva affiliation for the writer, and it is possible that some of the incomprehensible words in the text derive from Kannada or Telugu. The archaic language suggests the late sixteenth century as the latest likely date for the copper plate.

It is, however, clear that it did not originate in the chancery of any sultan but represents a historical consciousness working to generate authentic evidence for a tenaciously believed claim. The first name in the document is clearly the headman of the Cambhar (leather-worker) community of the township. I think it likely that the effort was to definitely establish the claims of a shrine dedicated to Dabad Cabār to certain specific lands and fees from the township of Miraj. This would explain the absence of any human recipient of the grant; it is to the dead man himself, who is seen as persisting beyond death as a custodian spirit of the ramparts. The author was likely a priest at the shrine, possibly a Virashaiva. We also have blood shed in a foundational moment being invoked in order to legitimate a current claim. The creation of a copper plate was done to authenticate its ancient provenance, at the very moment of foundation. Finally, we may note the narrator's unquestioning acceptance of the arbitrary way in which powerful nobles could cut short the lives of the poor and weak.

Dalits, like every other group in Maharashtrian society, aspired to *watan*, or hereditary patrimony. As mentioned, disputes over it generated much of the documentary record of the region, and Mahars were custodians of village gates and boundaries. In troubled times the patrolman was also a militiaman. This was especially true of those who served at the outposts around a fort. Their chiefs had the hereditary title of "Naik" and were men of status. A dispute over this post at the fort of Rohida was adjudicated in 1746–47 and Khandnak, son of Ramnak, explained how he was descended from a lineage that had served as fort guards from the time of the sultans (1650s?). They lived in villages near the fort. But the Mahar guards migrated, probably along with other villagers, during the time of troubles when Mughal and Maratha armies contended in the area. Two lineages disappeared. Then in 1674, Shivaji was crowned *chatrapati* (king) at Raigad, but there was further disruption, and after order was restored, Ramnak, the appellant's father, went to the (unnamed) king; the latter, having considered previous practice, reestablished eight guard stations and appointed Ramnak to oversee them. But after Ramnak's death, the appellant Khandnak allowed his father-in-law to act on his behalf, who (Khandnak states) then laid claim to the office. Khandnak (like other disputants that we have discussed) cited landmarks and practices as evidence for his claim: a reservoir, a house site, a temple. According to his evidence, after the revival of the office, his father Ramnak was allotted a water reservoir, built a house on the old site, and began working as outpost captain. He died and was buried under the Sarja tower, where a masonry grave marker was still found. Khandnak inherited the post, married, and moved into his father-in-law Bhojnak's house. After some time, Bhojnak persuaded Khandnak to allow him to officiate as captain. "Then differences emerged between us, and Bhojnak started a dispute. My father and, after him, I used to receive the head of the buffalo sacrificed at Dasera, but now Bhojnak began to take it. I protested and so now they have started burying the head in front of the temple of the Mother Goddess near the gateway."[54]

A similar foundational document was invoked by the Mahars of Sasvad, who had long claimed the traditional fifty-two rights. In the early nineteenth century, they produced a detailed document about this, of which framing narrative excerpts follow:

> Śrī
>
> Copy of a copy
>
> The Badshah's [initial] seal and terminal seal and the entries written in the hand of Damaji Pant Karkun. . . . Shets, Patils, Kulkarnis, Deshmukhs, and Deshpandes, and the twelve classes of village servants and the *qazi* and imam from Bedar and Ramji Patil and those of Delhi and Miraj, Khando Patil—under the gaze of all these and that of the headmen and accountants of the four quarters details [follow] . . .
>
> Thus the date Śake 1051 (1127–28 CE) Shravan bright half 13th day, Sunday, the paper was issued—attested Khando Narayan Kulkarni Dikshit Paithankar—at the camp of Pune attested by the honorable English general and Elphinstone sahib and Rabeson [Robertson?] sahib—if anyone wishes to contest this let him to go Pune and try.
>
> —This is a copy of a copy—copied according to order (exactly)[55]

This text clearly represented itself as written during early British rule: Mountstuart Elphinstone was the first commissioner administering the territory annexed in 1818, and H. D. Robertson was the Collector of Poona district under him. But it seeks to found itself deeply in the legendary history of Maharashtra, going back to the time of the last Hindu dynasty. It also founds itself on the authority of a hereditary official from Paithan, a Hindu sacred center often invoked as a southern Banaras. It also invokes Damaji Pant and his master, the Muslim Padshah of Bidar, and Islamic law officers under the latter. Overall, therefore, the authors were aware of the successive regimes that had governed the region and had a loose idea of their eras. Other documents of the late eighteenth or early nineteenth century also follow this pattern.[56]

Overall, then, what can we recover of the historical consciousness that underlay the documents we have been scrutinizing? There was, first of all, a telescoping process: various Islamic emperors were all rolled into one figure located in a single city. Equally, legitimate claims were those that came from him; we find no mention of previous rulers. In a way, the Islamic epoch was a yuga (eon) in itself, a new era in which all things began afresh. At least in Maharashtra, the rise of Shivaji Raje and his coronation (1674 CE) were similarly imprinted on the folk imagination. In conformity with the instrumental ends of such narration, authors were concerned with effective power rather than religious identity.

How did the historical consciousness of subaltern groups in India relate to that of other social classes? To begin with, there was a striking similarity in origin and purpose between elite and subaltern history. Subalterns too began to develop concrete narratives of past time in order to justify and contest claims in the present. They too used the legitimating strategy of harking back to the Padshah of Bidar as the founder of Islamic rule; they also introduced well-known themes from hagiographic tradition, as well as local monuments and markers in support of their claims. All of these would have been modes of authentication comprehensible to any village or district assembly in the region.

But we can also find differences in narrative expressive of the power relations in which different social groups were embedded. The Kolis and Ramoshis still wielded considerable military power. They controlled the environs of strategic fortresses and could threaten to devastate large tracts of country or block trade routes. They were, as I have shown elsewhere, extremely important in regional politics.[57] Their narratives reflect this role: they are stories of manly service and rich rewards; Dalit claims were often more modest.

Both the classes of subaltern narrative discussed are therefore realistic in that they connect the actual situation to the feasible aspirations of the people who generated them. New circumstances and new perceptions caused them to be made afresh. Subaltern groups drew on traditions and resources available to them to create social spaces for themselves under the constraints that larger social structures imposed on them. The evidence bears out Gautam Bhadra's observation that it would be an error "to think that there could be no exchange or sharing of ideals or ideas between classes, or that classes, even when they are in conflict, did not learn from each other."[58]

NATIONAL PROJECTS, MEMORY, AND FORGETTING

Spearheaded by the Bhosle dynasty, Maratha power rose within the frame of the sultanates of South India. Babaji Bhosle was an important chief under the early Nizamshahi sultans of Ahmadnagar. Shahaji Bhosle, father of the Chatrapati Shivaji, was a prominent Maratha noble whose career also began under the Nizamshahi sultanate of Ahmadnagar. In the early seventeenth century, the reduced remnant of this sultanate was controlled by Malik Ambar, who masterminded a decades-long resistance to the encroachments of the Mughal emperors from the north. Malik Ambar's crowning achievement was his victory at Bhatwadi in 1624. His army defeated the powerful southern Sultanate of Bijapur even though it was supported by an army sent by the Mughal emperor Jahangir. This remarkable victory utilized Maratha light cavalry to hamstring and ultimately rout the Mughal force. Those horsemen were raised and commanded by men from several Maratha gentry families, and Shahaji Raje, was one of the more prominent leaders.[59]

Malik Ambar died in 1626. Shahaji for some years led an effort to place an infant sultan on the throne and himself rule as regent, as Malik Ambar had done. The effort ultimately failed. In 1637, Shahaji was compelled by the joint pressure of the Mughals and the Adilshahi sultanate to accept the status of an Adilshahi jagirdar (military fief-holder). He spent the last decades of his life in central Karnataka warring with local chiefs as well as Qutbshahi commanders.[60] His son, Shivaji Raje, crowned himself *chatrapati* in 1674 and founded a powerful state. After withstanding decades of effort to crush them, the Marathas came to an accommodation with the Mughal Empire in 1719. They accepted the notional suzerainty of the Mughal emperors but increasingly functioned as an independent power across all parts of India. Maratha power then expanded to contend for effective control of much of the subcontinent by the mid-eighteenth century. They sought to use the Mughal emperors as a source of authority and legitimacy, even as they took effective control of much of South Asia.

These processes shaped memory and forgetting. I will show how memory was constructed around the project of inheriting the legitimacy and power of the Islamicate empires, especially the Mughal Empire. This served to connect with the most defiant of the Rajput lineages in the Mughal era, the famous Sisodiya Ranas of Mewar (in today's Rajasthan). This was already suggested in the panegyric to Shahaji Raje by composed by Jayaram Pindye in the 1650s, two generations earlier. The claimed connection between this dynasty and the Bhosle line was highlighted by Krishnaji Anant Sabhasad in the 1690s. His *bakhar* represents the Amber ruler, Jai Singh as sending a message to Chatrapati Shivaji saying, "You are a Śisode Rajput. You and I are verily as one. Come and negotiate." The genealogy was reemphasized in discussion of the royal coronation, where Gagabhat (aka Vishweshwara), a famous pandit from Banaras is said to have established that the Bhosles were descended from the only Sisodiya lineage to have come to the south.[61]

Factually oriented narratives also came to serve the identity of the Marathas as a rising regional and subcontinental elite. The above-cited officials of Anjanvel certainly saw the coronation of the Maratha sovereign Shivaji in 1674 as an epoch-making event. That act was the culmination of a campaign that both drew on and reinforced local and regional patriotism. He succeeded in founding an independent kingdom that survived a full-scale Mughal assault in the last 25 years of the Mughal emperor Aurangzeb's reign. The introductory chapter to the experienced minister Ramacandra Pant's treatise on statecraft was written in 1717. It began: "This is the kingdom that was assailed by a powerful enemy like [the Mughal emperor] Aurangzeb and still beat him back. Aurangzeb focused all his forces and expended all his resources against it, but failed to conquer; bootless, disheartened he took himself off to the land of death. And Aurangzeb was master of fifty-four kingdoms; endowed with wealth and soldiers second to none, of whom it was famously said 'either the lord of Delhi or the lord of the world' [are patrons comparable in wealth]."[62]

Dynastic identity thus merged with and built on regional pride, and the protean *bakhar* was turned to yet another narrative: the construction of a common glorious past. But it then began to diverge from the need to make a defensible argument that had constrained early narrators.

One of the most famous early historical *bakhar*s—that detailing the life and deeds of Chatrapati Shivaji—was written in 1694, during the hard days of the struggle with the Mughal emperor Aurangzeb, whose armies had overrun most of Maharashtra. Sabhasad, its author, framed the text as an answer to Chatrapati Rajaram's question: "My father achieved great feats of arms, confronted four empires—such was his valor. That being so, how has Aurangzeb been able to come and wreck fort after fort? You are an old and knowledgeable servant of the state—write an account of his [Shivaji's] deeds [*caritra*] from the very beginning."[63] Significantly enough, the text, while opening with an invocation of the deeds of the founder-hero, ends by speaking in terms of a regional patria ruled by a *Maratha* king: "He proclaimed his dominance from the Narmada river up to Ramesvara [the traditional southern extremity of India] and conquered the land. Adalshai, Kutubshai, Nizamshai, Moglai—these four empires as well as the twenty-two empires from beyond the seas were kept in check and a new empire founded; a Maratha Padshah seated himself on the throne as a chatrapati." It is perhaps not without significance that, while the work opens by describing itself as a *caritra* (biography), the closing sentences refer to it as a *bakhar*. The Maratha identity had been foregrounded from at least the 1670s, when a dependent of the newly crowned Chatrapati Shivaji wrote a Sanskrit epic on his career. It begins with Shahaji Raje's grandfather, Malavarman, who is emphatically described as a Maratha king ruling in Maharashtra.[64] The identity was also extensively invoked by Bhosle rulers during the darkest periods of the war with the Mughals.[65]

As we have already seen, the Marathi-speaking gentry had long written or dictated narrative histories for consumption in the regional political arena. They now expanded their horizons, aiming to dominate the peninsula and ultimately the entire Indian subcontinent. This added a fresh layer of macro-narratives to the local and particular histories that continued to be compiled. So, in 1813, we find a manuscript that applies the same term to what is clearly seen as a Maratha national history: *Svarājya mhanoñ Maharāṣṭarāje ajruyī bakhar*—a literal translation would be "the authentic history of our kingdom, that is, of the Maharashta kingdom."[66] The change first identified by Prachi Deshpande had occurred, and we now also need to view the *bakhar*s as "a popular historical memory of the Maratha political and military exploits."[67] The qualification that I would add to this formulation of the link between Maratha power and the *bakhar* genre is that only some select macro-*bakhar*s worked primarily with that goal, and a large number continued to build narratives centered on lesser lineages and local disputes, as well as the lives of worthy and holy personages and their doings.

Grant Duff, the first serious colonial historian of the Marathas, also used the longer *bakhar*s as a source.[68] He drew especially from one compiled at the beginning of the nineteenth century by Ramrao Chitnis, the hereditary holder of the office of secretary to the Maratha kings.[69] They continued to be written well after the imposition of colonial rule and the beginnings of Western education, and they differed little from the developed *bakhar*s of the eighteenth century. The loss of political power now seems to have sustained efforts at recording the past. Krishnaji Sohoni served the Maratha regime in its last decades; he subsequently became an ascetic and lived in the holy town of Vaijnatha, where his narrative of the period when the Brahman ministers were ascendant (c. 1720–1818) became sufficiently popular for at least two persons to compile it into history. Sohoni and presumably most of his audience were Brahmans, and their historical assessment is summed up in the disillusioned epilogue to the story:

> God granted a boon that Brahmans should rule the earth for a hundred years [even] in the Dark Age (*Kaliyuga*). This is in the Puranas and the words of [the ancient seer] Vyasa. So it happened. In Śake 1635 [1712–13] the

> Peśvas' government came into being; in Śake 1739 the kingdom fell. Until the time of Savai Madhavrao the kingdom was dominant. All its enemies lay underfoot with folded hands. Then, after Bajirao Raghunath came to the throne [1796], there were no more campaigns and expeditions, and the ruler saw no need to maintain armies. And so the present state of things has come about.[70]

It was clearly imprudent to say more.

Early colonial efforts to settle land tenure and limit tax exemptions also stimulated the writing of additional histories by landed families that needed to explain and justify their claims. Furthermore, as recently demonstrated in a penetrating article by Phillip Wagoner, early colonial narratives and reports were underpinned by the paleographic and linguistic work of traditional scholars, who often also wrote short histories.[71] Selections from this information were then seamlessly assimilated into the master narratives constructed in the colonial reports that provided the templates for most colonial history. We can see this happening by, for example, comparing the manuscript reports of Richard Jenkins's assistant Vinayakrao and Jenkins's own *Report on the Territories of the Rajah of Nagpore*.[72] The latter, in turn, was used in a multitude of colonial histories through the next century.

But now the new intelligentsia had to confront an inescapably powerful colonial tradition of history-writing. The responses to colonial history soon moved beyond oblique attacks such as that made in the last pages of Sohoni's *bakhar*. The new nationalist consciousness began to dovetail into an all-India narrative without losing its strong regional pride. At the same time, pride and interest in local history remained powerful.

Maharashtra- and Maratha-dominated states elsewhere also had recent memories of political greatness and a strong sense of identity that has survived powerfully into the present. The evolution of this identity in literature and history from the seventeenth century to the present is the subject of a brilliant monograph by Prachi Deshpande, a work indispensable to anyone who wants to understand this major Indian region. As Deshpande describes, "the pervasive presence of the past" is one of the most striking features of the public life of Maharashtra.[73] The claim to factual history has become a central part of the identity of the Marathi-speaking people, often strongly associated with the glorification of Shivaji, the first *chatrapati* and founder of the Maratha kingdom, or *Swarāj*. Its beginnings, like much else in the history of modern Maharashtra, go back to the seventeenth century. Sabhasad wrote a history of his recently deceased sovereign, the Chatrapati Shivaji, between

1694 and 1697. He remarked on the historic significance of the latter's imperial coronation: "A Marāṣta king mounted the throne as emperor (*chatrapati*)."[74] Nor was this just an encomium from an ardent royalist. British officials with long experience in India observed the same phenomenon. Almost a century later, the British Governor-General Warren Hastings was sailing to England soon after a long and bruising war against the Marathas. Musing upon affairs in the subcontinent, he wrote in 1786 that "the Mahrattas possess alone, of all the peoples of Indostan and Decan, a principle of national attachment which is strongly impressed on the minds of all individuals of the nation, and would probably unite their chiefs as in one common cause, if any great danger were to threaten the general state."[75]

What Hastings termed the "general state" was the Maratha *Swarāj*. The term *Swarāj* (literally, "own kingdom") became widely current through the eighteenth century, and while it sometimes only signaled the separation of authority and taxation in areas held as a condominium with the Nizam of Hyderabad, it also came to refer to the larger political formation dominated by Marathi-speaking warriors. Inside the softer boundaries of imperial claims was the hard definition of the "original kingdom" of the Maratha *chatrapatis*. A specific list of 252 subdivisions (parganas) that formed the home territory of the Maratha kings existed at least as early as 1720, when control over it was specified in a treaty with the Mughal emperors. Divisions were always present and had gone deep by 1802, when aggression by Jaswant Rao Holkar led the last peshwa to join hands with the British. But Holkar still hoped to mobilize Maratha solidarity to oppose the rising British. He wrote to a minor chief in 1803: "Due to [our] internal conflicts, the state (*daulat*) has been trapped and the foreign power has been emboldened to encroach on it. I came to the country [i.e., the Maratha home country, the *deś*] because of that and now seek to reassure the Śrīmant [peshwa] so as to end internal disputes, so that everyone can be united (*ekdil*) to consolidate the *śvarāj* and beat back the outsider."[76]

Nor was this a purely elite attitude. This is also noted by Elphinstone in his *Report*: the "Marratta peasantry have some pride in the triumphs of their nation and some ambition to partake in its military exploits."[77] This enmeshing of history and identity was unique in South Asia at the time.

FORGETTING VIJAYANAGARA

The opening chapters of this book addressed the issue of the institution of social memory. The preceding part of this chapter has looked at how the judicial settings of debates around the past meant that the invocation and critique of evidence became more deeply embedded in Maharashtra than elsewhere in South Asia. This rest of this chapter will reflect on what Maratha tradition chose *not* to embed in social memory. Not every past record was preserved or reconstructed. Indeed, historical memory is founded upon selective preservation and recall.[78] Pronouncing on nationhood in the era when ethnic and civic nationalisms jostled in Europe, Ernest Renan declared that "the essence of a nation is that all its citizens have many things in common, but also that they have forgotten a good many things."[79] This section will make this argument by studying how little memory of the great empire of Vijayanagara remained in the Marathi tradition in the centuries after that empire began its terminal decline after 1600. Records too disappeared as part of this process. This meant that later efforts at "remembering" could not find resources within the tradition and either gave up or relied on the common stock of Indic imaginative literature.

Legends about the great empire of Vijayanagara loomed large in popular and scholarly memory in South India for centuries after its passing. Legends about it crop up in many of the "local histories" collected by Colin Mackenzie's assistants around 1800. Its prominence could also lead to the careful construction of spurious narratives of its time, such as the *Rayavacakamu* so brilliantly analyzed by Wagoner,[80] who convincingly shows that faraway rulers of Madura were still enthralled by Vijayanagara fifty years after its fall, and an elaborate narrative was generated to link them to that empire. But the memory of Vijayanagara was not merely current among courtly literati. The name of Ramaraja (sometimes Rama Raya), its last ruler, also entered folk memory and crops up in some of the village histories and local histories collected for Mackenzie. Some were excerpted in the *Sources* and *Further Sources of Vijayanagar History*.[81] The city's fame (under the name Vidyanagara) extended to Bengal, where an anonymous devotee of Chaitanya (the founder of an important school of Krishna worship) composed a narrative about the latter's supposed southern travels. It was clearly written well after the period it purports to describe, because it includes Chaitanya meeting with the king, Pratapa Rudra—probably intended to be the ruler of Warangal deposed by the Tughlaqs in 1323! But the holy man also met Rama Raya (probably intended to be the regent of Vijayanagara, who was killed at Talikota in 1565). The latter is, however, represented as being a minister of the Warangal king: "From Rāipur, Chaitanya came to Vidyānagara, the town where Rāma Rāy, the minister of Pratāpa Rudra, lived. Chaitanya asked him to accompany him to Purī. Rāma Rāy said that important state business would keep him there for a few days more, but he would meet Chaitanya at Purī shortly."[82]

Common folk, like a community of barbers, might also explain a tax exemption by invoking the kings of Vijayanagara. So, for example, when the barbers of Utukuru in the district of Pottapinadu had to justify their tax exemption to the East India Company, they explained that "Koṇḍōjū, the barber gave Rāmarāja such a clean and comfortable shave at Vijayanagara that he won the royal approbation. Rāmarāja granted him graciously a charter as mark of his approbation of Koṇḍōjū's workmanship." The barbers were exempted from two taxes they had formerly paid.[83]

Vijayanagara was clearly a name to conjure with in the lands south of the Tungabhadra River. It was invoked to lend a unique sanctity and antiquity to local claims. Still, successor kingdoms gradually lost most concrete memory of the empire that Rama Raya had ruled until his death in battle in 1565. Robert Sewell (1866–1926), a Madras Presidency Indian Civil Service officer who became a historian of South India, referred to what he considered the absence of indigenous Hindu tradition when he titled his book *A Forgotten Empire*.[84]

Maratha memories of the same empire were scanty, despite the fact that the Bhosle regime was to campaign in and govern large parts of former Vijayanagara lands. If Shahaji Raje's panegyrist Jayaram Pindye is to be believed, one of those defeated by him was the Rayalu of Vidyanair (Vidyanagara, sixteenth-century synonym of Vijayanagara). The poet claims that the warrior caste of Vidyanair lost all shame and fled, abandoning their strongholds.[85] Following the retreat of the Mughals in the early eighteenth century, Maratha rulers were established in or sought to conquer a significant part of the former territory of that empire. A Bhosle dynasty ruled from the ancient city of Thanjavur, and the *chatrapati*'s warlords were striving to build appanages for themselves from the Krishna to Ramnad. In this they were reviving the example of Shahaji Bhosle half a century earlier. There can be little doubt that many of the same administrator-Brahman families served both the Nayaka successors of Vijayanagara and their Maratha competitors (not to mention other local rulers).

But Maratha historical memory was largely impervious to the appeal of Vijayanagara as a repository of ancestral glory. Indeed, while Jayaram Pindye had at least been aware of the legend linking Vidyaranya with the founding of Vijayanagara[86]—hence his adoption of Vidyanagara or Vidyanair as its name—later generations of Marathi speakers even forgot both famous names and referred to the kingdom of "Anagondi." Anagondi is a still-extant town on the northern bank of the Tungabhadra River, about five kilometers from the ruined city of Vijayanagara itself. A tradition reported by Nuniz in the early sixteenth century was that Deva Raya (Harihara?) lived in the fort there before moving upriver to found Vijayanagara. Anagondi was evidently a suburb of the great city in the days of its prosperity. In the eighteenth century, it was the seat of a local *rayalu*, or petty king, claiming descent from the Aravidu dynasty of Vijayanagara.[87] This ruler was recognized as the heir to Vijayanagara in Maratha tradition, but few concrete memories of that empire survived.

This is evidenced in the following entries in J. T. Molesworth's early (1831, 1857) *Dictionary* of the Marathi language. Molesworth lived and worked in Western India for several decades. He was assisted by the well-known orientalist John Wilson, John and Thomas Candy, and a team of seven local pandits. The compilers began by employing Brahmans to collect words and phrases "in several quarters of the Maratha territory." These were then scrutinized by a group of seven or eight other Brahmans and finally checked by other Indian scholars sitting with either Molesworth or one of the Candy brothers.[88] The entry for Anagondi in it is therefore a very good indication of the state of learned Marathi historical memory in the early nineteenth century:

> Anagondi *a[djective]* (From the name of a town of which, as the legend runs, the king or Raja used to call himself *sarvabhauma* or sovereign paramount, and divert himself with entering the revenues of the whole earth on the credit side of his ledger, expending them off again on the debit side.) Applied variously to as *Anagondi karkhana-karbhar-kharch-bak-sis-bolnem* &c. Disorderly business of proceedings; vast and foolish expenditures; lavish largesses or presents; wild extravagant speech &c. 2 *A[nagondi]ce rajya n[oun]* A name for any very confused and disorderly business or proceeding. *A[nagondi]ca raja m. A term for a soft fellow ready to give whatever is asked from him.*[89]

Going beyond the pandits who assisted Molesworth, we have separate evidence from the list of authoritative Sanskrit law books known to the Pandits of Pune as prepared by Vamana Shastri Satya "and corrected by reference to the Hindoo College and other Brahmuns who attended the distribution of the Dukshuna in 1825." It lists the "Madhwu," said to have been written about a thousand years ago (i.e., 800 CE!) by "Sayunacharya or Widyaruneswamee [Vidyaranya svami], a Sunyasee Brahmun of Anagoondy," and "Nundurajakrit, by Nunduraja of Anagoondy, of the Kshutryu caste."[90]

The decay of memory set in early. This is shown by a probably forged Sanskrit document produced by a learned Brahman family, the Padhyes of Golavalli around 1600 as evidence in a lawsuit. The Sanskrit text claimed to be a judicial verdict from Śake 1285 (1362–63) and alluded to the rule of a Yadava Ramaraja—obviously an impossible echo of Ramacandradeva of the Yadava dynasty, who had died in 1312 while a vassal of the Khalji sultans of Delhi. But the Marathi verdict rendered in 1600 seems to view it as a document originating from the much more recent Ramaraja of Vidyanagara or the Aliya Rama Raju killed in 1565![91] The Sardesai family who contested the Padhyes' claim also invoked the authority of Vidyanagara (Vijayanagara) but claimed their original grant came from Bukkanna, who, they declared, ruled the whole of South India up to the Narmada River. They at any rate knew the name of an early Vijayanagara monarch, even if they exaggerated his territories.[92] It is striking that both these literati lineages had little actual knowledge of the true history and chronology of the empire, or indeed of the Yadava dynasty of Devagiri that had ruled most of Maharashtra for two centuries.

These fading memories baffled the rare scholars who looked for some narrative of that empire. This is evident in a compilation of Marathi verses in a manuscript belonging to Satipa Kondkar, a resident of Loni in the Kadevala district. The manuscript was copied in 1738–39. It briefly narrates the story of Vidyanagara being founded under the patronage of the sage Vidyaranya, mentions some of the successive rulers, and states that Sadashiva, son of Acyuta, moved the capital from Vidyanagara to Anagondi. His son was Rama, who was unskilled in war and given to dissipation. Dandu, the Turk lord, was stupid by nature and could not learn Kannada. He knew that the emperor went on fixed days to bathe in the Krishna-tirtha at Rakshat-gadhi [*sic*]. He gathered three others and they killed the king with their swords. The king's army was left leaderless and was overcome by the Adal, Kutubaraya, and Nizamashaha in 1354 [1431–32 CE] *paradhavi abda*, on the fifth day in the bright half of Magha. But the author then adds, "the original manuscript is old and damaged; it does not match [other] evidence." He then provides three Sanskrit chronograms and Marathi verses, presumably from other manuscripts, which give three alternative dates. All of them are wrong. It is evident that the event was remembered only by its astrological conjunction, that is, by the month, day, and year of the sixty-year cycle.[93] Satipa's text represents a later attempt to work out the exact year. The author had clearly made a considerable effort at reconstructing the date of the fall of Vijayanagara. But he evidently found few resources in Marathi or Sanskrit beyond a simple dynastic list and a tale of Muslim treachery.

Likewise in the later eighteenth century, the Marathi narrative of the rise of the Bhosle kings—the *Shivadigvijaya*—stated that Ramaraja left for the south, after nominating a (nameless) merchant (*vaiśya*) to rule in his place. Six Yavana (Muslim) youths who had been raised by Ramaraja then decided to usurp the empire: they imprisoned the merchant and divided it among themselves, founding kingdoms at Anagondi, Bijapur, Bhaganagar (Hyderabad), Daulatabad, Amdabad, and Nagpur.[94] In this version, even the last Hindu ruler of Anagondi was now classed as a parvenu merchant, if not a usurper! The author clearly believed that the six subahs, or governorships, of the South in late Mughal times represented the original six parts into which the Vijayanagara Empire was divided but did not have an accurate list of these even as they had existed under Aurangzeb (d. 1707). So he extemporized by inserting the names of prominent cities of his own time, which was almost certainly after 1750 and probably nearer 1800.

A similar disregard was shown by the Maratha successors of Vijayanagara even in lands that had been important parts of that empire. In 1803, the last Bhosle Maratha ruler of Thanjavur had his personal secretary Bāburāya compose a long family history in Marathi that was then inscribed on the wall of the Brihadīśvara temple in that city. Vijayanagara-era frescoes still survive within the temple.[95] Yet even this southern ruler with a multilingual court slighted Vijayanagara in his origin myth.[96] Vijayanagara as point of origin—so important for many rulers of the same region—is here spurned in favor of an origin in Maharashtra and consequent affiliation to the anonymous Persianate *padshaha*.

In sum, therefore, the Maratha imperium invented little and knew less about their predecessors in the southern peninsula. Vijayanagara as point of origin does appear in an exceptionally contrarian narrative: the anonymous late eighteenth-century *More yanci choti bakhar*, glorifying the founding *chatrapati*'s enemy, Chandrarao More of Javli. It is probably a part of this contrarian stance that causes the text to state that all the noble Maratha lineages were originally in the service of Krishnadevaraya at "Vidyanagara." So, it adds, were those who were later to become sultans: Ibrahim, Ali Yedilshaha, and Bahirinizam [*sic*]. Ibrahim [Qutbshah] was appointed governor of Telangana and when out hunting on the banks of the Musi River encountered a hare that attacked his hunting dogs. He then founded Golkunda.[97] Vijayanagara finds no further mention in this narrative.

To sum up then, Maratha power as represented by the Bhosle dynasty rose within the frame of the sultanates of South India. In 1719, the declining Mughal Empire tacitly ceded the Marathas a condominium of the regions south of the Narmada River. With the further decline of Mughal power, Maratha generals extended theirs northward, securing effective control of the Mughal emperor by the 1770s. Memory was constructed around the project of inheriting the legitimacy and power of that empire. Vijayanagara was slighted.

We find similar failures of memory when we turn to local records kept by district hereditary recordkeepers. These were appointed custodians of local memory all over the subcontinent. Once again, we find that precious little of the great empire had passed into Maratha historical memory. Thus in 1823–24, the officials of the Anjanvel subdivision in southern Konkan were required to compile a detailed memorandum of the past revenue administration of their district. The memorandum shows considerable knowledge of past tax rates and practices and was clearly based on both memory and written records going back several centuries. They only had some hazy tradition of a "Kanada Ramaraja" as being an ancient ruler of their region: "Ali Idalshah and Bahiri Nizyamshah these two brothers killed the Kanada Ramaraja in the camp of Anagondi and seated Ali Idalshah on the throne of Vijyapur *san salas [3] tisa [and 9] maya [100] Śake* 1424 [1501–2 CE] *samvatsara* Dundubhi."[98]

As must be evident, little information had been transmitted through the centuries. The dates are wrong, and it is clear that the authors knew nothing of the great empire beyond its existence at some point in the hazy past and that "Ramaraja" had ruled it. This profound indifference was found even among the most learned. Historical memory of Vijayanagara was lost and proved irrecoverable even when actively sought. This is evident in the scantiness of the information available in a Marathi text produced at the end of the eighteenth century. This was copied into a set of Modi manuscripts that were then bound and transported to the India Office. There is no author name or colophon to this portion of the text; it is titled simply *Anego[n]dīcī kefiyat* and occupies five folios in a neat scribal hand, written on both sides of the paper. Wagoner has suggested in a personal communication that it might have been written at the instance of, or by Mackenzie's assistant Narain Rao, who was in the Bellari region in 1806–7.[99]

I published a free translation in 2009, and will therefore only comment on some important features here. It was written by a *karaṇam* (clerk) knowledgeable in Marathi and associated with the household of a claimant to Vijayanagara ancestry. The audience was clearly the British government: perhaps the object was to make a case for some claim in the aftermath of Tipu's defeat by the British in 1799. By this time, any clerk in touch with

Mackenzie or other administrators of the Madras Presidency would have known how important strict chronology and "factual" narration were for the new colonial government. One would expect every available historical resource to be deployed in these circumstances. Yet we can easily see that the writer had no information at his disposal beyond two legendary names. The folk tradition about the tax revenues of the earth being allotted in a fantasy ledger kept by the Anagondi raja is clearly echoed in the closing paragraph: "In our forefathers' time, the account papers for the entire realm of the South used to be regularly prepared." So the best that this *karaṇam* historian could do was to produce a rather thin pastiche of folklore and wonder-tale. There can be no better indication of how historical memory had decayed even in the heartland of the empire. Even those who most urgently needed to produce a convincing narrative lacked the evidence to do so. And that brings up a recurring point in this book: the preservation of a fraction of the immense world of human experience in the historical record depends on choices and resources, or else it perishes irretrievably.

These are among the very few Marathi historical sources that mention Vijayanagara at all. The deeply learned Datto Vamana Potdar was forced to end his survey of the Marathi sources with an expression of chagrin at the confused and obscure state of their knowledge of Vijayanagara: "In today's light this can only be a source of astonishment and regret. . . . It is our duty now to remedy the errors of the past."[100] He approached Vijayanagara from a different perspective than the eighteenth-century literati had done. Some later historians have been less cautious. A late expatriate effort to find yet another indigenous historical practice was made by V. Narayana Rao, David Shulman, and Sanjay Subrahmanyam in 2001.[101] They set out to "recover as history a significant body of literature from late medieval and early modern South India." This was to be done by reading texts exclusively through South Indian "society's visions and understandings of the past." The bearers of these visions were identified as members of the clerical classes (*karaṇams*). Relevant texts could be identified as factual by those (presumably the three authors) who are "at home in a culture have a natural sensitivity to texture. They *know* when the past is being treated in a factual manner."[102] This sensitivity (gullibility?) allowed them to paraphrase several late and fantastic narratives as "history." They were, as Sheldon Pollock wrote, misled into thinking the past was available to them, "altogether unmediated."[103] In fact, it never is.

This chapter explains how the social and political setting of early modern Maharashtra generated a unique genre of collective memory across the Marathi-speaking ecumene. The early emergence of a regional historical tradition in the Marathi language is explained by its social setting: strong and diverse local communities had demanded "commonsense" proofs even as the clerical intelligentsia sought documents and records. Thus narratives of this type had their beginnings in two related sources: lawsuits tried by the local community and inquests by incoming royal authority. By analyzing the setting of these narratives through the past six centuries, we gain a new perspective on the generative relations between the social framework on the one hand, and historical traditions and practices on the other.[104] But such narratives mutated as they became enmeshed in the Maratha imperial project of the eighteenth century before changing once again when their dominion was subverted by the incoming British.[105] Nonetheless, as C. H. Philips wrote, Marathi "alone among the mother tongues has carried over from its seventeenth century *bakhar* chronicles a fairly strong historical tradition."[106]

4 History and Memory through the Nineteenth and Twentieth Centuries

THE CONSTRUCTION OF NATIONAL PASTS TO REPLACE THE MANY local and community ones became a global anxiety in the nineteenth century. This anxiety began among the German intelligentsia in the eighteenth century and naturally intensified when almost all Europe was swiftly conquered, if but briefly ruled, by the Napoleonic Empire. It spread worldwide as Asia and Africa were slowly engulfed by Western empires. Western historical practice itself took institutional shape in the century after the French Revolution, an epoch marked by global imperialisms that were driven by metropolitan nationalisms, and soon opposed by emergent ones. As François Furet described it, history now became "the genealogical tree of European nations and of the civilization they bore."[1] The recovery of a historical past really gained significance with the worldwide spread of Western power in the nineteenth century. Its authenticity now had to be proved to the satisfaction of a wider community of historians supported by multiple states and universities. That meant that standards tended to converge on demanding authentic contemporary sources.

Demand often called forth supply. So in the early nineteenth century, some anonymous Czech patriot forged a set of allegedly ninth-century manuscripts. These were intended to demonstrate the antiquity of the language and nation as against the cultural and politically dominant German establishment.[2] In the British Isles, the long-suppressed strain of Welsh nationalism seized on medieval texts for an alternative narrative of the region's past.[3] Indeed, subregional pride led an early scholar of Welsh to forge a considerable body of texts in order to exalt the status of his native county, Glamorgan, as against the more celebrated North Wales.[4]

Securing claims to antiquity and continuity was even more important in the non-Western world, and nationalists were eager to recover and represent their own history. To be a nation, and not (as Winston Churchill famously described India) "merely a geographical expression," it was now necessary to have a historical consciousness expressed in a national history. As Prasenjit Duara has noted, "National history secures for the contested and contingent nation the false unity of the self-same, national subject evolving through time."[5]

The sudden rise of the West to near total dominance therefore created a crisis in historiography as in other fields of culture.[6] The eastern Mediterranean was first to feel this impact. The new national historiography began in Egypt but soon spread across the Arab world. After the French invasion of Algeria in 1830, French scholars made great efforts to recover the pre-Islamic past of the region. But their historical narrative showed the native peoples of the area as helpless victims of successive foreign civilizations. It consequently legitimized French rule and provoked a strong response from the local intelligentsia. They also turned to the same sources as the Europeans but claimed the Carthaginians as kin and allies of the local people. They represented the Arab conquest (complete by 700 CE) as a time when North Africa regained its true identity, a time when Arab and Berber all joined together in the glorious venture of Islam. Only the Byzantines and Romans were labeled enemies of the indigenes. This was an obvious parallel to the French. Thus North African "historians began to articulate an image of the long-forgotten past in national terms. They used the structure of French scholarship and turned its prototypes upside down."[7]

Across the colonized world, therefore, the power of Western narrative could not be denied, but chinks in it could be sought so as to turn it against the colonizer. Southern Africa felt the power of Europe much later than the north but had a similar response. "African historians turned to the past primarily to unearth the knowledge of greatness and to use the evidence to build sentiments of pride and nationalism."[8] In order to escape the domination of Western writing about Africa, its historians pioneered the use of oral sources, a practice that has now gained far wider acceptance in the academic profession.[9]

Even the matchless historical tradition of China had to be recast for the new epoch. Elman describes how institutions and libraries in the agrarian core of China were devastated by the Taiping Rebellion. The scholarly classes' self-confidence was also shattered by successive defeats by foreign powers. So, what China needed, the leading intellectual Hu Shih wrote in 1914, was: "1. the principle of inductive reasoning; 2. a sense of historical perspective; 3. the concept of progress."[10] Chinese historians had long characterized their writing as "national history," but Edward Wang shows that the term acquired a new meaning in the hands of early twentieth-century intellectuals. He argues that this modernizing intelligentsia was inspired by the novel Japanese definition of "national essence." For them, therefore, "historical study constituted an effective medium" through which to present the national characteristics of China's cultural tradition. But some of them argued that the Chinese people's lack of understanding of their own national essence was a problem that needed remedy. The influential Huang Chun-Chieh argued that the recovery of the national essence needed to reach back before the Qin dynasty, or over two thousand years. It was there that the early intellectuals found elements for the construction of the modern nation. But they rejected traditional historiography because of its deficiencies. The net effect of these, they declared, was that China had no adequate model of history writing. Teng Shih wrote "[w]ithout history there will be no scholarship and without scholarship there will be no national state."[11] This nation-building role for history was echoed by other leading members of the new intelligentsia. Liang Qichao wanted a new historiography to understand the laws of social evolution, promote nationalism, and "thereby ensure the survival of the Chinese people in the fierce competition of the nations of the world." He declared that without "a revolution in history, there would be no hope for the survival of our nation."[12] This was an anxiety shared across the non-Western world at the beginning of the twentieth century.

EARLY COLONIAL INDIA FROM INDOMANIA TO INDOPHOBIA[13]

The English East India Company initially entered government in South Asia as a subordinate of the enfeebled Mughal Empire. It officially had little to do with traditional learning as such. Individual officers, however, took an interest in indigenous learning during the eighteenth century, and the Asiatic Society was founded in Calcutta in 1784. Furthermore, the company was generally committed to maintaining established legal systems in the small coastal enclaves to which it was confined prior to its victories in the years 1757–64. That required its officials and judges to learn something of local law and practice. In the 1770s, the company gained direct control of taxation and judicial power across eastern India and sought to establish courts that enforced "traditional" laws. A handful of learned Hindus and Muslims then found influential positions advising English judges on the requirements of their respective judicial systems.[14] The education of this traditional intelligentsia was privately managed at home by tutors, at schools associated with religious foundations, and at small private schools. The same was true of the handful of minor officials, gentry, and clerks involved in government affairs.[15]

Englishmen in the East India Company service of the mid-eighteenth century had also been educated in a similar hit-or-miss way. They were often men with little money and few prospects sent out by families eager to unburden themselves of useless mouths. They picked up languages haphazardly and leaned on local culture brokers to manage their personal and official affairs. The wealth suddenly available after the conquest of Bengal led to a rush of upper-class appointees, many of whom had, however, had benefited little from their more protracted educations. All participated in a culture of "small salaries and immense perquisites" as Lord Cornwallis (Governor-General 1786–95) described it.[16] He sought to reform this by increasing and standardizing salaries and removing the most corrupt. His successor, Richard Wellesley (Governor-General 1798–1805) in 1799 established a college in Calcutta to educate the teenage boys sent out from England for the company civil service. But Wellesley's disastrous fiscal management ultimately led to his removal. Charles Grant and the Anglicists then ensured that trainees for the company service were educated not in India but in a new college called Haileybury (in Hertfordshire) in 1806.[17] But the institutions in Calcutta and Madras and their handfuls of indigenous scholars working in a hybrid "Anglo-Indian" style of learning survived some decades longer. Wellesley's initiative thus set off an academic institutionalization that created a small colonial public sphere by the 1820s.

The college in Calcutta and its peer in Madras offered specific sites that required the interaction of indigenous and Western scholars. These produced a new class of texts unknown to their regional vernacular traditions, such as the histories of Bengal that appeared soon after 1800.[18] Once colonial rule was firmly established in South Asia, the sense of lack felt by historians elsewhere quickly beset the Indian intelligentsia too. They turned instinctively to colonial discourse. Early European travelers had, of course, long recorded what they were told about the recent history of the subcontinent as part of the stock of information to be conveyed home. The first European empire—that of the Portuguese (established in Goa in 1510)—soon developed a providential, Christian narrative of its place and destiny in the world. For obvious political and military reasons, the Goa government also began compiling a record of neighboring and distant kings. The Portuguese controlled European access to the Indian Ocean through sixteenth but lost control during the seventeenth century. After the firm establishment of the English East India Company vis-à-vis its rivals (achieved around 1700),

European histories of "India" were often implicit or explicit contributions to then-current controversies regarding the past record and future status of the English East India Company.[19] By the later eighteenth century, the prosperous colonial city of Calcutta was the economic and intellectual center of the first major region colonized by the British Empire. Western modes of writing spread there at the very beginning of the nineteenth century. This was but a few decades after recognized histories such as Gibbon's *Decline and Fall* or David Hume's *History of England* were being written. British historians began writing on India in the modes then current in the West.

In the later decades of the eighteenth century, however, the old Hellenic fascination with the esoteric wisdom of India began to revive in "Anglo-Indian" circles. Translations of and studies in Indian sciences, literature, and religion made much of this lore available to educated Europeans. This was a period when what Trautmann has elegantly termed "Indomania" was widely prevalent in cultivated circles in Europe. The study of Sanskrit had opened new domains of knowledge, and a widely read essay by William Jones demonstrated the common descent of Greek, Latin, and Sanskrit from a lost ancestral language. Given the idolization of the classical Greco-Roman world in Enlightenment Europe, this naturally reopened the search for ancient Indian wisdom. That project was also promoted by Hellenic allusions to the esoteric knowledge of the Indians. It must be obvious that these lines of thought would appeal to the subjugated Indian intelligentsia. On the other hand, Jones still shoehorned Indian historical time into the frame of a secularized Mosaic chronology: events from Indic myth served to confirm the Old Testament narrative.[20]

But "Indophobia" soon arose to challenge Indomania. Its early manifestation was a long paper by the important East India Company potentate, Charles Grant (1746–1823).[21] Grant came from an impoverished Scottish family and, like many of that ilk, sought to improve his fortunes by going out to India. He went initially as a military cadet but then later secured a place in the much more lucrative East India Company's Covenanted (civil) Service. He made a fortune and returned to England in 1790 to become an important functionary in the East India Company's home establishment. He was at various times both a director and the chairman of the company. Always a committed Protestant, he joined the evangelical wing of the Church of England after his return. He then affiliated to the "Clapham Sect" and became a staunch opponent and critic of Indian (which was, for him, the same as "Hindu") religion, which he saw as intimately connected with India's culture and civilization.[22]

Trautmann has analyzed Grant's 1797 paper as a foundational text in the evangelical critique of Indomania. It was written soon after Jones's "Address" had strongly reinforced an already extant Indophilia. Grant's essay was to be frequently invoked to justify the anglicization of British India. It painted a dark picture of the moral depravity of the Hindus and attributed this to the uniformly despotic government that shaped their morals. That despotism, however, Grant argued, resulted from the intrinsic character of their religion. It was no accident that Grant, while citing the very lecture where Jones announced his discovery of the kinship of ancient Greek, Latin, and Sanskrit, completely omitted any mention of that proof. Jones had, in fact, gone beyond that linguistic connection to assert "what might be proved beyond controversy, that we now live among the adorers of those very deities who were worshiped under different names in old Greece and Italy; and among the professors of those philosophical tenets which the Ionic and Attic writers illustrated with all the beauties of their melodious language."[23]

Admitting that the Hindus worshiped the same gods as the Greeks had done would have threatened the genealogy that gave Christianity a unique connection with antique neo-Platonic philosophy. Furthermore, allowing India kinship with what Europeans saw as the Greek fount of republican virtue and democratic government would have wrecked Grant's focus on the spontaneously despotic nature of "Hindu" government.[24] That claim was the most important part of Grant's program. If despotism was an intrinsic quality of Hindu society, Grant could argue that the "benevolent despotism" that he advocated as active company policy was the best of all possible worlds. His implicit logic was that since Indian society was doomed to be despotic, it should have the best possible despotism—an English one. Indians would, he argued, attach themselves to it provided they were brought to share the Christian faith with their rulers. Indophobia and the project of an evangelical company empire thus went together.

Grant was not the only Scotsman in British India at the time. Well educated and politically connected but poor, it was natural that Scottish younger sons would be strongly represented in the growing military and civil establishments of the British Empire.[25] For some Scots, the seeds of Indophobia may have been sown before they left Britain by the lectures of the prominent and influential Scottish philosopher and mathematician Dugald Stewart. Stewart was a celebrity professor at the University of Edinburgh for fifty years. His ideas influenced the education of generations of Scots. He strongly rejected Jones's claims for the antiquity of Sanskrit and its being coeval with Greek. Stewart seriously advanced the bizarre claim that far from being contemporary to ancient Greek, Sanskrit had been concocted by a deceitful Indian priesthood when exposed to the elegance and beauty of Greek through Alexander's conquests in Asia.[26] Christian missionary denunciations of Brahmans as tricksters went back to at least (the future saint) Francis Xavier in 1544.[27] Stewart developed this idea further in order to refute Jones's ideas and was enthusiastically seconded by Charles Grant and later, James Mill.

Indophobia was thus buoyed by an odd alliance of philosophically incompatible evangelical and utilitarian interests in Britain and its empire. Trautmann sums it up: "The Indophobia that became the norm in early-nineteenth century Britain was constructed by Evangelicalism and Utilitarianism, and its chief architects were Charles Grant and James Mill."[28] Mill was a graduate of Edinburgh who initially eked out a living in London as an impoverished journalist. He never went to India or learned any Indian languages. But he was well grounded in the social theory of the Scottish Enlightenment and intelligently combined two rising (if mutually contradictory) currents: radical utilitarianism (which was the cutting-edge "theory" of its day) and an implicit apologia for Protestant evangelicalism. Both strains met in his *History of India*. It appeared in 1817, and conferred enough distinction to win him a lucrative and powerful appointment as Examiner of Accounts in the London offices of the East India Company.

But another, and ultimately more influential, Indophobic project had been simultaneously launched in India. The Baptist Christians Joshua Marshman and his colleagues William Carey and John Ward, sought in 1816 to raise money for a scheme of basic education in Indian languages. Like all publications by fund-seeking NGOs, the appeal began by painting a dark picture of current conditions. Money was needed for education to lift the Hindu people from a state where their "ignorance [was] not greatly exceeded by that of those savage hordes who have no written language." Hindus were indeed "below most savage nations in vice and immorality." Therefore, school lessons in history and chronology should begin with the Creation, describe the "primitive state of man, the entrance of evil, the corruption of the antediluvian age, the flood, and the peopling of the earth anew from one family" and proceed through the revelations after Abraham, Greece, and Rome, and conclude with "the reformation, the discovery of the passage to India by sea, and the various discoveries of modern science."[29] Thus, the strength of the providential Protestant narrative would be reinforced by a demonstration of the scientific triumphs that resulted from adherence to the one true faith, all unfolding in historical time in which Divine Providence granted Britain custody of India. Obscure India-based Baptists had thus anticipated the general thrust of Mill's *History*. But Mill's massive tomes gave evangelicals a powerful support in metropolitan circles, even if they were then little esteemed among established British officialdom in India.

Indeed, despite Mill's influential position at the center of power, the sharpest early criticism of his ideas came largely from experienced English officials in India. One of the earliest was Vans Kennedy (1783–1846), who pointed out the absurdity of Mill's claiming special authority *because* he had no direct knowledge. Kennedy derided those who "boast that they possess no personal knowledge whatever of the subject under discussion and urge this very ignorance as a proof that their opinions are most correct"[30] Kennedy had entered the East India Company's army in India in 1800 at the age of 17. He clearly had an aptitude for languages and was an official Persian translator from 1806. He later became "Oriental translator" to the government of Bombay and died in India in 1846. Kennedy quoted Thomas Munro (1761–1827; governor of Madras 1820–27), a prominent soldier-administrator, who had declared in the House of Commons a few years earlier that "if civilisation is to become an article of trade [between India and England], I am convinced that this country will gain by the import cargo."[31] (That remark was much excoriated by the evangelical establishment for decades after.)

Mill was also indirectly the target of historians like James Tod (1782–1835), whose extensive use of the Rajput annals obviously set a higher value on Indian learning than Mill was prepared to do. Furthermore, Mill was directly challenged by the ex-governor of Bombay, Mountstuart Elphinstone, who wrote his *History of India* soon after his own retirement from the company's service. No struggling scrivener, Elphinstone (1779–1859) came from an upper-class Scottish family, being the fourth son of the eleventh Lord Elphinstone. He was found a civil service appointment in India at the age of eighteen. He learned Persian by his twenties, rose to be governor of Bombay Presidency, and began accumulating materials later embodied in his histories, especially *The History of India*, published in 1841. Not surprisingly, it became the favored higher education textbook in Western India, where Elphinstone spent the culminating quarter-century of his Indian career. But it was popular even beyond the Bombay Presidency. Partha Chatterjee has pointed out that it remained the main university textbook through the nineteenth century.[32]

Elphinstone's *History of India* indeed went into several editions. As regards Mill, his preface was politer than Kennedy's review but made the same point. Elphinstone suggested that research conducted in Europe alone needed to be supplemented by the work of authors who had actually lived in India. Much of his chapter XI, for example, was a defense of Indians against sweeping moral denunciation by Englishmen such as Grant and Mill. He observed that "all persons who have retired from India think better of the people they have left after comparing them with others, even of the most justly admired nations."[33] But the objections of the Indophiles were ultimately silenced, even as grand theories such as those of Mill, Hegel, Marx, and Weber came to be put together out of the rejected fragments of their research.

Mill's massive text was to be a powerful source of Indophobia in Britain and Europe for half a century. Most importantly, it was read by impressionable English trainees destined to rule India when they underwent preliminary training in the college in Haileybury. It went into several editions in Britain.[34] Still, as we saw, despite its powerful supporters in England, Mill's *History* did not gain much traction among the English establishment *in India*. In its early decades, this would have been because it derided the hard-earned linguistic and local knowledge of English officials in India. Half a century after its publication, in an ironic twist of history, Mill was deemed too critical—not of the Indians but of the founders of British rule. In 1817, Mill was, we must remember, targeting important advocates of the idea that Indian civilization had much to offer the West. Warren Hastings had been sympathetic to this view. Discrediting Hastings (and by implication, men of his generation, like Thomas Munro) as corrupt and oppressive was a good way to illustrate how sympathy for Indian values would corrupt even virtuous Anglo-Saxon Protestants. Grant sent an effective ally out to India when he secured T. B. Macaulay (1800–1859) a lucrative appointment as the Law Member of the Governor-General's Council in India (1834–38).[35] Mill's polemic against Hastings was then recited with gusto by Macaulay. The latter also agreed with Mill in advocating a thoroughgoing Westernization of Indian education as the only solution for India's perceived social ills. While in India, he wrote a celebrated minute on Indian education that claimed that a single shelf of a good European library was more valuable than the entire classical literature of India and Arabia. Macaulay's collected essays were soon part of the curriculum of the new westernizing Indian universities established after 1857.

Then, however, only a few decades later, the Indian products of Macaulayan education used Mill's *History* and Macaulay's *Essays* as sources for a critique of the moral turpitude of the founders of the British Empire. John Strachey, erstwhile lieutenant governor, now termed Mill a "great criminal" for his biased and erroneous narrative of the rise of the British Empire in

India. Strachey quoted his ally, the important legal thinker and author, James F. Stephens, who wrote of Mill that his "excessive dryness and severity of style" produced "an impression of accuracy and labour which a study of original authorities does not by any means confirm. . . . His want of accuracy is nothing to his bad faith."[36] Furthermore, Mill was never (to my knowledge) translated into any Indian language, though his ideas were disseminated in the small higher education system through Macaulay's widely read essays on India.[37] School texts based on John C. Marshman's efforts, however, appeared early in territories dominated from Calcutta, while those drawing on Elphinstone's *History* predominated elsewhere. (School enrollments, of course, vastly exceeded the numbers attending the handful of colonial-era colleges.) While sharing Mill's outlook and consulting his book, Marshman also drew heavily on Stewart's *History of Bengal* (first published in 1813), Tod's *Annals and Antiquities*, and Grant Duff's *History of the Mahrattas* (1826).

British administrators of this era also had deep faith in the administrative acumen and statistical knowledge of the Mughal Empire. They uncritically accepted poorly founded data because they purported to come from the "registers" of that empire, especially if it appeared to show that the East India Company was collecting only a fraction of the tax to which it was entitled.[38] Thus Grant produced a large body of apocryphal revenue accounts intended to show that Bengal and Bihar under the East India Company were seriously undertaxed when compared to the supposed Mughal standard. Grant certainly had access to some assessment (not collection) records going back to the reign of Akbar and successively traced additions and changes made until the establishment of the company regime in 1765. He presented these records to Cornwallis as showing how under the Mughal Empire the gross produce of the land was "parcelled out in the smallest measured divisions of land by the sovereign, as sole virtual proprietor."[39] This was in fact an unfounded belief, but its acceptance shows how unquestioningly the myth of Mughal omniscience was accepted. Early British officials saw themselves as working a remodeled Mughal imperial system. An Indian official in fact wrote a Persian revenue manual titled *Diwan Pasand* for the benefit of British officials trying to revive Mughal practice. Persian histories and records and classical Mughal practices were seen as the core of a British empire in North India for some sixty years.

Persian had, of course, entered India along with the Turkish sultanates, but largely as a language of the courts and upper-class literati. It reached more deeply into local government with the Mughal emperor Akbar's decision to use it for administrative purposes down to (at least in theory) the village level. Its reach, like that of the emperors themselves, was uneven, and it may never have gone much beyond the core areas of the empire. It receded rapidly in Maratha lands and Central India and was never used beyond the governor's offices in the briefly occupied lands south of the Tungabhadra River (or most of today's Karnataka and Tamil Nadu states). It is possible that Persian underwent a revival when the colonial government adopted it as the official language in its eastern and northern territories (Bengal, Bihar, and the North-Western Provinces). That ended in 1837, but it was replaced by a heavily Persianized Urdu across the same region. Urdu was also extended to Panjab after the British annexation of the region in 1849.

It is not therefore unexpected that the historical culture of the Mughal imperial period provided the framework that early Western historians (usually all also full-time officials) found at hand when they arrived. What they perceived as "Hindu" history, on the other hand, was in many languages, including Sanskrit, a language to which very few had access. Much of the epigraphic record was undiscovered or illegible. Furthermore, the long spans and cyclical patterns of Indian chronology flatly contradicted biblical time, which reckoned that only 7,000 years had elapsed since the creation of the earth. Islamic chronology, however, came from the same Judaic tradition and fitted much better with Christian ideas. Duff and Elphinstone both relied heavily on Fereshte's *Gulshan* (completed around 1611). The early historian Mark Wilks in 1820 called him "the accurate Ferishta."[40] Persian literary traditions moreover provided a clear chronological sequence and a vivid narrative that underpinned much writing on South Asian history into the present. Authors down to the *Cambridge History of India* volume on the Mughals (1937) depended heavily on translations of medieval Persian works, adding only Western travelers' accounts to their main body of sources.[41]

We have already mentioned that John Briggs's 1829 multivolume translation of the Persian historian Astarabadi (Fereshte or Ferishta) became an important primary source for practically every historian of the time (and a few at present). Amazingly, it is still in print. This translation superseded early translations of parts of the text by Alexander Dow and others. But for a chronological and dynastic narrative, British writers of the nineteenth century were drawn to Briggs's translation of Fereshte. Briggs was a protégé of Elphinstone and, like him, proficient in Persian. Fereshte's own rendering begins with a lengthy dedication to his patron, Ibrahim Adil Shah. It opens with a short first chapter based, as he says, on a translation of the Mahabharata. It then moves to a chapter titled "The Rise of Islam in These Lands."[42] Clearly Briggs derived his title, *History of the Rise of the Mohammedan Power in India*, from there. Fereshte in Briggs's rendering, with its precise dates, clear succession of rulers, and matter-of-fact tone, established itself as key framing text for English histories as soon as they began to be written and is still frequently consulted by historians.

Many Rajput houses of Western and Central India had affiliated to and prospered under the Mughals. We have seen how the ecumenical histories written under that empire drew upon the historical memories of the major dynasties (as well as Sanskrit epics) in reconstructing earlier history of the Mughal dominions in South Asia. This earlier empire's recognition of the Rajputs as a kingly class made it easier for colonial officials to connect with such sources. That grew into an important strain of historical thought developed by the early colonial official James Tod. His much reprinted *Annals and Antiquities of Rajasthan* (1829, 1832) had a profound impact on later colonial and postcolonial memory across South Asia. Its tenacious imprint was found in nationalist lore and school textbooks across British India. It is, as Cynthia Talbot said, "difficult to exaggerate the importance of James Tod in shaping modern views of the Rajputs and their region." Tod spent the most of the last decade of his career in Western India and drew extensively on the traditional histories of the region.[43] Tod's dedication to King William IV demonstrates that his political project was to revive the Rajput kingdoms—or restore their "independence" under British protection. He was therefore particularly amenable to tales of ancient glory and sought to present the Puranas as well as bardic annals as types of "Hindu" historical practice, assimilating them to the monastic chronicles of medieval Europe. He wrote therefore that the "heroic poems of India constitute another resource for history. Bards may be regarded as the primitive historians of mankind."[44] His work has proved enormously influential in shaping both colonial and postcolonial historiography in India.

Briggs, Duff, Stewart, and Tod were all linguistically gifted army officers who came to India when young and became interested in the history of the regions where their careers lay. Stewart moved on to be professor of Persian at the East India Company College in England. His history was proudly founded on what were deemed the best indigenous authorities, meaning previous Persian histories.[45] Like Briggs's massive translation, it became raw material for later historians. Duff's career, on the other hand, ended as "resident" (effectively, superintendent) in the Maratha kingdom of Satara. He used his position there to seek out both Marathi texts and living eyewitnesses for the events he described in his two-volume *History of the Mahrattas*. Duff produced a work that, though now superseded by later scholarship, may yet still be profitably read as a source for the history of his times in Western India. Unlike Tod's *Annals*, Duff's history did not sell, and he lost money on its publication. But it was early translated (in 1830, into Marathi), and several reprints followed in later years. Prachi Deshpande has subtly delineated the varying levels of assistance and resistance of Indians whom Duff drew into this enterprise. She also points out the unchanging assumption of British superiority that permeates a work that remained the "standard work" in English and Marathi to the end of the nineteenth century.[46]

EARLY COLONIAL HISTORY IN BENGAL

English-language of histories of Indian regions, as well as the larger one by Elphinstone were initially intended for the English in India, incoming English officials, and the scholarly world of Europe. The triumph of the Anglicist program meant that a growing but always small number of Indians began to read these histories too. I have already alluded to the very different traditions of reconstructing past events in each part of India. The new colonial histories thus encountered distinct historical traditions, each structured by enduring features of the sociopolitical setting of its home terrain. The Bengal delta was a politically and religiously diverse region, with a corresponding variety of literary traditions. Mughal rule came later and sat lighter upon it. The Calcutta area became the bridgehead of British power in India, and a new urban center and corresponding hybrid cultural tradition sprang up there. The scribal intelligentsia of Calcutta were early adopters of a new historical style emerging from the interaction.

Madras and Calcutta were both initially small East India Company trading towns that grew into metropolitan centers of an emerging British empire around the Bay of Bengal. British Bombay, though older than Calcutta, had powerful Indian rivals in the area and only emerged as a significant territorial power after 1818. Calcutta was the biggest and wealthiest of the three cities in the early nineteenth century. It was also the seat of the governor-general, who came to control regional administrations across British Asia. New clerical and commercial classes closely intertwined with Western commerce and empire thrived there, and the largest and most complex bureaucratic and literary apparatus emerged in this city. Christian missionaries had long sought to influence elite and popular thought along the seaboard of the Bay of Bengal. The rise of evangelical interest in Britain (with which the politically networked East India Company director Charles Grant was affiliated) gradually gave the pro-missionary faction great power in the Bengal Presidency.

The small but energetic Baptist establishment at Serampore (near Calcutta) pioneered printing in Indian characters and printed a range of texts. They were thus ready when Western-style schools and a new curriculum began to require large numbers of cheap Indian-language histories.

We have already considered the two earliest Bengali-language histories, produced in 1801 and 1808 by teachers at the College of Fort William. Their authors, especially Ramram Basu, alluded to *kulaji* genealogical traditions, as did the earliest British authors, like John Marshman. But they were increasingly challenged by the gradual unearthing of copper-plate and lithic inscriptions, as well as other records that contradicted traditional caste legends. Efforts by Nagendranath Basu to incorporate new archaeological findings by announcing their "discovery" in supposedly ancient manuscripts only discredited the legends further. R. C. Majumdar published a series of articles on this debate in the Bengali journal *Bhāratavarṣa* during the 1930s and later reedited and printed them in 1973. He recalled that the debate grew heated but then largely died down thereafter. It was replaced by an archaeologically sustainable narrative of ancient Indian history to which Majumdar himself made large contributions.[47] The accumulating weight of these findings and the growing irrelevance of these minute gradations in the fluid postcolonial world gradually settled the controversy. But since Western dominance had resulted in every emerging nation seeking to have not merely a history but a unique one of its own, genealogical legends survived at the margins of scholarly thought in Bengal. The impulse to indigenist pride sustained them and then contributed to a late revival in the Western academy.[48]

Macaulay's victory over the advocates of the value of "Oriental learning" meant that the North Indian intelligentsia from Calcutta west to Agra were compelled to engage with British institutions, laws, and sciences. Old-school education was now disfavored in government employment. The stabilization of textual bodies of "Anglo-Hindu" and "Anglo-Mohammedan" law that judges began to consult reduced opportunities available to specialists in "Hindu" and "Muslim" law. Nor was it possible to maintain the hauteur with which Hindu and Muslim scholars had rebuffed early missionary attempts to debate their religious doctrines.[49] Now they *had* to respond to Western writings, because the emerging indigenous colonial intelligentsia was increasingly swayed by them.

The worldwide trend toward seeking an indigenous history reached India too, starting in Bengal. Initially, the Bengali intelligentsia began introducing critiques of the English into curricular materials supposedly complementary to the translated histories still read by students.[50] This was followed by exhortations, most famously by Bankim Chandra Chatterji (usually referred to as "Bankim Chandra"), to write authentic indigenous histories. The effort to find new sources thus gained a new importance for the nationalist project. The story of most Bengali Brahmans and Kayasthas being descended from ten ancestors brought from northern India by the mythic Adishura spread more widely. A reactive origin myth was developed by Muslim literati in Bengal. Upper-class Muslims in northern India had long seen themselves as descended from invading conquerors. So the learned Syed Ahmed Khan wrote in 1859 that the Muslims "are not the aborigines of this country. They came in the train of former conquerors and gradually domesticated themselves in India."[51] This idea of a conquering foreign origin was also current among the small Bengali Muslim upper class. The claim to West Asian ancestry was evidently current in the 1870s, since Bankim Chandra devoted a few contemptuous lines to rejecting it. He declared most Muslims were "lower-class peasants. It is impossible that the descendants of rulers should become peasants and the descendants of their subjects should become the upper classes."[52]

But more than Bankim Chandra's jibes, it was British colonizers' calm assumption that the majority of Bengali Muslims were descendants, not of former conquerors but of lower-caste Hindu converts that moved a Muslim aristocrat to compose a full-scale reply. Writing in 1895, Fuzle Rubbee drew on the emerging ethno-nationalist idea of nations as distinct descent groups to claim a completely foreign ancestry, not for an aristocracy but for all Bengali Muslims. His polemic was especially directed against the recently published ethnography of H. H. Risley, who had argued that the bulk of the Muslims of Bengal were low-caste converts from Hinduism. Rubbee's tract on the origins of Bengali Muslims indirectly drew on the genealogical folklore of upper-caste Hindus. After a long rehearsal of how innumerable West Asians were attracted by the wealth and generosity of the Bengal sultans, Rubbee concluded that

> it can safely, and without any fear of contradiction, be asserted that the ancestors of the present Musalmans of this country were certainly those Musalmans who came here from foreign parts during the rule of the former sovereigns, and that the present generation of Musalmans are the offspring of that dominant race who remained masters of the land for 562 years. Admitting, for the sake of argument, that the Musalmans of the present time are other than the descendants of those foreign Musalman rulers and settlers, who can then the progeny be of those foreign Musalmans and where have they gone to? Considering that the descendants

> of only five Brahmins and five Sudras who (as is said) originally came to Bengal from Kanauj could have multiplied to such an enormous extent, that they are to be found everywhere in the country, what impossibility is there in supposing that the descendants of the innumerable and countless Musalmans who came to this country, during long ages, have become more numerous than they.[53]

The advance of English histories (and Indian-language translations) led the novelist and colonial bureaucrat Bankim Chandra Chatterji to call for a collective Bengali enterprise to write the history of Bengal. His enterprise was, however, strictly ethnic and regional, as even a casual reading will show. He published several long essays in 1880. The first, titled "History of Bengal," was a review of a school textbook.[54] He began by declaring that the writing of history was an expression of national pride. Indians (*bhāratvarṣiya*) were too pious and lacked the arrogant pride so abundant in Europeans, "therefore we have no historical narrative." But then he quickly moved into lamenting the absence of historical memory specifically among the ethnic Bengalis. "There are one or two unfortunate nations (*jāti*) that do not know of the fame of their glorious ancestors, and the first among these unfortunates are the Bengalis; even the Oḍiyā people [of the neighboring region] have history." He then went on to draw selectively from the still ongoing reconstruction of early Indian history to declare that the Bengali people had defeated Mithila, Magadha, Kāśī, Prayāg, Utkala, etc. Sinhala was conquered by Bengali kings and ruled by their successors. He continued, "many believe that Bālī and Jāvā were Bengali colonies. The port of Tamralipti was the entry to the Indian Ocean. No other Indian nation showed such capacity for colonization [as the Bengalis did]." Around the same time (1880), he published another essay on history titled "A Few Words Concerning the History of Bengal." As this essay has lately been represented by Ranajit Guha, the founder of *Subaltern Studies*, as the fountainhead of the quest for an authentically Indian historiography of India, I will briefly consider its most striking features.

The essay reiterated that no nation that did not remember its past greatness could hope to achieve greatness in the future. Bankim Chandra sneered that English historians such as Stewart had written weighty books, and Lethbridge, Marshman, and others had all earned good money by dashing off cursory narratives. But these were not, he claimed, the authentic history of Bengal. If they contained any history, it was only the story of those in Muslim Bengal who took the titles of king or governor and spent their days in ease and indolence. It was the story of their births, deaths, and domestic trivia.

"It has no connection with the history of the Bengali nation. Any Bengali who accepts this as the history of Bengal is not a [true] Bengali." A person deficient in self-pride, who uncritically accepted the testimony of Hindu-hating Muslims as history "is not a Bengali." Bengal had no written history, he continued. What people read was not real history, "it was romantic tales (*upanyās*) or the biographies of callous, oppressive, foreign adherents of a foreign faith." He then laid out a long list of topics for investigation, such as the circumstance around the arrival of the Aryans from whom Brahmans and others were descended, as well as the origins of the lower castes. He went on to list questions such as governance under the Pala and Sena kings, kingship after the Afghan capture of Lakhnauti, the origin of the Bengali language, the pre-Aryan languages of Bengal, Todar Mall's land-tax system, the reasons for the conversion of half the population to Islam, and so on. All these were topics of research he recommended to his readers but did not undertake himself.[55]

As is often the case, the questions themselves reveal the findings that he sought from the new history. It should be the self-affirming history of the Bengali-speaking (and Hindu) peoples. But Bankim Chandra never wrote such a history; his longer works were in the more congenial medium of historical romance. His essays, insofar as they addressed historical matters, essentially selected tendentiously from the emerging finding of archaeology and Indology. But we can also see the beginnings of an epistemological nativism: only those who accepted his view of regional history were true Bengalis. This discredited narrative was, however, academically resurrected in Ronald Inden's early monograph, *Marriage and Rank in Bengali Culture* (1976), which blithely ignored the text-historical criticism of three generations of Bengali scholars to adopt and reproduce the whole mythic narrative of the origin of *kulin* lineages in Bengal. It also thereby incorporated Basu's anti-Muslim framing, one in which Hindu society was bereft of a righteous Hindu monarch after the alien conquest. Hindu upper castes then had to self-organize to prevent the abominable mixing of blood that might otherwise occur.[56] A variant of that position was to echo strangely a century after Bankim Chandra, when Ranajit Guha was to assimilate the former's Hindu Bengali nationalism into his own version of historical practice. This point was elided by Guha, who claimed that we should read Bankim Chandra's use of "Bengal and Bengali as notations often used by the author for India and Indians."[57] In this indigenist vein, Guha also claimed that anglophone education had hindered the development of a "distinctively Indian historiography of colonial India."[58]

Some of Bankim Chandra's contemporaries, however, were prepared to adopt new methods—and, while anxious to challenge English historians, also wanted to be viewed as scholars on par with Europeans. Rajendralal Mitra (1823/4–1891) is an early example. He became secretary of the Asiatic Society in Calcutta and then went on to work in the office of the Court of Wards. Honored by the British government, he was also active in the early meetings of the Indian National Congress (founded in 1885).[59] K. K. Dasgupta regards his debate with Burgess on the origins of Indian architecture as the first triumph of an Indian tradition of rigorous scholarship.[60] The development of a rigorous but Indian school of history thus became part of the nationalist enterprise.

This is exemplified by Ramaprasad Chanda (1873–1942) in Bengal. Born in modest circumstances, he began his research while still unemployed. After several years, he secured a modest income as a schoolteacher, first in Calcutta and then in Rajshahi (North Bengal, now Bangladesh). He helped found the Varendra Research Society there. Dineshchandra Sarkar's biographical preface to the reprint of Chanda's *Gauḍarājamāla* says of him that, though but a common schoolteacher, he rose to the first rank of historians though his intellectual brilliance and intensive research.[61] Chanda was in the second wave of Indian scholars who sought to rebut British narratives of Indian history. So when the colonial official H. H. Risley sought to apply the emerging European (pseudoscience) of craniology to analyze the "racial" composition of the peoples of eastern India, Chanda was the first to publish a response. It was Risley's craniological classification of Bengalis as "non-Aryan" that especially infuriated Chanda and led him to research and write a refutation. However, he used the same (now abandoned) skull-form comparison methods as Risley had done.[62]

More conventional and more cautious scholars like Jadunath Sarkar thought it too early to write alternative histories. Affirming the new empiricism, he wrote in 1909 that historians needed to reach "the bedrock of ascertainable and unassailable facts . . . on which alone the superstructure of history could be raised by our happier successors."[63] That enterprise occupied professional historians of Bengal for several decades, and the genealogical folklore of the *kulagrantha* tradition was gradually consigned to oblivion together with the hierarchies of social prestige that generated it. New nationalist, often Marxist, historians sought other phenomena in regional history, especially popular or plebeian movements against colonial rule. After 1947, the new Indian republic opened new archives and afforded fresh opportunities for the study of its own origins. Caste-rank snobbery seemed especially irrelevant in the new Nehruvian India. The regional historiography of Bengal gradually lost its distinctness and merged into the larger stream of nationalist historiography.

MARATHA HISTORY UNDER COLONIALISM

On the opposite side of the subcontinent, the colonized Maharashtrian intelligentsia soon absorbed the British sense that, whatever their elders might recollect, India lacked a sound historical tradition. By the 1860s the German tradition of text-critique that had lately overspread Europe also came to the Bombay Presidency, applied in the first instance, to Sanskrit manuscripts.[64] Recent history was still a sensitive topic. Mahadev Govind Ranade, the future high court judge and president of the Indian National Congress, was a teenage student at Elphinstone College, in Bombay, in the 1850s when he discovered the touchiness of the Bombay government firsthand. In 1859, he ventured to write an essay adversely comparing the British land-taxation system with the Maratha one. The principal, Alexander Grant, reprimanded him and suspended payment of his scholarship for six months. N. R. Phatak remarks that this early lesson taught Ranade to tread cautiously in what he said about the British regime.[65]

Another student, N. J. Kirtane, published the first Marathi critique of British historian Grant Duff's *History* in 1868 while a first year student in Deccan College, Pune. In his preface to the 1884 edition, Kirtane confessed that at the time of writing, he read Modi poorly, since his government school education had been in Devanagari script. But the famous intellectual Chiplunkar presided at the meeting where Kirtane criticized Duff and lavished praise on the speaker. Kirtane was then persuaded to print it in the journal *Induprakash*. It is likely, then, that as an argumentative youth, he was expressing ideas pleasing to his more cautious seniors. Kirtane began by lamenting that while the English had written many histories on Hindustan (India), there was but one history of the Marathas. He regretted that Duff had foregrounded the Muslim sultans and failed to trace how the impoverished Marathas had risen to subcontinental prominence. Duff was also charged with having neglected the origins of the Maratha lineages, such as the genealogical claims of the aristocratic thirty-six lineages and ninety-six lineages and to have insufficiently appreciated the first *chatrapati*'s achievements. Kirtane's attack on Duff's *History*, having been effusively praised by Chiplunkar, a founding figure of modern Marathi literary criticism, was reprinted several times. A. R. Kulkarni, who founded of the Department of History in the University of Pune, also authored a biography of Grant Duff. Kulkarni found various oversights and overstatements in Kirtane's text but credits his polemic with stimulating the search for, and publication of, Marathi historical texts in the 1870s.[66] But in Maharashtra all such efforts were politically fraught.

The civil servant Bankim Chandra could scoff at the battle of Plassey as a charade and no credit to English valor but still retire comfortably with the title of "Companion of the Indian Empire." But authorities in the Bombay Presidency were much warier of implied criticism written in Marathi. The region had been a source of anxiety during the great uprising of 1857–58. The exiled heir of the last peshwa, known as Nana Saheb, was one of the most prominent leaders of the rebellion in North India. Extra vigilance nonetheless helped ensure that the uprising of 1857 did not spread south of the Narmada River. A conspiracy in Western India was checked with several summary trials and executions in Bombay and Satara in mid-1857 itself. Furthermore, in the centuries of Maratha expansion, successful men had branched out from clerical office into banking and military command. Many soldier-officials accompanied and acquired hereditary offices in the new Maratha administrations scattered across the subcontinent from Thanjavur to Baroda, Indore, Gwalior, Delhi, and Jhansi. Many of the leaders of the revolt had come from the courts of displaced or threatened Maratha potentates. The most protracted campaign of the uprising was waged in Central India against Tatya Tope, a die-hard adherent of the deposed Peshwa dynasty, who was finally captured and executed in 1859. Other Maratha leaders vanished into the Nepal foothills at the end of the revolt, and their whereabouts were a nagging worry for the government of India for at least two decades thereafter. The suppression of the great uprising was followed by severe repression across much of India.

Even after the pall cast by the great revolt began to lift, "seditious" writing was further checked by the Vernacular Press Act of 1878. Then in the 1870s, the Brahman Wasudeo Balwant Phadke (1845–1883), a junior clerk in the army commissariat office, began the sort of conspiracy the post-Mutiny British always feared. He took several sick leaves during which (it was later revealed) he traveled around the country seeking funds and support for an anti-British uprising. He received funds, but the government could never establish where the money came from. In 1879 he led an uprising of Ramoshi and other hillmen that lasted several months and caused the British government considerable anxiety. He was finally captured and sentenced to life imprisonment in Aden, where his refusal of food resulted in an early death in 1883. It emerged that both before and during his short-lived revolt, Phadke had planned and reconnoitered under the guise of a Hindu ascetic. After intense pursuit by the mobilized police and paramilitary forces of the Bombay government dispersed his band, Phadke resumed his ascetic disguise. He was in fact ultimately captured in a temple town while planning a new outbreak.[67] This episode intensified British fears of devious plots by subtle Brahmans inspired by memories of past power and made them more suspicious of studies in Maratha history.[68]

Several Maratha kingdoms, large and small, survived under British hegemony until 1947. These establishments continued to provide support for the older clerical classes even as their governments reorganized under the impact of colonial modernity. It is perhaps not accidental that Kirtane went on to spend his career in the Baroda state service; it is unlikely he would have flourished in the British-run Bombay government. Justice Ranade had, as we saw, suffered a severe rebuke while a student; he waited until he had risen to the Bombay High Court bench before he ventured to publish history again. But Kirtane and many others were less immediately dependent on British favor.

Furthermore, it was not merely the distrust of any historical inquiry that might glorify the Maratha past that led the Bombay government to obstruct public access to historical records. In 1818 the incoming colonial government, wary of stoking fresh resistance, promised to maintain *all* established rights exactly as they had existed when it took power. What exactly those rights could be determined to have been immediately became at once a bureaucratic, justiciable, and historical question. A tight control on archives and documents was inaugurated in order to clamp down on contestations—and on the ever-present possibility of forged documents being added to the archive. Thus the first, and for decades the only, institutional user of the Maratha records was the government's Inam Commission. This was a body created to inquire into and, if appropriate, repossess all claims to tax-free lands, offices, pensions, and other such "alienations" from state taxes. (The body of records that it acquired was therefore initially labeled the Alienation Office.) Apart from political suspicion, the Bombay government had an obvious interest in controlling access to the many authentic documents found in the archives of the previous administration. They were also concerned with the use of evidence from there in civil litigation against the government. But the traditions of the older bureaucracy were maintained. The incoming government needed help with its inherited archives; it therefore sought to maintain some continuity with previous ones and especially guaranteed all previous grants of land or pensions. Determining exactly what these had been meant that older records and the protocols of interpreting them had to be sustained and thus that the importance of historical inquiry and knowledge of its techniques were transmitted to the emerging colonial intelligentsia in Western India. Even after older documents lost most of their relevance, the concern for documentation survived into postindependence India. The Marathi public sphere was never separated from the anglophone to the extent that it was in northern or eastern India.

It was, however, very cautiously indeed that local patriots ventured into the domain of history. The earliest venture after Kirtane was a periodical launched by K. N. Sane and others from Pune in 1878, titled *Kāvyetihās saṁgraha* (A Collection of Historical and Poetic Works). Lack of funding finally forced them to stop publishing in 1885. The preface to the first issue (January 1878) declared its aim to be the publication of Marathi and Sanskrit poetry. But it added a novel third category: historical writing extant in Marathi. It declared that the educated public would not contest the crying need for such publication. "Due to the foolishness, the ignorance and the misconceptions current among people, thousands of manuscripts have already gone to [package goods in] grocers' shops, and hundreds more are going there each year. At this rate, there will be few manuscripts left in fifteen or twenty years. And what a loss that will be for our country!"[69]

The preface to a text titled "A History of the Peshwas" in the first volume of *Kāvyetihās* began by praising Grant Duff's history as one of the best histories of India then extant, if not the best. It then went on however, to cautiously borrow from Kirtane's essay. It suggested that Duff's alien origin, limited acquaintance with the nuances of Marathi, and lack of sympathy with the subjects of his history could not but detract from the quality of the historical work. The editors added, however, that his research had not been superseded: "whoever has written anything about us Marathas has drawn from Duff's book. No one has written a distinct and independent text to date."[70] So far, this is also the complaint that Bankim Chandra was making in Bengal. But the response of the Maharashtrian intelligentsia was quite different. They sought documentation. The sources for it, *Kāvyetihās* declared, were unavailable, hence the need for their own project. This in turn reflected a still living tradition of bureaucratic scrutiny of documents.

Even if the great officeholders were replaced by English commissioners and collectors, many humbler functionaries in town and country continued to enroll their sons and relatives in the same government offices in time-honored fashion. I illustrate this continuity with the example of a minor Brahman family through two centuries. The Pendses were coastal Brahmans and lived for generations by combining clerical office and landlordship in the Konkan. Some migrated to the plateau region (Desh) by the eighteenth century and found work in the Pune government. One of these was Ganesh Krishna (also known as Raoji) Pendse, who was employed both by the last peshwa and the new colonial government. By 1846, he had retired and drew a pension from the latter. He was asked to verify a letter supposedly from the time of Madhavrao Ballal Peshwa (1760s). He declared that it did not seem to be either authentic or from Peshwa's government, saying that it was not in the correct handwriting; it did not show that the header was written by a different clerk than the body, as had been the practice; the correct seals had not been affixed; the polite phrases appropriate between the addressee and the supposed author were missing; and so on. For all these reasons, Raoji Pendse declared it was likely a forgery.[71] Thus when Maratha intelligentsia decided to challenge Duff and other colonial authors, they already had a full repertoire of critical techniques available to them.

We can these deployed by a later descendant. Narayan Vinayak Pendse had a minor post in the British Indian army and retired in the 1930s. A number of families were writing their lineage histories at this time, and the pensioner Pendse decided to devote himself to this task too. As would be expected, he began by determining the (Jāmadagnya) *gotra* to which his lineage belonged. This was something that would be traditionally preserved in order to ensure that marriage partners were appropriately selected. But he was prepared only go as far as records allowed and would not seek to interpolate generations. Thus he was able to cite a fourteenth-century stone inscription from the Konkan village of Mathagav that showed that at least five Jāmadagnya Brahmans were present. He suggested that the name Pendse was adopted by one of these Jāmadagnya Brahmans of the coastal region but scrupulously recognized that there were no recorded mentions of that surname for several centuries. The earliest he could trace was from 1598–99.[72] The historiographic consciousness deployed by Narayana Vinayak was both old and new: the hybrid tradition he adopted was already two generations old. As in Bengal, it began with hostile reactions to perceived denigration by new colonial masters. But it also drew upon more recent history and a combination of older clerical and newer critical methods.

K. N. Sane, as we saw, began the project in the periodical *Kāvyetihās saṁgraha* (1878–85). Others responded to the same challenge after it closed down. One of them was Dattatreya Balwant Parasnis (1870–1926), the son of a revenue officer. His formal education had ended with high school; nonetheless, he published a short-lived magazine before he was out of his teens. The historian and archivist V. G. Khobrekar describes how Parasnis established himself as an intermediary between many princes and senior British officials. His personal affability and diplomatic skills endeared him to many influential persons. He served as an intermediary between Indian gentry and the colonial establishment and benefited thereby. But he used his intellectual gifts and social skills not to enrich himself but for a larger purpose. He wanted to push forward research on the history of Western India and specifically on the Maratha people. "During the period of his visits to the [princely] courts and the [government] offices, Parasnis did not swerve from his most cherished aim: that of collecting and printing old historical papers, of publishing old pictures and providing material for historical research."[73]

Parasnis was not an eccentric. An episode in Pune when he was in his early twenties also shows how a keen public interest in the historical past and its appropriation for a nation-building future moved hand in hand, in Maharashtra and British India generally. A paraphrase of Parasnis's detailed account of the episode follows: During the spring festival of 1890 in Pune, one Pandit Vasantrao gave a public lecture titled "The History of the Provinces of the Northwest and Ayodhya in the Past Thirty Years." His talk contained many interesting stories about Lakshmibai, the widowed rani (queen) of Jhansi. The Pune newspaper *Kesarī* carried a summary of his lecture in its issue of May 27, 1890. Parasnis wrote: "Pandit Vasantrao had narrated this widely known story in a spicy, novelistic way. His delivery was also attractive and pleasing, and the listeners found it most enjoyable. Other inhabitants of Pune also enjoyed it through the newspaper *Kesarī*'s report. This revived interest in and appreciation of the Rani." Parasnis added that his own 1894 biography of the rani was an indirect result of this controversy.

Parasnis continued: People in Pune had not the least idea of the existence of the rani's adopted son, Damodar Rao. He was upset at false stories being spread about her and wrote a letter contesting them; *Kesarī* published the letter on June 10, 1890. He "demanded to see what evidence the pandit had to support them. The editor of *Kesarī* now apologized to the noble Damodar Rao for the false report." People waited to see what evidence the pandit would produce; "he had almost nothing and he too apologized in a letter to *Kesarī* on 23 September 1890." But all this only increased public desire for an authentic history of the rani, and Parasnis launched his project, beginning by contacting Damodar Rao.

Damodar Rao supplemented what he knew from his own experience with the recollections of aged servants and surviving documents and sent it all to the author. Comparing this with the works of Malleson and other

English historians showed many contradictions, "but the truth of either could not be determined solely by the sources obtained from Damodar Rao." Parasnis then collected other English works on the revolt and studied them for evidence on the queen. But they were also evidently biased. He therefore turned to a further search for Indian sources. He sought out Hindi and Bengali publications. He also traveled to North India, visiting Jhansi and other cities. But little evidence could be found there, and Jhansi itself was transformed. Still, more impartial histories were beginning to appear in English, and they contained new information. He based his biography on a critical reading of all the sources he could obtain.[74] Parasnis came from an old ministerial lineage in Satara and was adept at the scrutiny, comparison, and verification of documents, skills that had been developed by traditional officials who often had to adjudicate (or make) claims. But the episode and the keen interest in *Kesarī*, the foremost Marathi newspaper of the day, shows the presence of a widespread historical consciousness that sought to ground itself in a recent past.

Parasnis's contemporary Vishwanath Kashinath Rajwade (1864–1926) also decided that solidly grounding history in the latest methods of source criticism would enable India to recapture its own history. He commented that efforts like Kirtane's were hamstrung by a lack of dependable contemporary sources. Rajwade was scathing in his critique of the *bakhar*s that were slowly coming into the world of print, and devoted several pages of the introduction to his first volume of sources (published in 1898) to a denunciation of their exaggerations, anachronisms, chronological confusions, and love for fabulous stories. The truly important sources, he held, were contemporary letters, dispatches, and other documents, and he used a few of these to demonstrate triumphantly how Duff had been completely wrong in his account of the movements of the Maratha armies in 1754.[75]

This enterprise of gathering primary sources was carried forward by a number of other scholars. Their efforts culminated in 1910 with the creation of the Bhārāta Itihāsa Samśodhak Maṇḍal (Society for the Study of Indian History, henceforth the BISM). Its cause was furthered by the prominent nationalist politician Bal Gangadhar Tilak. In 1915, returning from a six-year sentence of exile, the founder of the newspaper *Kesarī* wrote: "The modern age demands evidence for everything that you say. Nobody would listen to your gossip. Your ancestors surrendered your kingdom and if you lose your history, your successors would destroy your religion and there would be every possibility of the effacement of the very name of Maharashtra."[76]

In 1921, the BISM began publishing an important quarterly that has, down to the present, printed a wide range of texts and articles that form an irreplaceable source for the history of the Marathas. Some activists of the BISM were associated with radical strains in Indian nationalist politics, but others were part of the new colonial bureaucracy.

A leading figure in the new enterprise for a national history was Rajwade, a fierce nationalist who forsook all gainful employment and devoted almost forty years of his life to locating, editing, and publishing primary sources for the history of the Marathas.[77] Rajwade came to the discipline of history in the 1880s. He was outraged by Duff's *History of the Mahrattas* and set out to correct its errors from primary sources, especially those in Marathi, and supplement these. He collected large numbers of documents, ultimately publishing twenty-two volumes of the *Sources of Maratha History* in his lifetime and four more posthumously. He also contributed to many journals and edited several old manuscripts. His introductions sometime dwarfed the text and were, in effect, short monographs.[78] He thus sought to displace colonial history by a more rigorous application of its own methods. Leopold von Ranke's doctrines may have reached him by indirect routes, but he was certain that their application would vindicate both Maratha and Indian nationalism. This was the atmosphere in which the early venture for a public *and* documented history was launched in the Marathi-speaking world.

And so Rajwade began the enterprise of defeating colonial knowledge by crushing it with a superior body of primary, contemporary sources. Denied access to the state archive inherited from the Peshwas, radical historians sought out private, temple, and priestly collections. At the same time, another response to colonial dominance came in the form of the historical novel and play. As Prachi Deshpande has pointed out, novelists and dramatists also drew heavily on historical documents to lend verisimilitude to their works.[79] Some indeed were major historians themselves.

The most illustrious of these was Vasudev Vaman Khare. He began his research supported only by his salary as a Sanskrit teacher. Finding that his official duties interfered with research, he retired early and lived in penury on a pension of fifteen rupees a month in order to pursue his mission. He secured and edited tens of thousands of eighteenth-century documents and published an unparalleled collection of records in a series titled *Aitihāsik lekha saṁgraha* from Miraj and Pune. His introductions to these go far beyond their modest titles and amount to short monographs. As another noted historian, T. S. Shejwalkar, wrote of him in 1930, "Undying recognition of his greatness is assured by the long poems, plays, biographies, historical essays and, above all, the historical papers that he edited." But Khare also wrote historical plays, one of which, titled *Śivasambhava* (The Rise of Shiva), Shejwalkar describes as an excellent introduction to the biography of the first Chatrapati Shivaji.[80]

Marathi historical novels also multiplied parallel to the new public interest in history. The major novelist Harinarayana Apte declared that the two pillars of the historical novel were oral traditions (*dantkaththā*) and (authentic) histories (*itihāsa*).[81] Such novels clearly inherited much of the color and anachronistic spirit of the traditional *bakhar*s. This was, of course, true of Bengal too, where Bankim Chandra began writing loosely historical novels in the last decades of the nineteenth century. But there was a notable difference between the regions: Khare saw his plays as potboilers needed to earn money to sustain the much more important task of editing and publishing tens of thousands of authentic documents he found neglected in the Patwardhan archives.

It was in the 1890s that Ranade, now firmly established on the uppermost rungs of the colonial judiciary, finally returned to publishing historical essays. He published a book of essays titled *Rise of the Maratha Power* in 1900. It was partly based on a recently compiled but still unpublished collection of documents from the Pune archives. His text was still too nationalist to please officialdom. This even though he declared that, while he wanted to present the Indian standpoint, he sought above all "to enlist the sympathy of the representatives of the conquering British power in the fortunes of its worsted rival."[82] As Ranade well knew, in colonized India, the need for state patronage (or at least avoidance of disfavor) excluded radical versions of nationalist history from the education system that took shape in the mid-nineteenth century. Nationalist history, however occasionally broke into print. An example of the latter was V. D. Savarkar's *The Indian War of Independence*, written in 1906–7.[83] Savarkar carefully mined standard British sources, like contemporary English memoirs and Kaye and Malleson's multivolume history of the great revolt of 1857–58. He also sought out Marathi manuscript sources, such as the yet unpublished memoir by Vishnubhat Godse.

Savarkar then carefully displayed his sources in text and footnotes—indeed, it might be said that he commanded a wider range of sources than many who publish about those events even in the present day. The book eschewed the prophetic or millenarian appeals that still resonated to many in the colonized world.[84] It drew most of its information from nineteenth-century British sources read "against the grain" and supplemented them with some similarly authentic Marathi documents.[85] Its most striking feature is how never-proven British theories of the uprising as originating in long-plotted conspiracies were consciously adopted by Savarkar. This was almost certainly so as to suggest to readers that this might be achieved again by a new generation in India. Savarkar's generation of nationalists looked to Mazzini's Young Italy and to the contemporary Irish nationalists and Russian revolutionary "People's Will" organization. Banned before its appearance, *The Indian War of Independence* was printed in France, and stray copies circulated illegally in India. A senior British official, Valentine Chirol, described the book as "combining considerable research with the grossest perversions of facts and great literary power with the most savage hatred."[86] With an eye to the turmoil of his own time, Savarkar recast the evidence into a narrative of a great cross-religious Indian conspiracy that almost succeeded before being derailed by fortuitous events and human weaknesses. Jawaharlal Nehru read the banned text in the 1920s. He thought it "a brilliant book" and judged that a new concise edition would be an ideal corrective to the English propaganda."[87] Thus one school of nationalist history unselfconsciously used the methods of Western historiography to develop a dominant national narrative engaged in a running polemic with "imperialist" history. It was therefore part of new pursuit of "scientific history" that, as Dipesh Chakrabarty observes, began in India in the 1880s and intensified in the early twentieth century. Chakrabarty notes that it was particularly intense in Bengal and Maharashtra.[88]

The BISM was founded in Pune in 1910. Many of early participants joined its efforts as a part of the patriotic enterprise that had gathered strength in the early twentieth century. A few began to be paid meager stipends after the institution's finances improved a little in the 1930s. The career of Ganesh Hari Khare (1901–1985) is a striking illustration of this. He volunteered at a night school while still a student himself (1916–19), joined the Non-Cooperation Movement in 1920, and subsequently participated in early agitations protesting the uncompensated displacement of rural people by large dam projects. The British government sentenced him to one year's imprisonment for his political activities. During the 1920s, he also taught himself paleography and came to Pune to join the newly commenced project of publishing primary sources from "the Shivaji period" of Maratha history. This was despite his having no regular income and usually eating just one meal a day. After six months, Khare was hired by the BISM for a small salary. He improved his paleographic skills and began working with Persian sources as well. He was a mainstay of the institute for many decades. He personally transcribed more than 75 percent of all *farmāns* from the Adilshahi Sultanate that have been published up to 2010. He also wrote hundreds of articles and many books in English and Marathi.[89] His life exemplifies the union of nationalism and historical research in Maharashtra.

Such associations made British authorities even more suspicious of requests to use official documents. When, therefore, no less than the Secretary of State for India, Robert Milnes, Marquess of Crewe, vehemently opposed opening government records to researchers in 1914, he was likely smarting from the use that Savarkar had made of the few records available to him.[90] Such official obstruction continued into the 1920s. The subtext to it can easily be seen in the ferocious response to F. W. Buckler, a junior academic at the University of Cambridge, when he ventured to suggest that the British assumption of sovereignty from the Mughal emperors was based on falsification of the historical record. What had happened in 1857, Buckler argued, was that the army "turned to its sovereign's allegiance against its rebel officer. Hence, in 1857 if there were any mutineer, it was the East India Company." That elicited a furious response from several veterans of the colonial establishment, including Douglas Dewar of the Indian Civil Service, jointly with H. L. Garrett of the Indian Education Service. The reply from another civil servant, S. M. Edwardes revealed the true source of their collective fury: "Indeed, had this pamphlet been published at the time when Vinayak Savarkar was compiling his *Indian War of Independence, 1857*, one can imagine that the Brahman rebel would have welcomed Mr. Buckler's theory, as lending some support to the views underlying his seditious publication." Edwardes added that the outbreak had nothing to do with Indian resentment of British usurpation but originated in the fundamental Hindu antagonism to Western civilization, "one of the mainsprings of anarchical conspiracies and non-cooperation movements."[91] The allusion to Gandhian noncooperation is unmistakable.

The devolution of authority from the central government to the provinces in the 1920s finally gave some real powers to Indian elected ministers. One of the results was that the government of Bombay came up with a small grant for the selection and editing of documents from the "Alienation Office." But even then it was Jadunath Sarkar who was asked to nominate an editor, as he was a government employee and not suspected of "excessive" nationalism. He nominated G. S. Sardesai, a careful historian, but also Sarkar's ally against the more nationalist scholars around the BISM.[92]

Meanwhile, Rajwade struggled with the difficulties of writing satisfying historical narratives in a rigorously documented mode. In his last years, he came to take a more sympathetic view of the *bakhars*—especially the *Mahikavatichi bakhar*, which he edited and published in 1924. In a lengthy introduction, he bent over backward to provide a factual basis for the diverse and contradictory narratives contained in it, and in his conclusion he cast two personages from it as heroes: Nayakorao, the warrior, and Keshavacharya, the Brahman preceptor.[93] (There is no evidence of their having been historical personages of any significance, or even having existed.) It is clear that he projected them as fifteenth-century forerunners of a Hindu nationalist movement that he desired in the colonized present. So the pioneer of the strict construction of verifiable history from contemporary sources found its results ultimately unsatisfying and returned to narrative modes far closer to those of the *bakhar*s he had formerly denounced. But though he was venerated by some and his compilations used by every historian of Maharashtra, the main currents of history had flowed past him. Not Rajwade or Savarkar but G. S. Sardesai wrote a definitive political history of the Maratha state from Shahaji Bhosle to the British, a work that is still in print.[94]

THE HINDU NATIONALIST PROJECT AND VIJAYANAGARA

Meanwhile, the emergence of Hindu-Muslim political tension in the 1920s contributed to a new interest in the Vijayanagara Empire. The outlines of a historical view of the empire as a defensive reaction to Muslim conquest had already been established by Robert Sewell in 1900. He established a narrative of Vijayanagara as a bastion of South Indian Hindu culture against alien Muslim invaders. He described the tide of Islamic conquest as overrunning the south until suddenly "about the year 1344 A.D., there was a check to this wave of foreign invasion—a stop—a halt—then a solid wall of opposition; and for 250 years Southern India was saved."[95] Sewell's history appeared at a key time for historians of South India. By the late nineteenth century, some Maratha historians were seeking "Hindu" rather than Islamicate roots for Maratha imperial formation. This was the path also taken by some of the earliest Tamil historians of the Vijayanagara Empire.[96] At the same time, they were engaged in finding indigenous (defined as Sanskrit, Tamil, or Telugu) sources of history to supplement or refute both the contemporary colonial as well as the medieval Persian sources of South Indian history.

An ambitious effort to connect Vijayanagara to the Marathi historical imagination was made near the commonly accepted sexcentenary of that empire's founding (1936). The Commemoration Committee contacted the

BISM and sought its cooperation in preparing a complete Marathi translation of the English volume being issued for that occasion.[97] The BISM made a considerable effort and complied with this request. In addition, it commissioned several additional chapters and a chronological table that were all added to the Marathi volume. Texts were also edited so as to be more accessible to the Marathi-reading public.[98]

A short preface titled "The Debt Owed to Vijayanagara," originally delivered as an address on December 26, 1936, by Shejwalkar, opened the volume. He began by arguing that while great civilizations like the Egyptian, Assyrian, Sumerian, and Iranian ones had disappeared from the earth, Indian civilization still lived. In medieval times, it had been forced to take shelter in the south before being taken into the hands of the Marathas and brought further north. "The protection of Vijayanagara gave this civilization its recent but crucial foothold, and it is the memory of this that we celebrate at this gathering today." He paid Vijayanagara the highest compliment available to him by declaring that its founding, six centuries before he was writing, had the same historic significance as the birth of the future Chatrapati Shivaji three centuries later.[99] His full-length essay in the same volume made an explicit effort to connect the two empires by arguing that Shivaji's object in his southern campaigns was to lay the foundation for a new empire like Vijayanagara, one which would be capable of confronting the Mughal emperor Aurangzeb. But he goes back to Shivaji's father, Shahaji. "From one point of view, Shahaji was grinding one Hindu empire into dust; from another point of view, he was laying the foundation of another Hindu empire."[100] But Shejwalkar's effort was an artifact of the religious politics of the 1930s. It was specifically an effort to construct a Hindu nationalist vision of a beleaguered civilization holding out against alien powers—explicitly, the Muslim sultanates and implicitly the British. But, as we have seen, the Maratha *Swarāj* (homeland) of the eighteenth century never constructed such a genealogy for itself.

The following narrative came to light in the effort to recover non-Persian accounts of the great Vijayanagara empire. It purported to be the story of the fall of Vijayanagara as written by an eyewitness to the battle of Rakshas-Tagdi, or Talikota. The incomplete Marathi text was first published by G. K. Chandorkar in the second annual volume of the *Proceedings of the BISM* in 1914. He lacked the first few pages, and they have never been found. In the 1990s, neither the Devanagari press copy nor the original manuscript used by Chandorkar could be located. Therefore, the Nagari printed text of 1914 is the only available copy of the Marathi version as it appeared in the early twentieth century.[101] Then various Kannada versions of what seemed to be the same story began to be located. S. Krishnaswamy Iyengar located a Kannada manuscript titled *Rāmrājana bakhairu* in the Oriental Manuscripts Library, Madras. That Kannada text was printed in 1922. Iyengar suggested that Chandorkar's Marathi work was an abridged translation of the Kannada original, which was itself written within a year of the great battle itself. This appealed to the growing effort to construct a succession of Hindu empires in southern India, whereby the legacy of Vijayanagara could be depicted as inherited by the Marathas. Iyengar published a summary in 1925.[102] An English translation from Kannada also lay unpublished in the India Office Collection. In 1946, a Kannada text and English translation appeared in *Further Sources of Vijayanagara History*.[103] Meanwhile the 1922 Kannada text had been studied by N. S. Rajpurohit as a guide to the location of the battlefield. He translated several passages into Marathi and paraphrased the rest. This article appeared in 1929.[104]

I will not enter into minute comparisons here, but it appears evident that several Kannada versions going back to (perhaps) 1800 were extant. Internal evidence and major inconsistencies show that none of these texts were even remotely contemporary to the battle. In fact, as I suggest below, it is more likely that the version available to Chandorkar (and through him, G. B. Gramopadhye) was written around 1800. This *bakhar*'s late southern origins are also evident in that "Akbar Jalaluddin Mughal Padshah" was shown as joining the coalition against Ramaraja, when he was in reality hundreds of miles away in North India that winter.

He is also referred to as ruling from Jalnapur, now the modest provincial town of Jalna (central Maharashtra, near Aurangabad) instead of Delhi or Agra! Jalna town was a strategic position for the Nizam of Hyderabad's campaigns against the Marathas, especially after he had lost the great fort of Ahmadnagar to the Peshwas in 1759. Jalna was later taken by the Marathas. The British forced its return to the Nizam in 1803.[105] But Maratha traditions—even the most fantastic ones—invariably visualize the Mughals as ruling from Delhi, and they would not have located the emperor Akbar in the obscure frontier town of Jalna. If, however, the only "Mogal" that the *bakhar*'s author knew was the Nizam of Hyderabad, the idea that the emperor Akbar ruled from Jalna becomes slightly less absurd. This is not to say that this text is devoid of fantasy; in fact, almost all of it is just that. So the scribe knew the names of ninety elephants and the number and type of fruits given by the king to his senior queen, possessed amazingly inflated military muster rolls, and counted that either four *million* or four *billion* (the text is confused) rockets were fired by the Karnatak army in one salvo. All this suggests that Chandorkar's text is a translation into Marathi of a late and fragmentary Kannada manuscript. It seems likely that a small core narrative was vastly inflated with fanciful details and a folk tale mocking Muslims for eating chicken, all perhaps to secure larger fee from colonial-era manuscript collectors.

Nonetheless, such was the hunger for authentically indigenous accounts of Vijayanagara that several historians accepted Chandorkar's text as entirely authentic. The text is in fact a testimony to the loss of real historical knowledge of the great empire among the successors to its former dominion. But the effort to find the story of Vijayanagara in the Marathi tradition led to the widespread adoption of the apocryphal text. In 1952 Gramopadhye, a professor of Marathi literature, produced a small volume of selections from different *bakhar*s, including this one.[106] But when editing his selection, Gramopadhye had largely omitted what he must have viewed as the "non-historical" or perhaps "fanciful" parts of the texts. This led to the omission of portions such as the lengthy descriptions of the emperor's visits to the palaces of his three principal queens and the highly imaginative list of fruits and other gifts that he distributed. The plainly fanciful list of military equipment is included because Gramopadhye evidently assumed it to be accurate. This presumption is reflected in his comment on the statement that there were oxen, each carrying twenty-eight projectiles (*bāṇa*). He remarks that each ox would easily have carried one or two hundred arrows. As later allusions to their being ignited for discharge clearly indicate, these were obviously supposed to be the simple rockets widely used in South Indian warfare during the eighteenth century. If so, then twenty-eight per bullock would be a reasonable load. But Gramopadhye interprets *bāṇa* in its original Sanskrit meaning of "arrow" and believes all these numbers to be factual. This is evident from his footnote "Why would each ox carry only 28 *bāṇa*? Each ox would easily carry one or two hundred *bāṇa*."[107] He thus rejected the one accurate detail in this farrago of fiction.[108]

The revival and reappropriation of this text in the 1930s was reflective of the effort to consolidate Hindus as a political community and enlist Maratha memory in that enterprise. That was tied into the larger narrative of Hindu nationalism that was taking organized shape in the twentieth century. Christophe Jaffrelot, one of the early analysts of this this phenomenon, observes that the movement "was born in Maharashtra in the 1920s."[109] Savarkar, author of *The Indian War of Independence*, went on to write *Hindu-padpadshahi*, a strident work of religious nationalism. An echo of the efforts of the 1930s came when the British-Caribbean author V. S. Naipaul visited Vijayanagara in 1976 and used its ruins to frame India as a "wounded civilization." "What happened in Vijayanagar happened, in varying degrees, in other parts of the country. In the north, ruin lies on ruin: Moslem ruin on Hindu ruin, Moslem on Moslem."[110]

But the appropriation of history to a Hindu nationalist project encountered considerable resistance in the Marathi-speaking public sphere. Jaffrelot has observed that resistance to an upper-caste project of Sanskritization also began in Western India far earlier than the north.[111] In Maharashtra, not surprisingly, this turned on the memory of the Chatrapati Shivaji. This reflected the unusually early rise of lower-caste politics in the region. This strain of thought began in Maharashtra with the Satyashodhak Samaj founded by Jyotirao Phule (usually referred to as Mahatma Phule) in the mid-nineteenth century. It reached India-wide stature under the leadership of Bhimrao Ambedkar in the twentieth century.[112] Deeper social histories as well as local histories began to be written. Alongside canonical works, a new Marathi-language historiography that was much more critical of the Brahmanical character of the Peshwas' regime also emerged. On the other hand, many currents of popular and academic history converged around the founder Chatrapati Shivaji. A more recent tacit critique of the Hindutva was written by the late A. R. Kulkarni, who founded the department of history in Pune University. While he was initially appropriated as a unifying transreligious ("secular") historical symbol, his very prominence also led to efforts at appropriating him for narrower causes, such as "sons of the soil" movements and Hindu nationalism. It has also in recent years led to politically motivated violence against anyone thought to have been disrespectful to his memory.

While Shivaji was celebrated across twentieth-century India, he was never lionized by the colonial establishment, which was still anxious about historical memory among the Marathi-speaking peoples. The kingdoms of Rajasthan were safer subjects, especially since they were being cultivated as allies against any resurgence of Maratha power. James Tod's *Annals and Antiquities of Rajasthan* (1829–32) was a success right at the outset. Tod was an army officer who served in Central India beginning in 1805, and a political agent (supervising envoy) to the western Rajput states from 1818 to 1823. His book was to prove profoundly influential in shaping the writing of colonial history and the nationalist narratives that followed it.

Talbot has recently traced the rise, through many metamorphoses of the public memory of Prithviraj Chauhan (historically Chahamana). The study of the creation of monuments and sites of memory was originally pioneered by the French historian Pierre Nora. Talbot uses Nora's wider definition of "site'" to include anything that has become a symbolic element of the material heritage of any community. These have been little studied in postcolonial India even though the country has seen a proliferation of such memorialization, with sites being rebuilt to fit the developing "memory." Talbot also mines the manuscript and inscriptional record in several languages and over several centuries to trace the early corpus of narratives in which Prithviraj appears, so as to narrate the metamorphoses his tale undergoes through the centuries. She begins with the earliest near-contemporary narratives of this king, written in Sanskrit and also in the distinct Persian historical tradition. Then she traces the emergence of a "standard narrative" that originated in the colonial retelling of Persian histories from the thirteenth and fourteenth centuries, and notes how later versions increasingly minimize Prithviraj's embedding in the central Rajasthan city of Ajmer to emphasize his role as king of Delhi. Thus Talbot carefully traces the creation of site of memory at the capital of late imperial India (1911–47) and the Republic of India.

But the monumental appropriation of Prithviraj was preceded by the discursive memorialization in Tod. Talbot shows that Tod largely accepted the traditions of the Rajputs as historical. Tod's romantic account of Rajput history loomed large not only in colonial texts but also later works by Indian authors.[113] It was to have a powerful effect on historical narrative in South Asia thereafter. Independent India's first Minister for Education, Abul Kalam Azad, saw the propagation of Tod's narratives as part of the British effort to set Hindus against Muslims. "There is enough material in Todd's Annals [*sic*] to colour the history of the middle ages in a way that would poison the relations of Hindus and Muslims."[114] But the great majority of each community probably came to Tod indirectly via versions of his legends embedded in school textbooks and the increasing number of plays and novels that featured episodes from his *Annals*.[115] It is to school texts that we now turn.

SCHOOLROOM HISTORY IN COLONIAL INDIA

The new British government reached into local society to a degree unmatched by previous administrations. Its functionaries were, therefore, more numerous and more powerful. At the same time, they were increasingly the products of the still-growing colonial educational establishment. Families from the older professional classes, as well as new men from the landed and business strata, began to send their sons to the new schools. Printing had been introduced early by European governments and missionaries in Asia, and by 1800, fonts had been created for several major languages. The new government used printing as an important technology of governance. The presses, for example, issued manuals and regulations and provided forms and registers for state functionaries and textbooks for the new schools. No longer was teaching to be done from random printed texts and such manuscripts as individual instructors had assembled to supplement their memories. It was this universal requirement that made textbooks so prominent in the gradual emergence of a "commonsense" history in British India.

The impact of colonial education was not limited to Bengal, where it first began. In 1803 the British seized control of the old Mughal cities of Delhi and Agra; their empire extended across the Panjab to the Khyber Pass by 1849. Missionary enterprise, patronized by powerful interests in Britain, pushed into these new territories too. They had been preceded, centuries earlier, by Roman Catholic preaching orders, such as the Capuchins and Jesuits. But none met with much success.[116] But the nineteenth-century Protestant missions were fueled by a new zeal and supported by the new bourgeois wealth of the early industrial revolution. By the 1840s, missionaries began pressing Islamic scholars for full-scale theological debate. Some debates were arranged, and Islamic scholarship generally held its own against evangelical challenge. The local Islamic intelligentsia's unease grew with the growing introduction of Western sciences and history into the curriculum of government-supported schools and colleges, for instance, at Delhi College. Furthermore, the expansion of printed polemic by the missionaries made responses in Urdu—the language of the literate across North India—all the more necessary. Some ulema (Islamic scholars) soon came to feel that the government was biased against them.[117] Syed Ahmed Khan stressed the widespread sense that the new education system was intended to subvert Islam, which manifested itself in the uprising of 1857–58.[118] The ruthless suppression of the revolt forced resistance into indirect channels. These included contesting textbooks and education. Syed Ahmed Khan, Munshi Zakaullah, Babu Raja (later Raja) Shiv Prasad, Bharatendu Harishchandra, and Swami Dayanand were some of the prominent participants in these polemics. The history that the educated public learned was not just from textbooks but, importantly, also in the counternarratives that these men (and others) produced and disseminated in the public sphere.

The growth of government bureaucracy and a growing insistence that its Indian personnel have some Western-style education soon enlarged the readership of the new histories, or schoolroom versions of them. Earlier generations of governors, such as Elphinstone or Munro, had felt that a reformed South Asian system was all that was needed for a successful administration. Consequently, indigenous education needed few changes beyond some limited financial support. But Macaulay's victory over the "Orientalist" school meant that Indian education had to be rebuilt from the ground up. East India Company parsimony meant that efforts at creating Western-style schools only intensified when it came under parliamentary scrutiny in the 1850s. Three universities were created in Calcutta, Bombay, and Madras in 1857. The royal government took direct charge of Indian administration in 1858. It pushed the same modernizing agenda. But the numbers educated were still tiny: in 1861–62, after the disruption of the great uprising had subsided, Calcutta University saw twenty-four successful BA students and yet smaller numbers for medicine and engineering. The total attendance at all government colleges in the five major provinces of British India was 2,712 (drawn from a population of about 250 million). Meanwhile, the attendance at all state-inspected primary schools in 1870 was 518,000. Schools were also thin on the ground, ranging from one per ninety-six square miles in Bengal province to one per twenty-two square miles in the North-Western Provinces.[119] In all parts of British India, local communities were expected to fund significant parts of the cost of lower-level schools. Teachers were correspondingly underpaid.

But the new education was seen as promising a share in government, with all the power and prestige that accompanied it. Initially, personal connections and apprenticeships were the commonest way that British Indian employees were recruited. Gradually, however, candidates with qualifications from the new schools and universities began to be preferred. That intensified after 1859 when the Secretary of State for India emphasized that a special permission would be needed to appoint anyone lacking an elementary education to any post with a salary exceeding six rupees a month.[120]

The case of the Tagores (discussed in chapter 2) was but one of the many that illustrated how British favor and bureaucratic success now played a large a part in the political economy that controlled status. It is not surprising, therefore, that English intervention in the history-writing process should have a great impact. English-language histories began to be gradually diluted down into Indian-language school and college textbooks. As we saw in chapter 1, Elphinstone, Marshman, and others of less note initially provided the master texts from which Indian-language textbooks began to be written. John C. Marshman, the son of the important Baptist missionary Joshua Marshman, did not belong to the aristocracy. He also did not share

Elphinstone's deist or perhaps Unitarian leanings. Joshua came from humble beginnings, being initially a Nonconformist weaver who nonetheless trained for the Baptist ministry and came out to India. His five year-old son John traveled with him. This John Marshman was for several decades closely connected with the Serampore Mission and its efforts at vernacular education. Marshman wrote several school histories; the earliest seems to have been *The History of India from Remote Antiquity to the Accession of the Mogul Dynasty*. It was printed in 1836 and initially met with a cold reception from the colonial establishment. Though it aimed to supply the perceived need for a school textbook, colonial educational authorities were far from eager to embrace it. Marshman wrote bitterly in the preface that he had not renewed an application for support from the Bombay government because of the insulting response received to an earlier communication, while the Madras administration had declared that it lacked the funds to assist his project. Finally, the Bengal government undertook to purchase one hundred copies for 150 rupees, a sum that Marshman described as far short of what was needed to even cover the cost of the books he had purchased for the project.[121]

But even if Marshman was initially rebuffed by officialdom, his text came to form the basis of early texts in Hindi (1846) as well as several in Bengali; Gopall Loll Mitra translated Marshman's history into Bengali in 1840. Marshman's criticisms of Hinduism certainly grated on his translator, whose preface complained that the author had, in some places, resorted to speculative inferences in order to criticize the Hindu faith. He had faithfully translated these passages but added his own refutations of these at the end.[122] The colonial project thus generated critical responses right from the outset. South Asians had ignored earlier European bizarrerie, such as the common Roman Catholic identification of Hindu gods with the devil and his infernal minions. The new historical challenge, supposedly founded on the superior Western knowledge that harnessed steam and made machines do unimaginable things, was harder to ignore. Still, beyond the English and Persian sources he cited, Marshman and his colleagues also drew on the folklore traditions of Bengal. The apocryphal King Adishura was, for example, accepted as authentic.[123] Marshman also learned the name of the Sena dynasty that ruled before the Turkish conquest (c. 1206). As "Sen" was in recent centuries a common last name among the Vaidya (or Baidya, nowadays meaning "physician") caste of the area, he probably followed contemporary informants and declared that Bengal had been ruled by "monarchs of the physician tribe."[124]

The demand for textbooks increased starting in the middle of the century as the new imperial government that replaced the East India Company accelerated projects of bureaucratic and educational modernization begun by Governor-General Lord Hardinge and Lord Dalhousie.[125] Thus the emerging Indian intelligentsia often read some version of Marshman in school. A tiny handful went to college or university and again encountered similar, more sophisticated anglophone histories. So they could not so easily ignore the new historical framing of their past and present. Furthermore, even under the early East India Company, traditional scholars had still possessed one prestigious refuge from Western education. Hindu and Muslim scholars were employed as experts in their respective legal traditions in the colonial judiciary. They were thus in a position to exert significant influence on that powerful institution. But a body of translations, and more importantly, a printed body of case law in English, took shape during the nineteenth century. The role of indigenous scholars withered away. On the other hand, English education allowed men to not just guide judges but rise to the bar and bench themselves. The colonial school thus became an indispensable gateway to social prominence and a secure livelihood. More or less successful residential versions modeled on English public schools were later created for the education of the indigenous aristocracy and princes. The first school history textbooks were a vital factor in forcing the budding intelligentsia into confronting the many fragmented traditions still current in the larger social milieu whence they came. They offered a powerfully persuasive new narrative. The resulting compulsory narrative integration was more pervasive, more homogenous, and more durable than the previous integration of histories undertaken in the Mughal epoch. It carried the prestige of the West, and its effects last to the present day. New textbooks written by select Indian intellectuals gradually replaced Marshman's schoolbooks from the 1850s, just as English-style education was being enlarged across North India.[126]

Avril Powell has published a richly textured study of the debates stirred up by two Hindi-Urdu school textbooks written by the Indians Raja Shiv Prasad and Karim al-Din. Those debates in turn contributed to the emerging Hindu-Muslim divide in northern India. Shiv Prasad's textbook came earlier and was adopted in the modern Uttar Pradesh area; Karim al-Din's was based on Shiv Prasad's. Both textbooks were in fact, heavily dependent on English language histories by Marshman and Elphinstone. But, as her careful analysis shows, each of these authors was a considerable scholar who added additional material from the major primary sources into the school texts.

Shiv Prasad was a protégé of Henry M. Elliot (1808–1853),[127] a powerful British official. Already proficient in "Oriental languages" when recruited,

Elliot pursued a research career alongside his official one and began compiling translations from the major Persian histories available to him. His translations had the embedded program of highlighting the virtue of British rule through a dark representation of Muslim rule in India. They were later edited in nine volumes by John Dowson from 1868 to 1877. They have remained in print ever since. Elliot had already declared in 1850 that the perusal of the Persian histories would serve to "dissipate the gorgeous illusions which are commonly entertained regarding the dynasties which have passed" and to show that the British had done more good in fifty years than their Muslim predecessors had in ten times that period. He added that while earlier historians wrote little about the conditions of the ruled, he would infer their condition from that of the contemporary subjects of the "Muhammedan kingdoms of India," whose rulers still emulated the worst of the Roman emperors.[128]

Elliot's ideas seeped into the world of colonial education even before Dowson printed the compilation. Elliot was Shiv Prasad's early patron in the emerging educational establishment. Another sponsor was William Edwards, also a secretary to the government of India. Shiv Prasad himself was a scholarly Oswal Jain who knew English, Sanskrit, and Persian, as well as other languages. He left British India to work in the state of Bharatpur at the age of sixteen but then secured an appointment as a scribe in the Rajputana Agency. In 1843 he left that post and returned to Banaras, his hometown. He was then employed successively by two important officials, Edwards and then Elliot, as a secretary. He then moved to a post in the emerging United Provinces Education Department. Shiv Prasad was initially employed only as a junior officer, but he ultimately rose to be Deputy Inspector of Schools. An early colonial intellectual, he was already connected with several influential officials.[129] That position, one would infer, gave him considerable power over the colonial vernacular intelligentsia employed in government-aided schools. He was also awarded the title of "Raja" by the government of India. Insofar as his reports might affect his superiors' decisions on grants-in-aid, he could indirectly dominate the trusts and sponsors who sustained non-government schools. Shiv Prasad wrote *Itihāsa timirnāśaka* (Dispeller of Historical Obscurity), a widely used history textbook in Hindi, and shortly thereafter translated it into Urdu with the title *A'inah-i tārīkh numa* (The Mirror of History). Elliot's agenda of highlighting British humaneness through lurid depictions of the debauchery and brutality of preceding Muslim rulers informed Shiv Prasad's textbooks. He discussed massacres in lurid detail, with repeated descriptions of how women and children—even breastfeeding infants—were not spared. He was also a leading protagonist in the Hindi-Urdu controversy in the 1870s.[130]

The contemporary Urdu history textbook used in the Panjab was written by Karim al-Din.[131] Karim al-Din came from a family of scholars in Panipat and was an important contributor to Persian and Urdu literary studies. He, like Shiv Prasad, rose high in the provincial educational establishment, in his case in the province of Panjab (which then extended from Delhi to Peshawar). Karim al-Din, Powell observes, reworked Shiv Prasad's textbook but based his text on Marshman's *History*. He also added information from the Persian histories of Abul Fazl and of Fereshte, as well Tabatabai's late eighteenth-century work. His work appeared with the title *Waqi'at-i Hind* (Indian Events).[132]

In order to understand why religious objections to both Shiv Prasad's *and* Karim al-Din's textbooks arose at this time, we have to step back and consider how Hindu sacred text was being historicized.[133] Initially, arguments turned around issues of the corporeal or incorporeal nature of the divine principle, the distasteful dietary habits of Christians, and similar themes.[134] But by the mid-nineteenth century, Vedic texts that traditional Hindu scholarship had deemed perfect and timeless were drawn into historical time by authorities closely associated with a powerful government. Furthermore, this government had a growing presence in education, and participation in that education was increasingly a prerequisite for state, or even private, employment. That inevitably required confronting newly aggressive, and sometimes disconcertingly erudite, Christian propagandists. For example, James Ballantyne was appointed principal of the Banaras Sanskrit College, an institution originally founded to sustain traditional Indian learning. Ballantyne was a vigorous advocate of Christianity and in 1859 published a work intended to strengthen Christian missionaries in debates with Hindu pandits. The book declared that the truth of Christianity was shown by Christ's miracles, which could only have been performed with authentic divine aid. The facticity of the miracles was attested by their witnesses being willing to suffer martyrdom in proof. "And all of this is founded on historical inference. . . . We therefore proceed to state what valid arguments, in respect of the fact that the Christian religion came from God, are derivable from the stores of history."[135]

Vasudha Dalmia cites this is as one example of how missionaries repeatedly brought forward the "*historical verifiability* of the incarnation of their god and the miracles he performed" as against the ahistorical Hindu accounts of their own gods.[136] The emerging British world-historical narrative soon also appeared in Indian-language textbooks and had to be learned by the budding colonial intelligentsia. It was also deployed in efforts at the "rectification" of historical memory. Shahid Amin has examined several Hindi tracts often written by men affiliated with the Arya Samaj in eastern Uttar Pradesh. One began by declaring that the man who does not know his own history cannot understand how to move along "the path of progress."[137]

It was thus impossible for scholars to ignore history as a source of authority without being dismissed as ignoramuses. Indian scholars who wished to defend any given position could no longer rely upon traditional forms of exegesis and proof. Hence even the most overtly dismissive of the West had to provide arguments grounded in Western-style history and framed within a universal chronology. Asia has had an ancient tradition of religious debate founded on philosophical reasoning. Nineteenth-century Christian missionaries introduced a new trope. Christian polemic partly grounded its arguments in the *historical* veracity of events such as miracles. Both Muslims and Hindus then responded with new historical as well as older philosophical defenses of their own beliefs. An early example of this process was Vishnubawa Brahmachari in Maharashtra. He started to respond actively to the growing presence of aggressively polemical Christian missionaries in the region by taking up their tactics starting in about 1850. These included public debates. These debates were often held on Back Bay beach in Bombay before audiences of up to two thousand. He invoked the Veda as the fount of all knowledge. To blunt missionary attacks on "superstition and idolatry," he was quite prepared to treat many Hindu practices as merely pedagogic stages to true insight.

But beyond the philosophical and scriptural, his defense depended on an invocation of history and on recent European advances in it. The Indo-European languages, he claimed, were all descended from Sanskrit, which was the fount of all true knowledge. Furthermore, he countered English claims that cited industrial and scientific leadership as demonstrating the superiority of Christianity by claiming that Vedic Indians already had steamships, telescopes, printing presses, and so on. Thus "all the great material accomplishments, which in modern times the Europeans claimed as their own, originally existed in India." As Conlon describes, Vishnubawa's "great strength lay in his readiness to adapt new information into a rather inchoate mass of facts and fables, secured by an overarching belief in an idealized Vedic age and sustained by his own rhetorical powers." He also deployed the new medium of print and a long exposition of his monist version of the Vedas was published in 1859.[138] Nor is he likely to have been the only Indian to respond in the same way. Krishna Kumar has perceptively traced the beginning of a new traditionalism or "revivalism" to late nineteenth-century responses to colonial education.[139]

That response, however, would meet with an obvious retort from the protagonists of Western civilization. They could legitimately ask why had it proved necessary for European engineers and technicians to introduce modern technologies to India if they were long known there? At that point, the premolded work of Elliot and others could be invoked to explain the low state of India at the outset of British rule. British historians' depiction of "Muslim rule" thus came to be used to explain conditions at the beginning of British rule and, indeed, to implicitly see the conquest as a redeeming force. That pro-British, but anti-Muslim, stance was especially valuable for those seeking lodgment in the emerging colonial educational establishment as it displaced responsibility for backwardness from the British on to their "Muslim" predecessors. Indeed, it tapped into the already extant western Indophile narrative of the British as rescuers of oppressed Indians.

INDIGENIST RESPONSES IN COLONIAL EDUCATION

Even after the expansion of primary education in the twentieth century, it only reached a small fraction of the population. R. V. Parulekar calculated that the 1911 census only enumerated 5.4 percent of the population in British India as literate, and by 1931 this had risen to a mere 6.9 percent.[140] But the uppermost fraction of this small elite was to shape the politics of South Asia into the twentieth century and after. Its members also participated in crafting institutional responses to the challenge of what seemed to be the conjoined forces of Westernization and Christianity. Some forty years ago, Kenneth Jones and Barbara Metcalf separately presented an institutional history of two important North Indian responses to that challenge.[141] These were the Arya Samaj and the Dar al-Ulum in Deoband. Barbara Metcalf wrote of the latter that "schools became their characteristic institution. Their dominant activities were education and propaganda." It slowly implanted a uniformly trained Islamic intelligentsia in little schools and informal instructional settings across South Asia. It also depended (like the more elite Aligarh College) on a network of donors and alumni. This new pattern of funding again intensified its networking effect across British India and beyond. Metcalf also notes its parallels with the Arya Samaj and the new organizational methods learned from Christian missions.[142] "More and more Muslims shared a common language in Urdu: the language of the new schools, of the books and pamphlets and translations of religious classics, and of ever more popular public debate. They shared greater concern with the sources of the faith, the "high tradition" to which increasing numbers assimilated."[143]

But the two institutional projects were differently placed with regard to the European narrative of South Asian history. Colonial textbooks already drew liberally upon Persian histories written under the patronage of Muslim rulers. Several textbooks and research monographs were being written by leading members of the new indigenous intelligentsia, like Munshi Zakaullah (1832–1910). He had been educated at Delhi College in a combination of Islamicate and Western sciences. He later served as inspector of schools and ended his government career as professor at Muir Central College at Allahabad. He could declare that he had composed the Mughal empire chapters of his history of India mainly from the best contemporary Persian historians before resorting to less dependable European texts.[144] Furthermore, monuments to Mughal rule were still visible across the Indian subcontinent; it was easy to demonstrate their achievements. Colonial textbooks already demarcated history into Hindu, Muslim and British periods. Students, both Muslim and others, would easily (and falsely) extrapolate "Muslim" rule with their own lived experience of subjection in colonial South Asia. They observed a few thousand British officials and seventy thousand soldiers lording it over millions of Indians. The gradual embedding of that delusion in the "commonsense" past of literate and illiterate alike was to have vast political consequences that have endured to the present.[145]

The Arya Samaj loomed large across the cultural and religious landscape of North India from the 1870s. Krishna Kumar found that it had an important place in the biographies of many litterateurs and social leaders of the time. It was important in that it united several modes of intervention and deployed them in the new colonial public sphere. First of all, it tapped into much older oral practices of memory maintained by communities of religious practice across South Asia. Second, it employed the institutional methods of the Christian missionary networks that it sought to counter, including public debates and full-time preachers. It also reached across the British Empire to preach to the emerging Indian diaspora elsewhere. Third, the Samaj also skillfully used the power of the printing press to spread its ideas. Finally, it constructed a parallel network of schools and colleges across northern India. Educational institutions, Kumar noted, became a "favorite sphere of revivalist mobilization." This whole project involved an "interplay of political, religious and pedagogic strategies" through a whole century.[146]

As a result, revivalism sank deep roots among the emerging Hindu middle classes in the central Indo-Gangetic Plain. This area—stretching roughly from Srinagar to Ajmer and from Peshawar to Allahabad—contained the agricultural and military core of British India. It was the seat of its most explosive twentieth-century political confrontations. The Samaj deeply shaped the practices of memory in this vital heartland in a way that has lasted to the present day. The effort began in the late nineteenth century and has persisted since. Shahid Amin perceptively described these processes at one site, the shrine at Bahraich, as an effort to remedy a perceived "'failure' of Hindu memory."[147] These newly installed social memories, in turn, later helped fuel what Jaffrelot has called an "ethno-nationalist" project for India.[148] I will now look at the shaping of the project and the place of historiography within it.

The Hindu nationalist movement was ready to accept the darkest colonial version of "Muslim" rule. But it could not accept the same colonial textbooks' accounts of the ancient or "Hindu" period. It needed to establish "narratives of pride" as polemical responses to Christian denigration of the Hindu faith. The strongest such "historical" response came from the Arya Samaj. The Samaj was a Hindu reformist organization founded in 1874–75 by Swami Dayanand, a Gujarati Brahman who, dissatisfied with the secluded life of a traditional Sanskrit scholar in his home region, set out across India in the mid-nineteenth century. He met and argued with many in the new intelligentsia of the day, the lay public, missionaries, and members of the colonial educational establishment alike. He and his early followers clearly understood the power of the nascent colonial educational system, the value of print media, and the importance of lay organizations.

Their institutional success meant that the Arya Samaj is a still extant and powerful organization today. It was, at one time, bitterly opposed by many orthodox Hindus and itself divided into two factions soon after the death of the founder. But many of its early reforms, such as acceptance of cross-caste interdining and a wholly new "Vedic" marriage rite, lost their radical edge many years ago. It appealed considerably to the new professional and trading classes of North India. At the same time, it also attracted support from some Indian chiefs and rulers. Crucially, it cemented its institutional presence and cultivated a capacity to shape the new "common sense" of the past through the establishment of recognized schools and colleges on the pattern of the Christian missions. This newly conceived religious community claimed (as we shall see) to aim at a return to the pristine ways of life of the Arya-s (the Sanskrit word anglicized as "Aryans") of a putative golden age before the Mahabharata War.[149]

Their narrative began with the fall of Vedic learning as a consequence of the Mahabharata War five thousand years ago. Authentic Vedic knowledge was lost for many centuries. Its destruction was (again, in Swami Dayanand's telling) completed by Muslim invasions, but British rule marked a possible turn for the better. The Samaj was hopeful of enlisting the colonial educational establishment in its favor. Its effort to capture the emerging colonial educational establishment is also evident from the conciliatory citation of Western Sanskrit scholarship in a long letter from the Lahore Arya Samaj to Gottlieb W. Leitner, who controlled government education in the province of Panjab.[150] My translation follows:

> It was during the Dark Age that the [presently] authoritative commentaries on the Veda, such as that by Sāyana, by Mahidhara and others were written. However, at the end of the previous [eighteenth] century, the greatness of Sanskrit language and literature attracted the attention of notable scholars such as Colebrooke, Jones, and Carey. That impetus not only worked wonders in linguistics, not only begot the leading lights of Western science such as Bopp, Burnouf, Schlegel, Wilson, Weber, and Max Mueller and gave us Rajendralal Mitra but it is also expected [the letter continues] that *this impulse will reach maturity in the [new] Vedic commentary of Dayānand Sarasvatī.*[151]

As this text has been included in the *Laghu grantha* (Shorter Works) of Swami Dayanand, one must assume that he at least authorized it, though he did not sign it and it speaks of him in the third person. We may note the important role posited for Western scholars and the potential role of Leitner, the addressee, in bringing this great revival to fruition.

The Theosophical Society had, for example, already developed the idea of a community of divinely inspired sages who lived in Tibet. That was also where Swami Dayanand placed the first emergence of the "Aryyas." In the eighth chapter of *Satyārtha Prakāśah*, Swami Dayanand is asked by a student where the first creation of humans occurred. The reply is "Trivishtap, or what is called Tibbat." On account of the continual wars between the wise and the wicked, the Aryya folk left their ancestral homeland and, choosing the best part of the world, came and settled in it. "In the beginning the land had no name and had no inhabitants. Early in the era of creation, the Aryya-s came from Tibet to live here." They were, the text claimed, its first inhabitants. This was, of course, a rejection of the idea of "migration of the Aryans" (or Nordic peoples) that had become accepted doctrine among European ethnologists by this time. But if anyone sought to adduce evidence that contradicted Swami Dayanand, it could be dismissed by invoking his reading of the Veda. This method is deployed throughout his work; for example,

"When the Veda says this, why would intelligent people adopt the delusions of some foreigner?"[152]

Swami Dayanand also made an unusual distinction by classifying some texts as the *authentically* divine parts of the Veda. These were the hymns, which he described as uttered by God. The remaining parts of the Vedic text were prose instructions and commentaries, that (he thought) were added later by mortals, albeit wise and good mortals. He was challenged on this by the important education department official and historian Shiv Prasad, who asked him what texts he considered to be the Veda. Did he consider the Brahmanas (commentaries and instructions) to be Vedas? He responded that only the *Saṁhita*, the hymns, were uttered by God (*Īsvarokta*). They were true Vedas whose truth he acknowledged. The Upanishads and prose commentaries of instruction were acceptable only if they did not contradict the hymns of the Rigveda. Elsewhere he responded to Griffith, then principal of the Banaras Sanskrit College:

> Vedic knowledge has been shrinking for about five thousand years. Before the Mahabharata all the sciences were properly taught in this country. But after that texts and methods of study all changed completely. That corrupted tradition has prevailed from that time to the present. This is despite the fact that some people here and there do memorize the true Vedic texts, but no one understands the meanings of the words themselves. Nor are any grammatical texts meaningfully taught so that it would be possible for a trained person to understand the meaning of the Veda. Modern commentaries such as those Mahidhara and others are utterly corrupt and obscurantist. Those who read them can never understand my commentary on the Veda.[153]

The Samaj's purified "Vedic" Hinduism thus rejected the later body of traditional learning and practice embodied in the texts such as the Puranas. Swami Dayanand especially disliked the *Bhagavata Purana*, a foundational text for the widespread Vaishnava tradition of devotion to Krishna. It encouraged ecstatic *bhakti* forms of life and worship that he abhorred. The Puranas and many other texts also often contained *mahātmyas*, narratives explaining the value of particular pilgrimages or the worship of specific deities. These frequently advocated religious practices that were the special targets of missionary polemic against "idolatry and superstition." The Arya Samaj rejected traditional post-Vedic Puranas as inauthentic. These, *Satyārtha Prakāśah* declared, were later fabrications by a designing priesthood. This heterodox idea was faithfully transmitted by the Arya Samaj thereafter. Thus the prominent Arya Samaj activist and nationalist political leader Lajpat Rai wrote in his account of the Samaj's doctrines: "The Puranas (ancient commentaries on the Vedas and other works on theology) are the Aitreya Brahmanas and similar compositions by the great Rishis like Brahma and others. In Itihas or history I include *Kalpa*, *Gâthâ*, and *Nârâshansi*. The *Bhâgwat* and other books of that sort are not the Puranas."[154]

The difficulty with this is, of course, that *if we accept the premise of a linear time*, the value of the Veda as a historical source cannot extend beyond the period of its own composition. (Indeed, the Mahabharata War was obviously post-Vedic.) Furthermore, the history of the five millennia of decay after the supposed collapse of Vedic learning would have to be written from limited sources. Exclusive or extensive recourse to Vedic sources then also implicitly accepted the premise of an unchanging post-Vedic India where change only occurred under external impact. In a way, this was also the Western Orientalists' vision. For example, Max Mueller, the second Boden Professor at Oxford, wrote in 1890: "The Hindus were a nation of philosophers. Their struggles were the struggles of thought. . . . It might justly be said that India has no place in the political history of the world."[155]

But for nationalists the pitfall here was that accepting this argument could justify colonial rule as a necessary "guardianship" of the apolitical Hindus. So it could not satisfy the Arya Samaj. Like Lajpat Rai, who had been prosecuted the government for sedition, many of its members were prominent in the nationalist movement in North India. They were therefore impelled to develop a historiography of the more recent era ending in the twentieth century. For that period, they had no recourse beyond producing rewritten versions of select Western-style histories, whether written by Indians or Europeans. Western histories of conquest and colonization were obviously the model for another Arya Samaj text that declared ancient Indian kings had directly ruled Afghanistan, Baluchistan, and Tibet, and that "Indian colonists colonized Egypt, Rome, Greece, Peru, and Mexico."[156]

The same impulse had inspired Bankim Chandra's near-contemporary essays that claimed that the Bengalis had colonized much of Southeast Asia. Both originated in the effort to match the colonial narrative of English prowess by claiming equal "achievements" for ancient Indians/Hindus. This line of thought was sustained by a network of schools and colleges in North India funded by the Arya Samaj and their bitter rivals, the Sanatan Dharmis, or followers of "ancient tradition." It therefore remained a powerful unofficial presence in the construction of the "new" Indian past among the emerging neo-Hindu intelligentsia in North India. It was also nested in a powerful institutional structure, that very network of schools, colleges, and trusts across northern India.[157]

Furthermore, as Krishna Kumar's important article demonstrated, this institutional network was tied into the project of developing a new Sanskritized Hindi as the national language of a revived India. Kumar traces the beginning of this project to the 1870s, when the Samaj adopted Hindi as its lingua franca. This was also time when the enlargement of printing and colonial school education meant that the choice of language used in school and government could advantage or disadvantage rival segments of the intelligentsia. The new Hindi project soon had a specifically Hindu revivalist character.[158] It also collided with the expansion and consolidation of Urdu as the language of educated Muslims that Barbara Metcalf has discussed. These strains were to emerge strongly into anglophone public discourse in India in the 1980s and 1990s.

Within the upper Anglosphere, however, the disciplinary standards and findings of mainstream Western historians were felt to be too strong to oppose, especially in state-controlled institutions. State pressure for conformity intensified after the suppression of the uprising of 1857. Despite being a considerable scholar of Islamic sciences, Muhammad Husain Azad (1829–1910), for example, only found employment in the Panjab education department at fifteen rupees a month in 1864. He later impressed his English superiors and was given another post that paid seventy-five rupees.[159] The colonial educational establishment offered one of the few stable and well-paid careers available to the South Asian intelligentsia. But South Asians held few of the best posts, those in the selective and well-paid Indian Education Service (starting at 500 rupees a month, rising to 1,000 in ten years).[160] (Jadunath Sarkar, the pioneer historian of Mughal India, was one of the few indigenous employees.) Those salaries had been set in order to attract Englishmen, and only Indians of exceptional talent could be hired in such posts. All state employees were bound by the general service rules and unwritten conventions that governed their working. In general, fear of government displeasure meant that historians tended to shy away from study of the "British" period. Sarkar's great work was on the Mughal Empire. Several others researched the sultanates that preceded that empire, or aspects of the political and religious life of the medieval period. Yet other historians focused on the ancient period and on deep regional histories. The writing of the history of British India was left largely to Englishmen associated with the colonial government, such as Vincent Smith and H. H. Dodwell.[161]

An alternative meliorist narration was represented in work such as Surendranath Banerjea's *A Nation in the Making*. This accepted the educative role of British rule and merely advanced a claim for equality within the empire, on par with self-governing dominions.[162] When first published in 1925, its program had already been overtaken by the more populist agenda of Gandhi and the left-wing nationalism of Jawaharlal Nehru. More critical works could only be written by men who had severed ties with the British establishment. These included G. T. Garratt, who resigned from the Indian Civil Service in 1921 in protest at wasteful expenditure in a time of famine, and Edward J. Thompson, who became a journalist after quitting his post at the Wesleyan College in Bankura (Bengal). They were prepared to argue that Indian unrest represented the stirring of a national movement. As liberal Englishmen they invoked the idea that World War I had radically changed the world and that Britain's mission in India was coming to an end. In 1935, Garratt and Thompson published a history titled *The Rise and Fulfillment of British Rule in India*. They anticipated the possibility that "the great sub-continent of India [would] form part of a noble comity of nations within the British Commonwealth." If their title invoked Macaulay's "proudest moment," the authors—both admirers of Gandhi—also faintly echoed the Indophilia that Macaulay had rejected. In the foreword, they declared that "love of England cannot blind us to the dangers which beset Western civilization, and we are convinced of the immense influence that India, called to a reinvigorated existence, could exert in solving those problems which now oppress the mind of man."[163] Other critical traditions were developed entirely outside the official education system. B. D. Basu, for example, was a retired army medical officer. He logically extended the religious periodization found colonial textbooks to characterize the British too and published a two-volume *Rise of the Christian Power in India*, as well as a work on the ruin of Indian industries by colonial rule.[164]

The imperial apparatus that was shaken—indeed fractured—by World War I had come of age after the suppression of the great uprising of 1857–58. It emerged through a reconquest of India and a reestablishment of the Indian Empire on a new foundation. Queen Victoria's Proclamation of 1858 promised (among other things) that all her subjects would have equal access to state employment, regardless of race, color, or religion. New elites, civil and military, found niches in the formative period of the new apparatus and sought to widen them in the new dispensation. Their efforts led to a gradually widening recruitment of Indians in the civil wing (and during World War II, to the military wing) of the imperial government.

ALTERNATE PASTS, CONTRADICTORY FUTURES

The version of British imperial history implanted in textbooks and curricula always had its critics, going back to the first translators. Tacit resistance and selective appropriation were used to build alternative narratives. Much social memory was, in any case, formed outside the classroom. Krishna Kumar is a leading Indian professor of education, and to my knowledge the only academic to have published a comparative study of historical memory among school students in India and Pakistan. He observed that long "before children have the capacity, and find the opportunities, to make sense of the past, they are socialized into its many legacies." That socialization is an amalgam of school, home, and societal setting.[165]

Elements of the imperial factual frame developed to legitimize British India were increasingly culled and deployed in alternative narratives by various nationalist critics. Nor indeed did the imperial narrative lack internal critics in Britain and beyond. All this enabled alternative social pasts and corresponding projected futures to emerge in British India and fuel nationalist movements. Major political currents of the period between World Wars I and II began to place themselves firmly in a historical frame. Unreconstructed Conservatives like Winston Churchill drew dark visions of India regressing historically and falling into a brutal anarchy if the British left.

Indeed, it was only in the period between the two world wars that a foreseeable end to the British empire in India began to seem realistic. Many political currents debated the arrangements that should succeed this hitherto unshakable empire. Jawaharlal Nehru, soon to be prime minister, developed his ideas of the past and future of India in the interwar period. Nehru's narrative saw India as distinguished by the continuity of its cultural tradition "through five thousand years of history, a tradition which was widespread among the masses and powerfully influenced them." But he went on to argue that the spirit of the modern age sought equality and that India's social and economic system had to be remodeled to conform. It would, he thought, already have happened but for the reactionary bent of colonial authority.[166]

World War II—and the signal defeats inflicted on all the colonial empires in Asia by the Japanese—seemed to portend an imminent collapse of all empires. By 1940, the two major political formations that were to create successor states—the Indian National Congress and the Muslim League—increasingly grounded themselves in claims on the future based on historical narratives of nationhood. M. A. Jinnah enunciated his ideas in March 1940, at the Lahore session of the All-India Muslim League. The argument made in his address was historical from the outset. In his understanding, Muslims had been separate from Hindus through the twelve centuries from the earliest Arab conquests in Sindh up to his time. Therefore, they could not simply become citizens of a multireligious republic after the British left. If British rule were to end, Hindus and Muslims could either live in a condominium of two equal nations within a very loose system of "autonomous national states" or as entirely separate nation-states bound by future treaties with each other. The 1940 speech developed an extended historical argument for this separateness in the Indian subcontinent: "It is quite clear that Hindus and Musalmans derive their inspiration from different sources of history. They have different epics, different heroes and different episodes. Very often the hero of one is a foe of the other, and likewise, their victories and defeats overlap. . . . We know that the history of the last twelve hundred years has failed to achieve unity and has witnessed, during the ages, India always divided into Hindu India and Muslim India."[167]

A few months later, the Islamic scholar Abul Kalam Azad responded in his capacity as president of the session of the Indian National Congress at Ramgarh in December 1940. Islam, he said, had come to India centuries ago and had now melded with the extant traditions. "This fusion was a notable event in history. . . . These thousand years of our joint life has moulded us into a common nationality. This cannot be done artificially."[168] It is not surprising that Jinnah's argument was strongly contested from the outset, not only by his political antagonists but also academic historians sympathetic to the Indian National Congress.

The success of the Muslim League in the elections of 1946, Britain's rush to leave its South Asian empire, and the inability of political leaders to achieve a workable compromise led to the partition of British India into India and Pakistan in 1947. Brutal violence accompanied the partition and led to the flight of millions in both directions. The newly independent states had to strengthen their new national identities through (among other projects) the writing of history. New nationalist projects had grown within and finally captured the apparatus of the late British Empire in India. The transfer of power in 1947 essentially handed over two parts of a functioning imperial apparatus to India and Pakistan. Each country received a specific fraction of the funds, personnel, equipment, and records of the old empire.

But they did not inherit its already decaying legitimacy. Therefore, like all the new nations that emerged after World War II, these two saw their task as that of making new citizens by implanting the national narrative more deeply among them. There was a considerable injection of resources into education, much of which found its way into higher education, including history. The new states had, therefore, to build their own identities as nation-states in a new global setting. After the end of empire, the new nation-states therefore enlarged their educational and ideological apparatuses and the dissemination of new national narratives. The outlines of each had been crafted in the late colonial period. India thus had several narratives developing since the late nineteenth century. The last seventeen years of colonial rule saw a growing divergence between two "master narratives."[169]

The Indian nationalist vision of the past was crafted in the interwar period and most vividly expressed by Jawaharlal Nehru. His ideas fitted well with left liberal currents in world thought and were widely adopted among the intelligentsia even before his rise to political office. The broadly liberal character of his regime and its alliance with the left allowed many find niches in the rapidly growing educational establishment of independent India. But the Indian nationalist narrative was deeply shaped by a number of thinkers. Gandhi was among Congress Party leaders who (at least rhetorically) rejected the sciences and techniques that had come from the West.

He rejected the historical past as being any basis of a projected future. He generally argued that individuals and communities should make ethically valid choices, regardless of the past. Gandhi's close ally and ultimate successor was, however, Nehru, who was enamored of modernity even as he rejected market capitalism as an economic system. Gandhi's assassination by a Hindu nationalist in 1948 left Nehru the dominant figure in Indian political life. His thought drew on a longer tradition of nationalist critique going back to South Asian claimants to equality in a liberal empire. That school had shaped an economic critique of British policy which was, however, premised on the possibility of a voluntary policy change by the government.[170] In the 1930s, Nehru refounded this argument on the Marxist theory of economic imperialism, which analyzed that social formation was exploitative by its very nature, incapable of reform. As far as the identity of India was concerned, he invoked a fundamental geographical and cultural identity that had existed through millennia and accommodated new faiths and peoples through time. Islam was one of the newer faiths but could not, in his view, be the basis of a national community. Many Indian historians endorsed this. Speaking as president of the Indian History Congress in December 1947, the distinguished Aligarh Muslim University historian Mohammad Habib hailed the newly created Nehru cabinet as giving a "a fine vision of the future National Governments of India." He continued that "the country has always been one and indivisible, and will always continue to be so. The unity of India is one of the fundamental postulates of Indian moral consciousness, and the longing for a centralized administration has been one of the most visible and persistent demands of the political spirit of the Indians throughout the ages. . . . *The advent of Islam made no essential difference to the character of our country.*"[171]

This official view was given an academic presentation in *History of the Freedom Movement in India* by Tara Chand. Its first volume was published in 1962 by the Ministry of Information and Broadcasting. The Nehru government was, however, exceptionally tolerant of criticism, and counter-arguments also appeared freely. R. C. Majumdar was initially involved in the history project. By his own account, he was forced out because of his dissenting views on the origins of the nationalist movement.[172] The Congress governments maintained only a loose control over the official production of memory. Different Indian states developed their own somewhat variant narratives, generally tending to glorify important regional figures, especially those who had resisted the British in some way. Meanwhile, folk and local traditions continued their own reproduction. Finally, at least until 1999, Indian history textbooks ended at independence. As Krishna Kumar wryly remarked, "not just the narrative of the freedom struggle but history itself comes to an end in 1947." He added that this framing had had the unintended consequence of presenting the division of British India into India and Pakistan as "the last major event to have occurred in India's long history." It also had the unintended effect of giving it an evocative freshness, making it a key part of "children's socialization into a political legacy."[173]

On the other side of the newly drawn border, Pakistan had had less time to develop an official historiography. After 1947, the newly formed Pakistani historical establishment began strengthening the narrative outlined by Jinnah. The distinguished historian I. H. Qureshi (soon to be education minister in Pakistan) published a learned treatise in 1962 arguing that the Hindu and Muslim communities had always had a distinct identity. As a careful historian, he recognized that the Muslims of South Asia had not *begun* as a single community; they were initially of diverse geographical origins, spoke different languages, and descended from "different racial stocks." But, he continued, they had gradually melded into one community, something that (he claimed) had not happened to the Muslims of West Asia.

This was because the South Asian Muslims lived in a Hindu environment. All Hindus, he believed, shared a common ethos. That gave the qualities Muslims borrowed from their habitat "a quality of uniformity. This has at once created homogeneity among them and made them distinct from other Muslim peoples without in any way alienating them from the Muslim world." This, he continued, also minimized the sectarian differences that sometimes beset Muslims elsewhere. Every denomination, he declared, ranging from the Ismailis and Ahmediyyas to the most orthodox Sunnis, contributed to the leadership of the new Pakistan. But since the majority of the aristocracy was of foreign origin, it was the Central Asian region that shaped Muslim culture as a whole. "The dominant foreign element is Central Asian because the conquerors after the tenth century were mostly of Turkic origin."[174] Thus Qureshi's argument sought to explain why all Muslims in the subcontinent—regardless of home language, "racial" stock, or location—belonged to a single nationality. At the same time, it also explained why they could not simply merge into other Muslim nations to their west (or conceivably, for East Pakistan, to the east). Simpler texts sought to present more accessible versions of his thesis to undergraduates.[175]

Early efforts at creating a historical society and a history congress began in Pakistan too. A meeting of historians in 1950 resolved to establish them both. A History Congress was held in 1951, and the Pakistan Historical Society officially came into being in 1953. Compilations of sources and scholarly histories also began to appear, notably a *History of the Freedom Movement* that began at the death of the Mughal emperor Aurangzeb in 1707 and continued to the creation of Pakistan in 1947.[176] Difficulties in implanting the new narrative manifested themselves by the late 1960s. The conflict resulted ultimately in the emergence of another South Asian nation-state, Bangladesh, with its own new set of social memories and state institutions. The divergent narratives of school textbooks in India and Pakistan up to 1999 have been so thoroughly analyzed by Krishna Kumar that no purpose is served by my repeating his ideas. The later period of textbook controversies has been comprehensively presented by the contributors to a special issue of the *Journal of Educational Media*, and once again, it would serve no purpose for me to attempt a summary of Fuchs and Nair's articles here.[177]

THE ANGLOSPHERE IN THE IVORY TOWER

In the early Nehruvian period, the Republic of India faced many challenges but seemingly surmounted them better than many of its contemporary emerging nations. Mass illiteracy, however, remained, and so did English as a language of privilege. History departments in the few but comparatively well-funded Indian universities controlled by the central government were confident, indeed complacent, in their authority. Even though English-medium education expanded dramatically after India became independent, few of its people were literate enough in English to participate in academic debates on history. The narrow circle of specialists could still, in principle, resolve disputes by reference to sources and documents, as in the standard model. This gave its members an undue sense of their own grip on the past. Satish Chandra, a professor of history and later the powerful chairman of the University Grants Commission, wrote in 1972 that national historians in India "command a measure of public esteem which is becoming rare elsewhere."[178] In fact, this mainly reflected the indifference of the larger public to seemingly arcane anglophone debates.

English had been the language of imperial administration and political life since the nineteenth century. Early histories written in India were mainly intended for officials and the upper political establishment in Britain. Public figures in the Asian territories of the empire wrote as much, if not more, for the policy-makers in Britain as anyone in their home countries.[179] The postcolonial metropolitan intelligentsia, such as Satish Chandra, mistook indifference for assent. Looking back at the early decades of the Republic, Neeladri Bhattacharya later recognized that the strength of the liberal consensus had been "illusory." Beneath the anglophone world, "a range of alternative narratives of the past undercut the new nationalist history that was taking shape." Tanika Sarkar and Nita Kumar demonstrated the mechanisms of embedding. They both studied how alternative narratives were imparted in schools run by religiously affiliated organizations. Kumar, however, went further and also observed the survival of "local history not explicitly taught anywhere but known and cherished by children." These histories, she declared, are what they share with the very numerous illiterates.[180]

Strains of Hindu nationalism emerged strongly into anglophone public discourse in India in the 1980s and 1990s. One early response, in 1992, was to point to the illicit roots of Hindu nationalist images of the past in imperial historical practice as established under British rule.[181] Partha Chatterjee himself moved beyond this early and ineffectual response to argue for academic historians' need for an appropriate incorporation of the popular historical narrative. He added that if this history could have been written in the Nehruvian university, it would not have had to seek validation "from forces in the domain of the popular."[182] But we should note that "the popular" now includes for many of "the people" an unfounded narrative of a glorious temple in Ayodhya demolished by a sixteenth-century conqueror. The strong electoral presence of right-wing parties in state and national government from that time has served to further entrench such narratives. But their origins lie deep in the emerging vernacular tradition of the colonial period.

The unification of the Indian-language public sphere resulting from increased participation by plebeian strata in a volatile political life revealed the shallow roots of academic history in India. An early sign of this was, perhaps, that the removal of colonial statuary—usually located at prominent places in major colonial cities—was a much more potent source of popular mobilization and a source of greater anxiety to the government than historical writing as such. The renaming of streets and even entire cities has been a sporadic concern of governments thereafter. The erection of statues and monuments, the reconstruction of temples—in short, the implanting of places of memory across the land—has followed. Furors now occur over "historical" Bollywood film content. Academic historians have been left with little role in the shaping of social memory. The mass consumption of television starting in the 1990s and the internet after 2000 has allowed a further fragmentation of discourses, the enclaving of information now bemoaned as "tribalism" in American public life. A recent survey found that even among the English-reading public in India, 68 percent received their news through smartphones—mainly routed via Facebook and WhatsApp—and not directly from newspapers or their websites.[183]

THE POPULAR AND THE PROFESSIONAL IN INDIA

Although Gandhi and Nehru had very distinct ideas of what a secular politics entailed, their joint legacy controlled early tendencies toward Hindu nationalism on the Indian political scene for several decades. Indira Gandhi, who dominated national politics from 1969 to 1975, deployed an especially strident combination of anti-imperialist nationalism and radical Nehruvian economics to sustain her career. But Congress hegemony began to crumble after 1975, and Indira Gandhi fell from office in 1977. The Rudolphs, writing at the end of that decade, presciently observed that the "elites of the founding generation used but did not replenish the political and cultural capital which Nehru's and Gandhi's leadership created."[184] Ashis Nandy, in flight from inescapable facts of the South Asian present, claimed that in the 1980s a large segment of the people of India still lived outside history. History, for him, was a

Western intrusion that the idyllic world of the premodern had never known. Innocent of that knowledge, Indians had seen no need for projects such as religious nationalism, or nationalism at all. Only colonialism brought this dangerous gift to the subcontinent and produced nationalism and the idea of a determinate national history. What Nehru had seen as part of the precious scientific legacy of the West, Nandy evaluated as a poisoned chalice.[185] More than a decade later, the political scientist Sudipta Kaviraj recognized that the original cultural capital had depended on an easy multilingualism, on "the political diglossia of the national movement." By the 1990s (Kaviraj wrote with some exaggeration), monolingual speakers of regional languages were cut off from a "unilingual English-speaking elite."[186] This phenomenon (even if exaggerated) contributed to the disjuncture between university historians and popular conceptions of the past.

Conclusion

THE POST-TRUTH ERA HAS BEEN, AMONG OTHER THINGS, DEFINED by a rejection of experts, historians included. This was brought sharply home to the Indian metropolitan historical establishment in the early 1990s. Concerted efforts by leading historians could not undermine the Hindu nationalist (and largely unsubstantiated) narrative of the earlier history of the Babari Masjid in Ayodhya. A narrative going back to Henry M. Elliot and Raja Shiv Prasad had been gradually entrenched in the vernacular-using North India. The academic elite then awoke to the long-extant gulf between popular conceptions of the past and "secular" anglophone history.[1] But the "popular" is not a changeless entity. Its social memories have been created by past historical processes such as those traced here. The people who Ashis Nandy claimed still lived without "history" nonetheless had fully developed collective memories parallel to the ones that the new nation-state was seeking to implant. This book has devoted considerable space to describing the social frames of the popular and the scholarly alike. Neither of these is permanent. The collective shapes memory, memory constitutes the collective. Scholarship must strive to build on evidence. We have entered a post-truth world through many paths. One of those brought us here by arguing that all narratives were constructed, and consequently all are equally valid.

This book has obviously rejected the idea that South Asians before colonialism were somehow devoid of socially constructed memories of collective pasts. It is true that they were not all uniformly concerned with these, nor did each region or community have the same protocols for finding socially important facts about itself. I have shown the diversity through time and space of South Asian approaches to the past and compared them to those elsewhere in the world. Some regions knew factual history and often cared passionately about it. They developed, argued, and fought over rival versions of the past. Elsewhere, detailed knowledge was entrusted to professional custodians, such as genealogists and marriage brokers—but then these were subject to the pressures of popularity and patronage. British colonial rule, like other colonizing empires, imposed a new uniformity. It also gave history a new legitimating role in public and national life. The new colonial educational system became a novel gateway into office and honor.

By the mid-nineteenth century, traditions of criticism and debate grew up to contest colonial renderings of the South Asian past. We have seen how by the 1880s, colonial potentates such as John Strachey began to regret the historical memory that Edmund Burke and Thomas Macaulay had left for India. The historical record was being turned to anticolonial purposes. The colonial government therefore maintained its control over access to records and archives. Officially patronized historians also had to steer clear of anticolonial narrative even as nationalists pursued historical research as a nation-building vocation, independent of whatever career actually sustained them. Regional variation in the protocols of debate and the narratives constructed persisted, reflecting the persistent variations in social organization and intellectual life across the subcontinent.

Independent India enlarged the resources available to recognized historians and opened many archives to them. A standard conventional narrative dominated state power for three decades after the coming of Indian independence and the establishment of the Nehruvian consensus. The inheritors of the Raj also increasingly wrote to each other, and the wider anglophone world, in English. But beneath the world of Nehruvian history, older strains persisted in an increasingly separate Indian-language public space. How far the two had diverged was revealed in the early 1990s: a distinctly post-truth discourse mobilized masses of Indians around a narrative of past religious violence originally shaped by a handful of colonial intellectuals of the nineteenth century. The political convulsions that resulted can be said to have transformed the modern political life of the Republic of India; paradoxically, that has made control of the past more important to those in control of the present. As in the United States, the past is simultaneously perceived as embodied in statues—in the Indian case, increasingly larger ones.

Finally, who frames the framer himself? I hope this book has not appeared reductionist: the social frame is what enables history to live and historians to practice. But the frame does not make the painting, even though a canvas will fall limply underfoot without a frame to hold it. We academics often take a grandiose view of our part in shaping discourse. "Crucial," "vital," "critical," and "central" are some of the terms routinely seen in descriptions of obscure and illustrious texts alike. New visions are more frequent in academic blurbs than in optometric clinics. We should take a more modest outlook on our craft, like the great poet Auden, who wrote of his own vocation that "poetry makes nothing happen, it survives." History makes nothing happen—but it will survive! A conceived past informs every lived present—and the present in turn is where historians live and practice. And because it is evident that the living demand for history as truth is too deeply planted in contemporary culture to be soon uprooted, let me plead that we continue to strive for an evidence-based mode of writing it.

Notes

Preface

1 Oxford Dictionaries, "Word of the Year 2016."

2 Suskind, "Faith, Certainty and the Presidency." "The aide said that guys like me were 'in what we call the reality-based community,' which he defined as people who 'believe that solutions emerge from your judicious study of discernible reality.' I nodded and murmured something about enlightenment principles and empiricism. He cut me off. 'That's not the way the world really works anymore,' he continued. 'We're an empire now, and when we act, we create our own reality. And while you're studying that reality—judiciously, as you will—we'll act again, creating other new realities, which you can study too, and that's how things will sort out. We're history's actors . . . and you, all of you, will be left to just study what we do.'"

3 An early example was a protest against a projected American film (*Guardian*, "British war veterans"). This use of "revisionist" would never be accepted by professional historians whose trade it is to scrutinize and revise previous narratives.

4 Osborne, "Supporters, opponents."

5 Wemple, "The Post's bizarre story."

6 AHA, https://www.historians.org/news-and-advocacy/statements-and-resolutions-of-support-and-protest/aha-condemns-second-draft-of-executive-travel-ban.

Introduction

1 Novick, *That Noble Dream*, 372–73.

2 Novick, *That Noble Dream*, and "My Correct Views on Everything," 703.

3 The site's home page offers for $99 to "Uncover your ethnic mix, discover distant relatives, and find new details about your unique family history with a simple DNA test." It states that two million people have taken the said DNA test so far. www.ancestry.com/dna_(FAQ section), accessed January 9, 2017. Subscribers are offered access to millions of historical records, including more than three billion birth, marriage, and other records. www.ancestry.com/cs/offers/subscribe?sub=1, accessed January 9, 2017.

4 I use "lineage" in its sociological sense, as a socially recognized descent group that transfers property or prosecutes blood feuds for its recognized members. Believing oneself a descendant of Attila has no social effect today, nor does a Y-chromosome DNA match to John Churchill, first Duke of Marlborough (1650–1722), entitle one to live in Blenheim Palace.

5 This point is further elaborated in chapter 1 of this book. Contributions to the debate include Grafton, *What Was History?*; Smith, *Gender of History*; Chakrabarty, *Calling of History*; Thapar, *Past Before Us*; Iggers and Wang, *Turning Points in Historiography*; and Chatterjee and Ghosh, *History and the Present*.

6 Chakrabarty, *Calling of History*, 11.

7 This is the classical epistemological problem of self-reference, now prominent for neuroscientists too.

8 Chakrabarty, *Provincializing Europe*, 32–34, 255.

9 Partha Chatterjee, "History and the Domain of the Popular," 31–34.

10 Pollock, *Literary Cultures in History*, 1–36.

11 Philips, *Historians of India*, 9. Philips wrote that "Marāthī, alone among the mother tongues has carried over from its seventeenth century *bakhar* chronicles a fairly strong historical tradition."

12 Spivak, "Can the Subaltern Speak?," 271–314.

1. The Construction of Collective Memory

1 This argument is not original. It is a familiar one in the philosophy of history. But philosophy is rarely written and little read by practicing historians, hence this excursus. For predecessors, see, for example, the special issue of *History and Theory* 16, no. 4 (1977), titled "The Constitution of the Historical Past."

2 I realize that I have slipped here from an ontological argument (about being) to an epistemological argument (about knowledge). My answer to that objection is that an unknowable but extant past cannot be an object of present knowledge. It is therefore irrecoverable historically. Believers in a transcendent God may believe that that such a being would indeed know the entire past. The past would therefore ontologically exist in the mind of God. But obviously, no created being can enter the mind of a transcendent God; still less can a humble historian do so. So God's knowledge is, by definition, unavailable to the minds of real human beings or to the recording systems that they have made, whether clay tablets or computer data banks.

3 This paragraph is based on Balslev, *Time in Indian Philosophy*, 26–69.

4 Trautmann, "Indian time, European time," 175–78.

5 Ricoeur, *Reality*, 1–36, especially 7, 11 (emphasis added).

6 An example of how the beleaguered inhabitants of the academic cloister eschew those in adjoining cells, even as they discuss them.

7 Collini and Williams, "Collingwood, Robin George,"; Collingwood, *Idea of History*, 212–16. This was not even a good description of historical practice when *he* wrote. Numa Denis Fustel de Coulanges had studied variants in harnessing techniques a half-century earlier; Marc Bloch was using French rural topography to understand property tenures in long-vanished agrarian societies.

8 Editorial introduction to Halbwachs, *On Collective Memory*. Maurice Halbwachs (1877–1945) was a professor at the University of Strasbourg when he was arrested for protesting the occupation regime and deported to Auschwitz, where he perished.

9 Halbwachs, *Social Frameworks of Memory*, 51. He added: "Society from time to time, obligates people not just to reproduce in thought previous events of their lives, but also to touch them up, or to complete them so that, however convinced we are that our memories are exact, we give them a prestige that reality did not possess."

10 For a quick overview of false memory, see Loftus, "Creating False Memories," 70–75.

11 Loftus and Doyle, *Eyewitness Testimony*, 53.

12 Halbwachs, cited in Apfelbaum, "Halbwachs and the Social Properties of Memory," 77–92 (emphasis added).

13 Halbwachs, *On Collective Memory*, 182–83. He writes: "Society tends to erase from its memory all that might separate individuals, or might distance groups from each other."

14 Editorial introduction to Siu, Crossley, and Sutton, *Empire*, 2 (emphasis added).

15 Yerushalmi, *Zakhor*, xxxiv–xxxv.

16 Yerushalmi, *Zakhor*, postscript, 109.

17 Halbwachs, *On Collective Memory*, 215. "The Christian collective memory could annex a part of the Jewish collective memory only by appropriating part of the latter's local remembrance while at the same time transforming its entire perspective of historical space." See also Zerubavel, *Time-Maps*, 3–10.

18 Yerushalmi, *Zakhor*, 20–23.

19 Halbwachs's professorship was at the University of Strasbourg, in a region that twice changed sovereigns through successive annexation by Germany and France between 1870 and 1945. Each regime had its own narrative of the past, of Louis XIV and Napoleon, not to speak of Frederick II and Bismarck.

20 Halbwachs, *On Collective Memory*, 193–235 (quote from 235).

21 The last decades of the twentieth century also saw the composition of several providential "Rise of the West" texts that variously interpreted the then current world situation as a result of intrinsic cultural traits.

22 Assmann, *Cultural Memory and Early Civilization*, 143.

23 Boone and Mignolo, *Writing Without Words*; Boone, *Cycles of Time*.

24 Albiruni, *Chronology of Ancient Nations*, 42. All spelling and diacriticals as in the original.

25 Assmann, *Cultural Memory*, 268. Recent research shows that the story was more complicated.

26 Porten, "Exile, Babylonian"; Bagg, "Palestine under Assyrian Rule," 119–44.

27 Haeem S. Kehimkar terms this *keriyath Shema*. He reports that as they knew no other, this prayer was repeated at every ceremony, whether marriage, circumcision, or burial. Kehimkar, *Bene Israel*, 40; for Marathi names of important days in the religious calendar, see 22.

28 Cited in Isenberg, *India's Bene Israel*, 23 (emphasis added).

29 Isenberg, *India's Bene Israel*, 10–11, 98–107.

30 I take this idea of performative memory from the profoundly original work of Novetzke, *Religion and Public Memory*, chs. 1–3, especially 122–31.

31 Chakrabarty, *Calling of History*, 8. "Historical writings end up being embedded in different public contexts in very different ways. . . . The valence of even the basic categories of the discipline—such as 'research,' 'facts,' 'truth,' 'evidence,' 'archives'—can be molded by the interaction between history's cloistered and public lives." They can also be extinguished by changes in the public sphere, or by a social collapse that ruins the cloister itself.

32 See Verbrugghe and Wickersham, *Berossos and Manetho*, 8.

33 Pingree, "Hellenophilia," 556.

34 Blyth, *Karnak*, xviii-xix.

35 Dillery, *Clio's Other Sons*, 56–57. Over two thousand years ago, Berossos and Manetho, both priests—one in Babylon and the other in Egypt—wrote histories of their ancient

civilizations. Their narrative built around the framework of the "king-list" but were written in Greek for the benefit of their Hellenic rulers.

36 Monson, *From the Ptolemies to the Romans*, 76–80, 94, 134–37.

37 Blyth, *Karnak*, xviii–xx, 225–36.

38 Bickerman, "Origines Gentium," 65–81 (quotes from 73–74).

39 Verbrugghe and Wickersham, *Berossos and Manetho*, 1–6.

40 Davies, "Liber Landavensis," 340.

41 Yarshater, *Cambridge History of Iran*, 344–70 (quote from 368).

42 Chitrarekha Gupta, *Brahmanas*, 167–71.

43 Pathak, *Ancient Historians of India*, 1–11. Considering the word *āsa*, we should note that the object was clearly singular—the verb (√*as*, meaning "to be") is in the singular third-person past perfect. This would mean that there was only *one* historical past.

44 "Mucyate sarvapāpebhyo rāhunā candramāyathā / jayonāmetihāsa ayam śrotavya vijigiṣunā //" My translation, undated text.

45 Pathak, *Ancient Historians of India*, 8–29, 74–83. He writes: "Religion standardised the *itihāsa* tradition, but it also destroyed the historical character of the tradition by inundating it with accounts of practices and philosophies of various cults" (18).

46 Pathak, *Ancient Historians of India*, 74–76, 104–5.

47 Pollock, "Mīmāṃsā" (quotes from 607, 608). There are obvious parallels with and divergences from the rabbinical tradition described by Yerushalmi and summarized earlier in this chapter.

48 Kane, *History of Dharmaśāstra*, 334–66.

49 Vad, Mawjee, and Parasnis, *Sanads and Letters*, doc. 32, 144. "Thereupon the judicial assembly asked the headmen of the sixteen villages to remember their forty-two ancestors and provide an authentic narration of the history of the dispute."

50 Sumit Guha, "Speaking Historically," 1094.

51 Mate, "Hero-Stones," 79–82; Sontheimer, "On memorials to the dead," 87–99; Settar and Sontheimer, "Hero and Sati Stones of Maharashtra," 261–81.

52 Duff, *History of the Mahrattas*, I, 19.

53 Durrant et al., *Letter to Ren An*, 4–5, 20. Here and elsewhere, I have transcribed Chinese names as they appear in the sources I cite, though this introduces inconsistencies in the text.

54 Elman, *From Philosophy to Philology*, 105.

55 Iggers, "What is so uniquely Western," 101–110.

56 Zhang, "In and Out of the West," 50.

57 Lieberman, *Strange Parallels*, 716–36. I am indebted to Azfar Moin for bringing this argument to my attention.

58 Johnson, "Epic and History in Early China," 255–71.

59 Johnson, "Communication, Class and Consciousness in Late Imperial China," 71.

60 Kulke, *Kings and Cults*, 114–136.

61 Boone and Mignolo, *Writing Without Words*.

62 Culbert, *Classic Maya Political History*.

63 Vansina, *Oral Tradition*, 97.

64 Quilter and Urton, *Narrative Threads*, xiii–xix; Cummins, "Representation in the Sixteenth Century," 188–219 and 24n. My translation of the Spanish quotation.

65 Julien, *Reading Inca History*, 5, 89.

66 Ossio A., "Guamán Poma," 153–213. An earlier statement is in Zuidema, *Ceque System of Cuzco*.

67 Every entry in the *Armorial général* is accompanied by a sketch and a description of the family's coat of arms. "Scandalous words" was a common phrase in the case reports in Squibb, *Heraldic Cases*. We should remember that only "gentlemen" were entitled to fight duels.

68 Sircar, *Indian Epigraphy*, 89; Sontheimer, "Hero and Sati Stones of Maharashtra," 261–81; Eysenbach, *Histoire du blason*.

69 Sherlock, "The Reformation of Memory," 31–40, cited 33. "Site of memory" is a term coined by the French historian Pierre Nora.

70 Barlow, "Becket, Thomas," for example.

71 https://networks.h-net.org/node/28765/discussions/166559/obituary-jan-vansina. Jan Vansina (1929–2017) trained in European medieval history but began his career in African studies in 1952 in what was then Belgian Congo.

72 Vansina, *Oral Tradition as History*, preface to new edition, xii–xiii.

73 Folkenflik, "Macpherson, Chatterton, Blake," 378–391.

74 Henige, *Oral Historiography*, 2, 80–105.

75 Vansina, *Oral Tradition*, ch. 4, esp. 114–116.

76 Vansina, *Oral Tradition*, 117–19.

77 Fox, "A Rotinese Dynastic Genealogy," 37–79. Leach is quoted on p. 38.

78 Rosenthal, *Muslim Historiography*, 11–21.

79 Rosenthal, *Muslim Historiography*, 11–21.

80 Elphinstone, *Kingdom of Caubul*, 158 (emphasis added).

81 The highly influential Henry M. Elliot (published 1850) denounced historians of medieval India as sycophants lacking the "fidelity of Suetonius . . ." and entirely deficient in philosophical understanding. *Bibliographical Index*, xi–xvii. This was also the time when Macaulay was listing Herodotus and Tacitus as the only historians he admired.

82 Hartog, "The Invention of History," 21.

83 Robertson, "David Hume."

84 Eysenbach, *Histoire du blason*, 13–15; D'Hozier, *Armorial général*, part I, x. In the *Armorial*, the D'Hoziers state that before the sixteenth century, heralds had jurisdiction over single provinces, but migration and mixing made it necessary to centralize the function under Royal control.

85 Wagner, *Heralds and Heraldry*, 28–45, 64–68.

86 Guenée, 450–52, 460–61, 464–65.

87 Henneman, "'Enquêteurs-Réformateurs.'"

88 D'Hozier, *Armorial général* complement to part VII, 775–80; the verdict of December 19, 1658, is on 780–83.

89 D'Hozier, "Dedication," *Armorial général*, n.p.

90 D'Hozier, *Armorial général*, pt. I, i–v.

91 Henneman, "'Enquêteurs-Réformateurs.'"

92 Printed in full in Wagner, *Heralds and Heraldry*, 3–5.

93 More status-obsessed societies like Spain saw innumerable disputes around honorific forms of address. The royal court developed complex codes of etiquette for headwear

worn in royal palaces, for example. García Hernán, *La nobleza en la España moderna*, 43, endnotes.

94 Squibb, *Reports*, 43–47. Squibb reprints several more cases.

95 Gerbet, *Les noblesses espagnoles*, 56–58. Gerbet's book also describes the many regional and accidental variations in recruitment and continued membership.

96 *Las Siete Partidas*, vol. II, 70–71.

97 García Hernán, *La nobleza en la España moderna*, 21; the excerpt of *Pragmática* is taken from pp. 105–106.

98 Sicroff, *Les controverse des statuts*, 26–36, 39–40, 69–99. The affirmation required of witnesses is on p. 97, note 9.

99 Gerbet, *Les noblesses*, 47, 56–58, 233–36. Gerbet remarks that the nobility were long hostile to statutes that exalted racial criteria as an addition to caste. The book also describes the many regional and accidental variations in recruitment and continued membership.

100 Gerbet, *Les noblesses*, 47, 233–36.

101 Martínez, "Language, Genealogy and Classification," 25–42.

102 Twinam, *Purchasing Whiteness*, 116–19.

103 Crick, *Historia*, 1.

104 Crick, *Historia*, 220.

105 Crick, "Monmouth, Geoffrey"; Crick, *Historia*, 1–18.

106 Guenée, "La culture historique des nobles," 265.

107 Nutt, "History, Tradition, and Historic Myths," 337. For his biography, see Tedder, "Alfred Trübner Nutt."

108 In 1186, Rigord composed a genealogy of the French kings, which began with Priam, king of Troy (whose fugitive son Aeneas had been celebrated by the Latin poet Virgil as ancestor of the Romans). See Guenée, "Les généalogies entre l'histoire et la politique," 450–77.

109 Crick, *Historia*, 3.

110 Grafton, *What Was History?*, 193.

111 Grafton, *What Was History?*, 146–49.

112 Wongcha-um, "Thai court." Not many Western monarchies survive, and their executive power is negligible. But at the end of 2017 a Thai Buddhist historian was prosecuted and faced prison for questioning the facticity of a military feat attributed to the King Naresuan, who ruled c. 1590–1650.

113 Heerenden,"Camden, William."

114 Wheare, *Method and Order of Reading*.

115 Swain, "Theory of the Four Monarchies," 1–21; also Beverley, *The Kingdom of Jesus Christ*. The four monarchies were those foretold in Daniel's dream in the Old Testament, where the sequence culminated in the Jewish Messiah. The idea had appeared in the late Hellenic period before it was borrowed by the Romans and then by the Christians. Previous monarchies were regarded as secular and impermanent, but Christ would return to establish the fifth and eternal monarchy.

116 Breisach, "From Ancient to Medieval Historical Thinking," 45–57.

117 Furet, "The Birth of History in France," 78–79.

118 Burke, *History and Social Theory*, esp. 15.
119 Novick, *That Noble Dream*, 26.
120 Hamilton, *Hitler Diaries*, 66–74.
121 Trautmann, *Aryans and British India*, 42–43. The major scholar William Jones was also, as Trautmann points out, a defender of the biblical account of early human history.
122 Cited in Sumit Guha, "Lower Strata, Older Races," 425.
123 Marshman, *History of India*, 3, 8–9 shows that as late as 1836, a serious scholar could dismiss all non-Christian chronologies as false.
124 Trautmann, *Aryans and British India*.
125 Renfrew, *Archaeology and Language*.
126 Ehret, *Civilizations of Africa*; Ehret, "Language and History."
127 For an overview of these and many other cases, see Williams, *Forensic Historian*.
128 Bartlett, *Trial by Fire and Water*.
129 Gordon-Reed, *Thomas Jefferson and Sally Hemings*.
130 Novick's *That Noble Dream* has documented this dominance and shown both the subtle and crude methods by which it was maintained well into the 1950s. See especially pp. 72–85.
131 Williams, *Forensic Historian*, 71–73.
132 www.innocenceproject.org, accessed September 12, 2016.
133 Bolnick, "Individual Ancestry Inference and the Reification of Race."
134 Financial bias has especially been recognized in the medical sciences and resulted in stringent requirements for the disclosure of funding sources.
135 Donovan, Pasquetto, and Pierre, "Cracking Open the Black Box" (emphasis added). Cited with the authors' permission. A prescient early discussion by Gary Younge appeared in the *Guardian* in 2006 (www.theguardian.com/science/2006/feb/17/comment.columnists).

2. The Many Pasts of the Indian Subcontinent

1 Trautmann, *Aryans and British India*, 30. As Trautmann writes, "In the beginning, Persian was the principal medium through which the approaches to India's ancient past were made."
2 Rosenthal, *History of Muslim Historiography*, 47n2. The historical success of Islam seemed to demonstrate its superiority to other religions.
3 Humphreys. "Turning Points in Islamic Historical Practice," 89–100, quote on 91.
4 Robinson, *Islamic Historiography*, xx.
5 Robinson, *Islamic Historiography*, 134–35.
6 Albiruni, *Chronology of Ancient Nations*, 39.
7 Rosenthal, *Muslim Historiography*, 30–44.
8 Meisami, *Persian Historiography*, 9.
9 Siddiqi, *Indo-Persian Historiography*, 17–28, shows how Fakhr-i Mudabbir pioneered both approaches.
10 Jackson, *Delhi Sultanate*, 151–70; Siddiqi, *Indo-Persian Historiography*, 9–15.

11 Bosworth, "Abū 'Abdallāh al-Khwārazmī," 113–164.

12 Albiruni, *Chronology of Ancient Nations*; also see Yano, "al-Bīrūnī."

13 Aerts, "Canon and Canonisation of Ḥadīth."

14 Bosworth, "Heritage of Rulership," 51–62, esp. 52–53.

15 Trautmann, *India: Brief History of a Civilization*, 156–57.

16 Jackson, *Delhi Sultanate*.

17 Siddiqi, *Indo-Persian Historiography*, 7–9; Meisami, "Past in Service of the Present," 250.

18 Rosenthal, *Muslim Historiography*, 48–51.

19 Albiruni, *Chronology of Ancient Nations*, 47–48.

20 Bosworth, "Heritage," 54–55.

21 Auer, *Symbols of Authority*, 39–41. "At the origin of the pious ruler there was frequently a narrative in which the stature of the youth was recognized by a Sufi shaykh" (87).

22 Rosenthal, *Muslim Historiography*, 35–42.

23 Talbot, *Last Hindu Emperor*, 49.

24 Trautmann, *Aryans and British India*.

25 Marshman, *History of India from Remote Antiquity*, 3–7.

26 Kuiters, "Alexander Dow"; Truschke, *Culture of Encounters*, 217–21.

27 Powell, "History Textbooks," 97.

28 Fereshte, *Târîkh-e Fereshte*, 1–29 covers the period up to Noah (Nuh).

29 The *Rajatarangini* written in Kashmir was the major exception. The source of its historiographic method is still uncertain.

30 Amartya Sen, "India: The Stormy Revival."

31 Pathak, *Ancient Historians of India*, 120–21.

32 Ibn Baṭṭuṭa, *Travels of Ibn Battuta*, 740.

33 Irfan Habib, *Cambridge Economic History of India*, 48–76; Qureshi, *Administration*, 238–40.

34 Cort, "Jain Knowledge Warehouses," 77–87. The richness of the Jain tradition as a historical source has been known to outsiders since the late nineteenth century. Sufi stories are discussed in Nizami, *On History*, 163–97; the traditions of Namadeva are considered in the innovative work *Religion and Public Memory* by Christian L. Novetzke; and John Cort gives a fascinating account of the long preservation and reproduction of ancient manuscripts in Jain monastic collections. Talbot, *Last Hindu Emperor*, 50–61 shows how Jain narratives diverged from both Indo-Persian and Rajasthani vernacular versions of the story of Prithviraj.

35 Nahata, *Ṭhakkura Pherū*, editorial introduction, 12–13.

36 Talbot, *Last Hindu Emperor*; Ratnawat and Sharma, *Cāraṇ Sāhitya paramparā*.

37 Joiya, "Cāraṇīk abhilekha sāṁsan bahi," 390–95.

38 Marwar, *Riporṭ mardumśumārī Rāj Mārwāṛ*, 326–27.

39 Ibbetson, *Tribes and Castes*, 231–34. Bhats were a caste of bard-genealogists.

40 Nesfield, *Caste System*, 46. He remarked that the growing prestige of the colonial honorific system was reducing their influence, so landed men now sought prestige in colonially invented titles (such as "Rai Bahadur" or "Khan Bahadur," etc).

41 *Report of Mr H. Rivett-Carnac*, 30–31.

42 "Collection of Songs Made by Radhakrishna," 383b, 384a.

43 Mukta, *Mirabai*. See Lorenzen, *Kabir Legends*, where Kabir repeatedly defies a historical sultan of Delhi, Sikandar Lodi. Likewise, Mirabai was said to have escaped unscathed from efforts by the royal family she had abandoned to poison her. For Muin al-Din Chishti's defiance of the local Hindu king of Ajmer, see Currie, *Shrine and Cult*, 76–81; Siddiqi, "Early Chishti Dargahs," 1–23. For a story of how the confronting the founder of the shrine of Bu Adam in Rampal (in the modern Dhaka district) led to the downfall of the legendary Hindu monarch Ballal Sena, see Ashutosh Gupta, "Ruins and Antiquities of Rampal."

44 See, for example, the references to *mahatmya* texts in Khare, *Mahārāṣṭrācī cār daivaten*. For the growth of stories around the saint of Ajmer, see Currie, *Shrine and Cult*, 66–96.

45 See, for example, Mann, "Religion, Money and Status," 145–171.

46 Vad, *SSRPD*, vol. 7, part 2, 359.

47 Currie, *Shrine and Cult*; Mohammad Habib, "Chishti Mystic Records," 436–94.

48 Amin, *Conquest and Community*, esp. 10–14.

49 Sontheimer, "Forest and Pastoral Peoples," 100–29, and "Origin, Structure and Transformation of the Cults of Birobā, Mhaskobā and Khandobā," 185–206.

50 Amin, *Conquest and Community*, map 16.1; Babur, *Baburnama*, 335.

51 Halbwachs, *Social Frameworks of Memory*, 199.

52 Halbwachs, *Social Frameworks of Memory*, 92. Was this perhaps an example of a phenomenon of religious memory described by Halbwachs? He wrote that "while the memories of other social groups permeate each other mutually and tend to correspond, the memory of religious groups tends to be fixed once and for all. It either obliges others to adapt themselves to its dominant representations, or it systematically ignores them; contrasting its own permanence with the instability of others, it relegates them to an inferior rank."

53 Amin, *Conquest and Community*. Much of the preceding paragraph is drawn from Amin's monograph.

54 Amin, *Conquest and Community*, 177–78.

55 Amin, *Conquest and Community*, 159.

56 Roy-Burman, *Hindu-Muslim Syncretic Shrines and Communities*.

57 All information on Khandoba is taken from deeply researched study by Khare, *Mahārāṣṭrācī cār daivaten*, 69–152.

58 Khare, *Persian Sources*, vol. 6, doc. 89.

59 Talbot, *Last Hindu Emperor*, 198–201.

60 Babur, *Baburnama*, 330, 355. See p. 387 for the ratio of land assessed at a thousand *tankas* paying one horseman.

61 Scott, *Seeing Like a State*, 18–19.

62 This argument in fleshed out in Sumit Guha, "Rethinking the Economy of Mughal India."

63 Ernst, "Muslim Studies of Hinduism?," 179; Ali, "Translations of Sanskrit Works," 171–80.

64 Truschke, *Culture of Encounters*, 26–54, 101–104, 137–39, 142–65.

65 Truschke, *Culture of Encounters*, 232–33.

66 Rashid, "Treatment of History," 139–51; Nizami, *On History*, 224–44; Abu'l Fazl, *History of Akbar*, vol. 1, xi.

67 Ziegler, "Marwari Historical Chronicles," 219–50, esp. 232–34.

68 Abul Fazl Ạllámi, *Aín i Akbari*, 115–414.

69 Talbot, *Last Hindu Emperor*, 93–103; Truschke, *Culture of Encounters*, 202–27.

70 Abu'l Fazl, *History of Akbar*, vol. 1, x–xi, 33–34, Indian and Chinese chronologies, 167–77.

71 Siddiqi, *Indo-Persian Historiography*, 6–7 describes how travelers' tales and salacious gossip were incorporated by the historian Ibn al-Asir.

72 Talbot, *Last Hindu Emperor*, 93–106.

73 Ziegler, "Marwari Historical Chronicles," 234–47.

74 Perhaps this marked the decay of patronage?

75 Rajnish, *Lok mahākāvya Ālhā*, preface, 1–12.

76 Talbot, *Last Hindu Emperor*, 202–206.

77 Amin, *Conquest and Community*, 19–40; quote on 22.

78 Amin, *Conquest and Community*, 55–70.

79 For a longer discussion of these patterns in North India, see Sumit Guha, *Beyond Caste*, ch. 2, esp. 88–91.

80 Cited in Cohn, "Camars of Senapur," 12.

81 Cohn, "Pasts of an Indian Village," 243–44, 248.

82 Kasturi, *Embattled Identities*, 1–38, quote on 5.

83 Malcolm, *Memoir of Central India*, vol. II, 140 and footnote (for quote), vol. I, 507, 546 (for background).

84 Elliott, *Chronicles of Oonao*, vii.

85 Elliott, *Chronicles of Oonao*, 36, 42, 53.

86 Benett, *Report on the Family History*, 3–8 (including annotations).

87 Babur, *Baburnama*, 328–33, 355–57; cf. Benett, *Report on the Family History*, 18–21 for the Tilokchand legend.

88 Benett, *Report on the Family History*, appendix I (separately paginated), 6.

89 Malcolm, *Memoir of Central India*, vol. II, 140.

90 Talbot, *Last Hindu Emperor*, 183–218; Śekhāvat, "Rājasthānī itihāsa kā ek srot," 116–25.

91 Talbot, *Last Hindu Emperor*, 185–89.

92 Führer, *Inscriptions*, 314–15, 320, 323–34. Orthography as in the source.

93 Kulke, *Kings and Cults*, 189–91. Kulke also cites Sircar on the writing of similar temple-centered histories in the Tamil regions, as an example of how a cultural and political setting actuated a similar effort at building a historical past (188n).

94 This account of the social frame of historical memory in Odisha is drawn entirely from Kulke, *Kings and Cults*, especially "King Anangabhima" (17–32), "Jagannatha under Muslim Rule" (33–50), "The Chronicles and Temple Records of the Mādaḷā Pāñji of Puri" (136–58), and "Reflections on the Sources" (159–91).

95 Abul Fazl Ạllámi, *Aín i Akbari*, 144–47 for Bengal.

96 Salim, *Riyaẓu-s-Salātin*.

97 Karim, *Social History of the Muslims*, 6–16.

98 Karim, "Did Ibn Battuta Meet," 290–96; for the forgery, see Karim, *Social History of the Muslims*, 92–93.

99 Ashutosh Gupta, "Ruins and Antiquities of Rampal," 12–27.

100 Bhatia, *Unforgetting Chaitanya*, 171–73.

101 Ram Ram Basu, *Rājā Pratāpāditya Caritra*. Biographical information from the appendix, titled "Analysis," 175–89, Carey quote (English in the original) from 187. Basu resigned from the College some time before 1818.

102 Ram Ram Basu, *Rājā Pratāpāditya Caritra*, quote from 1 (emphasis added).

103 Ram Ram Basu, *Rājā Pratāpāditya Caritra*, 1–23, 62–65. This is taken from the Bangabasi Press edition of 1912–13, edited, annotated, and supplemented by Nikhilnath Ray. It lacks a title page and publication information, which I have gathered from internal evidence and Ray's biographical data in *Sahitya Manjusa*.

104 Endnotes to Ram Ram Basu, *Rājā Pratāpāditya Caritra*, 110, 165–67.

105 Vidyalankar and Banerjee, *Mrityuñjaya Granthāvalī*, 117–39. I am indebted to Gautam Bhadra for supplying me a photocopy of this rare publication.

106 Vidyalankar and Banerjee, *Mrityuñjaya Granthāvalī*, 136–39.

107 Partha Chatterjee, "History and the Nationalization of Hinduism," 111–49, esp. 114–15.

108 Many viewed these traditions as authentic ancient history. The newspaper *Ananda Bazar Patrika* said of the 1898 edition of *Sambandhanirṇaya*: "The wealth of information this book contains is simply marvelous. The materials collected in it go a great way to furnish us with a real social history of Bengal" (front matter, III). Bankim Chandra wrote of the first volume that, had it been published in Europe, it would have had a tumultuous reception, and that for some time its praise would have been heard on every side (front matter, X). By implication, it had not been adequately appreciated in Bengal. Not coincidentally, his family prided themselves on being descended from one of the five mythic elite Brahmans (Shastri, *Racanā samagra*, 794–98; 1894 obituary notice for Bankim Chandra).

109 Jogendra Nath Bhattacharya, *Hindu Castes and Sects*, 41–42.

110 Endorsements included one from H. H. Risley, the author of *Castes and Tribes of Bengal*, famous for his claim that one could rank castes according to the ratio of the breadth and length of their heads. See prefatory matter to the appendix of Vidyanidhi, *Sambandhanirṇaya*.

111 Ramesh C. Majumdar, *Baṃgīya kulaśāstra*.

112 Ramesh C. Majumdar, *History of Ancient Bengal*, 469–70.

113 Mukherjee, "Class, Caste and Politics," 33–78.

114 See the story of the Tagore lineage in Jogendra Nath Bhattacharya, *Hindu Castes and Sects*, 122–24. Satyendranath Tagore passed the Indian Civil Service exam in 1863.

115 Girishchandra Basu, *Sekāler dārogār kāhiniī*, vol. 3, 211–12. The author (1824–1898) was posted in central Bengal in the 1850s and 1860s. The verse read: *mūḍāle māthā uṭhībe cūl / tabu nā hobe Mustauphīr kūl* ("If the head is shaved, hair will fly / but still the Mustaufis will not be aristocrats"). This bit of doggerel was apparently thought sufficient to degrade a powerful landed lineage.

116 Śen, *Banga sāhitya paricaya*, vol. 2, 1695.

117 Ramesh C. Majumdar, *Baṃgīya kulaśāstra*, 6–8.
118 Kumkum Chatterjee, "King of Controversy," 1454–75.

3. Social Structure and Historical Narration in Western India

1 "An Account of Shahaji and His Son Shivaji," in Forrest, *Selections from the Letters*, 1–22.
2 Cited in Kulkarni, *James Cunningham Grant Duff*, 127n.
3 Dhundhiraja, *Rajavyavaharakosha*, manuscript composed c. 1676 and edited by Kailash N. Sane, in Mujumdar and Apte, *Sivacaritrapradipa*, 169.
4 Amarasimha, *Amarakośah*, vol. 1, 58.
5 An argument made in Meisami, *Persian Historiography*.
6 Verdicts from judicial assemblies often ended with the warning "whoever violates this will be a wrong-doer before the community and punishable by the Diwan."
7 Potdar and Mujumdar, *Śivacaritrasāhitya*, 113–18.
8 This interesting manuscript is in the British Library, London, Mss Mar A-7 pt. 1, ch. 6, verses 40–41, 48: "tenen svamate lihilī bakhar."
9 Potdar and Mujumdar, *Śivacaritrasāhitya*, 113–18.
10 Coats, "Account of the Township of Lony," 192. He adds, "The cultivators . . . form almost the whole of the population of the Township. . . . A school is established in the town, where reading, writing and arithmetic are taught; but it is only attended by the children of brahmins, shopkeepers and patails [headmen], so that scarcely any of the cultivators can either read or write." Coats was a medical officer for the government of Bombay. He served as a vaccinator and also a surgeon attached to the British mission (the Residency) at the Pune court from at least 1806 to 1817. His duties gave him unusual access to rural life and enabled him to write the first study of an Indian village ever written.
11 Anant, *Sabhāsad bakhar*, 2.
12 Printed in *Ramdas ani Ramdasi* 27 (1958–59): 239.
13 Gune, *Judicial System of the Marathas*, 10–25. Here I depend heavily on the still unsurpassed work of the historian V. T. Gune, who was the first to argue for and substantiate the persistence of a customary land law through successive political regimes in this region.
14 Skaria, "Forest Polity in Western India," 45. "Indeed, it seems that Dangi historical imagination is most concerned with the what-really-happened in situations where there is a degree of contestation. In other words, the need to prove legitimacy has led to a more detailed remembering of the past." Consulted with the author's permission.
15 One manuscript was edited and printed by Rajwade, *Mahikāvatīcī bakhar*. Others exist; a slightly variant one is *Mahikāvatīcī bakhar*, British Library, London, Add Mss 26494 B.
16 Rajwade, *Mahikāvatīcī bakhar*, 41. The two dates do not match.
17 Sardesai, *Selections from the Peshwa Daftar*, vol. 31, 21.
18 Sardesai, *Selections from the Peshwa Daftar*, vol. 31, 88–90.
19 BISM, *Vārṣika itivṛtta*, 360–72.

20 Vad, *SSRPD*, vol. 1, 224–25.

21 For an excellent account with many documents attached, see Gune, *Judicial System*.

22 Kulkarni, *Jedhe sakavali-karina*. *Karina*, an Arabic loanword, is derived from *qrn*, meaning "to join or connect" (Platts, *Dictionary of Urdu*); it is here applied to an explanatory history.

23 BISM, *Vārṣika itivṛtta*, 42–44.

24 Avalaskar, *Āngrekālina aṣṭāgār*, 36–37, 120, 122.

25 "Parasnis transcripts," fols. 22–23.

26 Halbwachs, *On Collective Memory*, 40.

27 "Parasnis transcripts," fol. 87.

28 Complaint made in 1757 CE, printed in Pendse, *Pendse Kulavṛttānta*, 33.

29 These two paragraphs depend entirely on the painstaking work of the historian Gajanan B. Mehendale, author of *Śrī Rājā Śivachatrapatī*. Vol. II, appendix 29, 899–936 contains a discussion of this problem and suggests the reasons for the forgeries.

30 A key term found in one of these forgeries is "Hindavi swaraj," translatable as "Indian kingdom" or even "Hindu kingdom." Hindavi is a Persian construction that may be read either way. I have myself been misled into reading it as an expression from the mid-seventeenth century rather than from around 1800.

31 Sardesai, *Selections from the Peshwa Daftar*, vol. 31, 67–69.

32 Rajwade, *Maraṭhyāncyā itihāsācī sādhane*, vol. 2 in the new series, 86–89; Pavar, *Tārābāīkalīna Kāgadpatre*, vol. 1, 189–203. I owe this idea to Prachi Deshpande (personal communication).

33 A full history of the community was written by Alexander Mackintosh, captain in the Ahmednagar Local Corps, who spent several years in operations against them, and interrogated many. See Mackintosh, *Sketch of the History of the Ramoossies*, in *Madras Journal*, 232–35.

34 The Padshah of Bidar was firmly lodged in popular memory as founder of the first Islamic dynasty in southern India. The later Bahmani sultans did in fact rule from Bidar in the fifteenth century, and it remained the center of the rump kingdom after provincial governors in Bijapur, Elichpur, Ahmadnagar, and Golkunda became independent. But the first major center of that sultanate was at Gulbarga.

35 Devle, *Mahipatibuvā Tahrabādkar racita śrībhaktavijaya*, 387–94. This was an extremely popular legend and was rendered into verse by Mahipati (among others). The text was completed in 1762; Mahipati died in 1790.

36 The Chivhe lineage were Kolis, the Khomnes Ramoshis. The two tribal groups were rivals for dominance in the same hill region. Some of the spellings used suggest that there really was an original Persian text: thus "Essoojee" and "Chooha" make sense as an English rendering of the sequences ye-sin-vav-jim-ye and chim-vav-he, the latter being "Chivhe" with the short vowel left unmarked.

37 Mackintosh, *Sketch of the History of the Ramoossies* in *Madras Journal*, no. 7 (April 1835), 107–9. The killing of Afzal Khan after he tried to overpower Shivaji during a parley was followed by the rout of the Bijapur army accompanying the khan. It was one of the most famous episodes in the early history of the Maratha kingdom.

38 Athavale, *Umājī Rāje*, 183–84, appendix.

39 Athavale, *Umājī Rāje*, 213, appendix.

40 For a complete background to the sociopolitical order in the western mountains, see Sumit Guha, *Environment and Ethnicity*, ch. 4.

41 Elliott, *Chronicles of Oonao*, 64, note 9. In a forged *sanad* presented to Charles A. Elliott in the Unnao district of Uttar Pradesh around 1860, the forger sought to validate a claim to its being issued by "Rai Prithora" (Prithviraj) in 582 Hijri, or the year popularly thought to mark the death of that king.

42 Elphinstone, *Report on the Territories*, xiv.

43 Coats, "Township of Lony," 189.

44 Atre, *Gāṁva-gāḍā*, 91.

45 Moon, *Growing Up Untouchable.*

46 Kulkarni, *Maharashtra*, 1–62.

47 Jenkins, *Report on the Territories*, 54 (emphasis added).

48 Spivak, "Can the Subaltern Speak?," 308. The Italian Gramsci scholar Guido Liguori believes this essay to be the single most widely read and translated text of the Subaltern School. In an email to me in 2017, Professor Spivak added the clarification that she did not ask "Can the subaltern talk?" because the answer to that would be yes. I will not pronounce on whether "speaking" was more difficult than "talking." But I do argue that the utterances of subalterns, such as the barber-woman cited below, were as authentic as those of anyone else in that time—or, indeed, now. She spoke from her recognized place as a mother and a member of village community. These were indeed socially constructed roles, but then so is any role.

49 Vad, *SSRPD*, vol. 1, 186–87.

50 Oturkar, *Peśvekālīn*, 25–26.

51 Vad, *SSRPD*, vol. 1, 161–64.

52 Gokhale, "Matwan Plates." Shobhana Gokhale found the Matwan plates included in the daily worship of rural household.

53 Rajwade, *Itihāsācārya Vi. Ka. Rājwāḍe*, vol. 4, 46–47 (author's translation). Rajvade boldly identifies the ruler as Yusuf Adilshah, whose second regnal year would fall in 1486–87.

54 Joshi and Khare, *Śivacaritrasāhitya*, 197–98.

55 Gavli, *Pesvékālina gulamgirī va aspruśyata*, 97–106. I have not inserted diacriticals in this quote as the official titles here all familiar ones.

56 Oturkar, *Peśvekālīn*, 69–71.

57 Sumit Guha, *Environment and Ethnicity*, 62–105.

58 Bhadra, "Mentality of Subalternity," 91.

59 Bendre, *Māloji Rāje*, 224–28.

60 Sardesai, *Marathi Riyasat*, vol. 1, 89–109.

61 Pindye, *Rādhāmādhavavilāsacampu*; Anant, *Sabhasad bakhar*, 34, 74.

62 Pant, *Ājñāpatra*, 59.

63 Anant, *Sabhāsad bakhar*, 1, 100.

64 Paramananda, *Śivabhāratam*, ch. 1, verses 42–43.

65 Pagdi, *Hindvī svarājya ani Mogal*, 17–18.

66 British Library, London, Mss Mar D.31, fol. 126.

67 This most important insight is from Prachi Deshpande, *Creative Pasts*, 70.

68 Prachi Deshpande, *Creative Pasts*, ch. 2 and ch. 3 cover much of this ground too.

69 Duff, *History of the Mahrattas*, vii–viii. The Marathi translation appeared in 1829–30 and became a required schoolbook, reprinted eleven times by 1838 (Jog, *Marāṭhī vangmayācā itihāsa*, pt. 4, 553–54). Duff's sources are listed in Kulkarni, *James Cunningham Grant Duff*, 118.

70 Sohoni, *Peśvyāncī bakhar*, 240. This text has been more fully analyzed by Prachi Deshpande in ch. 2 of *Creative Pasts*, especially 45–46.

71 Wagoner, "Precolonial Intellectuals," 783–814; also Dirks, "Colonial Histories and Native Informants," 279–313.

72 Jenkins's *Report on the Territories* acknowledges his British assistants but never mentions Vinayakrao. Hundreds of folios of Vinayakrao's Modi script field notes, tour diaries, and transcriptions from 1808 to 1823 are in the British Library, London, Marathi Mss D.35 to D.46.

73 Prachi Deshpande, *Creative Pasts*, 1.

74 Anant, *Sabhāsad bakhar*, 100.

75 Hastings, *Memoirs Relative to the State of India*, 89.

76 Khare and Joshi, *Aitihāsik Marāṭhī sādhane*, 56–57.

77 Elphinstone, *Report on the Territories*, 7.

78 Julien, *Reading Inca History*, 293. As Catherine Julien put it: "It should not be lost on the reader that a study of memory is intimately bound to a story of what was forgotten."

79 Renan, *Qu'est ce qu'une nation?*, 9.

80 Wagoner, *Tidings of the King*.

81 Iyengar, *Sources of Vijayanagar History*.

82 Dinesh Chandra Sen, *Chaitanya and His Companions*, 267.

83 Sastri and Venkataramanayya, *Further Sources of Vijayanagar History*, vol. 3, 197. Attested by inscriptions in *South Indian Inscriptions, vol. XV. Part II*, 314–15.

84 Sewell, *Forgotten Empire*, 2. "And yet in the present day, the very existence of this kingdom is hardly remembered in India. . . . Even the name has died out in men's minds and memories, and the remains that mark its site are known only as the ruins lying near the little village of Hampe."

85 Pindye, *Rādhāmādhavavilāsacampu*, 256–57.

86 For background, see Kulke, *Kings and Cults*, 208–39.

87 Tobert, *Anegondi*, x–xii, 192–96.

88 Molesworth, *Dictionary of Marathi and English*. preface to the second edition, xviii–xxi.

89 Molesworth, *Dictionary of Marathi and English*, 28 (emphasis added).

90 Steele, *Law and Custom of Hindoo Castes*, ix–xii, 1–22.

91 Potdar and Mujumdar, *Śivacaritrasāhitya*, 333–38. I located this reference via the valuable article by Potdar, "Marathit Vijayanagara," 338–50.

92 Cited in Potdar, "Marathit Vijayanagara," 339–40.

93 Y. Khu Deshpande, "Vijayanagarce Rājānca ullekha," 113–15.

94 Potdar, "Marathit Vijayanagara," 343–44.

95 Paramashivan, "Vijayanagarakālīn citrakalā," 208–9.

96 Row, *Marathi Historical Inscription*, 1–2.

97 Incomplete text by Anonymous, "Aitihasik sphuta lekha," 21–29.

98 Potdar, "Anjanvela tālukyācī vahivaṭa," 318–20. The Arabic numbers are obviously garbled. In the sixty-year cycle, Dundubhi should be 1502–3, so this is evidently elapsed-year reckoning. But the date is obviously wrong.

99 Sumit Guha, "Frontiers of Memory," 265–68.

100 Potdar, "Marathit Vijayanagara," 350.

101 Rao, *Textures of Time*, 226–34 pronounce on *bakhars* largely through ponderous paraphrases of Raeside's readily available English translation of one text.

102 Rao, *Textures of Time*, 2–5.

103 See Pollock, "Pretextures of Time," quote from 372. Sheldon Pollock long ago pointed to the many contradictions that arise with the authors' naïve and underthought use of the opposition of "factual" and "mythic" and from the nativist notion of possessing unmediated access to the past.

104 To avoid confusion, let me clarify that "Marathi" is the language; "Maratha" is sometimes the name of the ethnic community, and sometimes refers only to the land-owning castes within it. "Maharashtra" is the name of the Indian state predominantly inhabited by speakers of Marathi.

105 I take this idea from Prachi Deshpande, *Creative Pasts*.

106 Philips, *Historians of India*, 9.

4. History and Memory through the Nineteenth and Twentieth Centuries

1 Furet, *Workshop of History*, 98.

2 Novak, *On Masaryk*, 271–72. The scholarly nationalist Masaryk denied the manuscript's authenticity and was, as a consequence, violently attacked in the Czech press.

3 Davies, "Liber Landavensis," 335–51.

4 Lloyd, "Geoffrey of Monmouth," 460–68.

5 Duara, *Rescuing History from the Nation*, 4.

6 This paragraph is drawn from Humphreys, "Turning Points in Islamic Historical Practice," 89–100 (quotes on 92, 97).

7 This paragraph is based on Choueiri, *Modern Arab Historiography*; and Gordon, *Self-Determination and History*.

8 Falola, "Nationalism and African Historiography," 217.

9 Vansina, "Afterthoughts on the Historiography of Oral Tradition," 105–10.

10 Cited in Chou, *Hu Shih*, 168; see also 196.

11 Wang, "China's Search for a National History"; the telling quote from Teng Shih is on 196.

12 Li, *Reinventing Modern China*, 32, for the quote from Liang Qichao.

13 These terms, as well much of the argument of this section, are derived from Trautmann, *Aryans and British India*, 62–130.

14 Misra, *Judicial Administration of the East India Company*.

15 Adam, *Report on the State of Education in Bengal*, 1835.

16 Kaye, *Lives of Indian Officers*, vol. I, 128.

17 Danvers, *Memorials of Old Haileybury College*, 11–30.

18 Gash, Norman, "Wellesley [formerly Wesley], Arthur"; Trautmann, *Madras School.*

19 Auber, *An analysis of the constitution.* Peter Auber was commissioned by the English East India Company to compile an official record, and his book included a short history.

20 Trautmann, "Indian Time, European Time," 172–73.

21 Trautmann, *Aryans and British India*, 99–103.

22 Carson, "Grant, Charles."

23 William Jones, *Discourses Delivered before the Asiatic Society*, vol. 1, 30.

24 Trautmann, *Aryans and British India*, 101–9.

25 The Oxford Dictionary of National Biography (2004) wrote of Henry Dundas, first Viscount Melville: "Where he impressed his countrymen was by supplying them with official patronage in Britain and the empire, which they thought had been wanting so far." Three of Dundas's brothers were found jobs in India, and two of them died there.

26 The description of the careers of Dugald Stewart and James Mill is based on their entries in the Oxford Dictionary of National Biography. Other information is taken from Trautmann, *Aryans and British India*, ch. 4.

27 Ines Županov cited in Sumit Guha, "Conviviality," 278.

28 Trautmann, *Aryans and British India*, 99.

29 Carey, Marshman, and Ward, *Hints Relative to Native Schools*, 8–16.

30 Vans Kennedy, "Remarks on the Sixth and Seventh Chapters," 169–70.

31 Beveridge, "Kennedy, Vans"; Munro quote is from Vans Kennedy, "Remarks on the Sixth and Seventh Chapters," 169.

32 Bayly, "Elphinstone, Mountstuart"; Partha Chatterjee, "History and the Nationalization of Hinduism," 137–38. Elphinstone was also the history textbook at Haileybury in the 1840s. Danvers, *Memorials*, 70.

33 Elphinstone, *History of India: The Hindu and Mahometan Periods*, 194–95.

34 Trautmann, *Aryans and British India*, 118.

35 Thomas, "Macaulay, Thomas Babington, Baron Macaulay."

36 Strachey, *India*, 194 (emphasis added).

37 Strachey, *India*, 193–96. Strachey lamented that through Macaulay *Essays*, Mill's "false history is systematically taught by us and believed by the educated Natives of India to be true."

38 Sumit Guha, "Economy of Mughal India," 535–56.

39 James Grant is cited and discussed in Sumit Guha, "Rethinking the Economy of Mughal India," 536. Grant's report of 1788 was deemed valuable enough to be printed in the Parliamentary Papers of the 1812 session. It occupies 205 large folio pages in print.

40 Wilks, *Historical Sketches*, vol. I, 10n.

41 Hardy, *Historians of Medieval India*, 1–3. Hardy is, however, too sweeping in condemning earlier historians for assuming that one could craft a reliable narrative by the comparison of authorities. He resorts to the same technique himself, as, for example, when discussing the artificial sequence of events in Afif's history of Feroz Shah Tughlaq. For Afif, see 48–49.

42 Fereshte, *Târîkh-e Fereshte*, 1–12.

43 Talbot, *Last Hindu Emperor*, esp. 15, 186–96.

44 Tod, *Annals and Antiquities* vol. I, introduction, x. The unpaginated dedication to King George IV, June 20, 1829, said: "The Rajpoot princes, happily rescued, by the triumph of the British arms, from the yoke of lawless oppression, are now the most remote tributaries to Your Majesty's extensive empire; and their admirer and annalist may, perhaps, be permitted to hope, that the sighs of this ancient and interesting race for the restoration of their former independence, which it would suit our wisest policy to grant, may be deemed not undeserving Your Majesty's regard."

45 Stewart, *History of Bengal*, 2 and list of Persian sources.

46 See Prachi Deshpande, *Creative Pasts*, 71–80 for a full account.

47 Ramesh C. Majumdar, *Baṁgīya kulaśāstra*, esp. the introduction, 1–2, and 88–107.

48 Kumkum Chatterjee, "The King of Controversy," 1454–75.

49 Powell, *Muslims and Missionaries*; Dodson, "Contesting Translations," 43–59.

50 Partha Chatterjee, "History and the Nationalization of Hinduism" 125–28.

51 Syed Ahmed Khan, *Causes of the Indian Revolt*, 45.

52 Bankim Chandra, *Racanāvalī*, vol. 2, 340.

53 Rubbee, *Origin of the Musalmans of Bengal*, 53–54.

54 Bankim Chandra, *Racanāvalī*, vol. 2, 330–33.

55 Bankim Chandra, *Racanāvalī*, vol. 2, 336–40.

56 Inden, *Marriage and Rank*.

57 Ranajit Guha, *Indian Historiography of India*, 1. In fact, what Bankim Chandra actually meant can easily be inferred from many of his writings, and is enumerated in the famous patriotic song "Vande Mataram," which speaks of "seven crore pairs" of arms raised to defend the Mother. Seventy million (or seven crores) was the population of the Bengal Presidency (Bengal, Bihar, Orissa, and Assam) enumerated in the 1872 census, if rounded to the nearest ten million (one crore). The hymn, both text and translation, may be found in Bose, *Artist in Chains*, 228–29.

58 Ranajit Guha, *Indian Historiography of India*, 1, 26, 67–69. Only in the first decade of the twentieth century, Ranajit Guha continued, did Indians move to implement this agenda—but their (unnamed) works were often proscribed by the colonial government.

59 Dasgupta, *Indian Historiography*; and Banglapedia, "Raja Rajendralal Mitra."

60 Dasgupta, *Indian Historiography*, 7.

61 Chanda, *Gauḍarājamāla*, i. After 1920, it should be noted, he held more prestigious positions at the University of Calcutta, the Indian Museum, and elsewhere. But he had already established his reputation by then.

62 Banglapedia, "Ramaprasad Chanda"; Kenneth A. R. Kennedy, "Have Aryans been identified," 48–49; Chanda, *Indo-Aryan Races*, 62–65, 253ff. The statistical appendix sought to test the hypothesis that Bengali Brahmans were descended from five ancestors who came from Kanauj (present-day Uttar Pradesh); he compared the head measurements of Brahmans from the two regions.

63 Cited in Chakrabarty, *Calling of History*, 64.

64 This is almost entirely based on Prachi Deshpande, *Creative Pasts*, 97–100. She describes this as a method evolved by philologists studying older texts. Versions were

compared, copyists' errors and forgers' mistakes sought out. By this means, manuscript traditions were established. The method was imported into historical practice by the German historical schools. "Scientific" source criticism thus "legitimated history as an independent profession" (Evans, *In Defence of History*, 18–20).

65 Phatak, *Nyāyamūrti Mahādeva Govind Rāṇaḍe*, 14–15.

66 Kirtane, *Grantdufkruta Marathyance bakharivar tika*; Jog, *Marāṭhī vangmayācā itihāsa*, part 4, 556; Kulkarni, *James Cunningham Grant Duff*, 212–13.

67 A selection from the original Bombay government records about Phadke, as well as his own journal, is printed in Government of Bombay, *Source Material for the History*, 73–129.

68 Phadke's travels in the guise of a religious mendicant bore an eerie parallel to the imagined leader of the insurgents in Bankim Chandra's novel *Ananda Math*. Sisir Kumar Bose reports that news of Phadke's rebellion was heard even in Bengal. The possibility of appearing to sympathize with him so alarmed Bankim Chandra that he removed even minor anti-British utterances in his novel. The book therefore acquired a more marked anti-Muslim tone. Bose, *Artist in Chains*, 141–47.

69 *Kāvyetihās Saṁgraha* 1, no.1 (January 1878): 3–10.

70 *Kāvyetihās Saṁgraha* 1, no.1 (January 1878): 3–10; Sohoni, *Peśvyāncī bakhar*, 3–5.

71 Pendse, *Pendse Kulavṛttānta*, 55.

72 Pendse, *Pendse Kulavṛttānta*, 1–15.

73 V. G. Khobrekar in S. P. Sen, *Historians and Historiography*, 207–14, quote from 208.

74 Parasnis, *Jhānśī saṁsthānacyā*, 7–19.

75 Rajwade, *Itihāsācārya Vi. Ka. Rājwaḍe*, vol. 10, 1–8, 24–25.

76 Cited in Kulkarni, *Maratha Historiography*, 127.

77 See Joshi's introduction to his edition of *Rajvade lekhasangraha*, 1–13.

78 A valuable English account of Rajwade is Kulkarni, *Maratha Historiography*, 136–68.

79 Prachi Deshpande, *Creative Pasts*, 154–64.

80 This account is based in Tryambak S. Shejwalkar's essay in *Nivaḍak lekha saṃgraha*, compiled and published by H. V. Mote, 380–84.

81 I rely here on Jog, *Marāṭhī vangmayācā itihāsa*, pt. 5, vol. 1, 448–49. Prachi Deshpande, "Narratives of Pride," 155–56 cites the popular novelist V. V. Hadap: he claimed to use his imagination only where "historical evidence had *failed* in its task" (Deshpande's translation; my emphasis).

82 For a full account, see Kulkarni, *Maratha Historiography*, 198–223; Ranade, *Rise of the Maratha Power*, ii.

83 I need to stipulate that this was written during Savarkar's revolutionary nationalist phase before World War I. The writing of that time had a tone quite different from his later Hindu nationalist works following his return from prison.

84 For prophetic revolts, see Adas, *Prophets of Rebellion*.

85 Savarkar, *Indian War of Independence*.

86 Chirol, *Indian Unrest*.

87 Nehru, *Essential Writings*, vol. I, 639–41.

88 Chakrabarty, *Calling of History*, 38–39.

89 This description is entirely based on the biographical note by Gajanan Mehendale's preface of the new edition of Khare's *Saṁśodhakāca Mitra*, 1–10.

90 For Crewe's scathing comments, naturally echoed by all junior bureaucrats, see Chakrabarty, *Calling of History*, 44–47.

91 All the articles are conveniently reprinted in Pearson, *Legitimacy and Symbols*. Buckler's "The Political Theory of the Indian Mutiny" is on 43–74, Edwardes on 75–84, and Dewar and Garrett on 85–119. Quotes are successively from 46, 76, and 79.

92 Chakrabarty, *Calling of History*, 154–55.

93 Rajwade, *Mahikāvatīcī bakhar*, introduction, esp. 109–10.

94 Sardesai, *Marathi Riyasat*. The first edition of 1,500 sold out in 1991 and was followed by a second printing of 1,000 copies. As of 2016, plans are afoot to reissue it. (Information courtesy of Anjali Nerlekar)

95 Robert Sewell was a scholarly Indian Civil Service officer from the Madras Presidency. He titled his history of Vijayanagara *A Forgotten Empire*.

96 An excellent survey is Stein, *Vijayanagara*, 4–7.

97 On the political and cultural significance of the BISM, see Prachi Deshpande, *Creative Pasts*, 117–20.

98 Karmarkar and Oturkar, *Vijayanagara smāraka grantha*, 1–2.

99 Karmarkar and Oturkar, *Vijayanagara smāraka grantha*, 1–7.

100 Shejwalkar, "Vijayanagara Samrajyace Maratheshahivarila parinama," 64–65.

101 This information is derived from the introduction to the reprinted text in Sovani, *Aitihasika bakhari*, part 1, 12, 13–23. For an earlier published and longer discussion of these materials see Sumit Guha, "Frontiers of Memory," 269–88; and Sumit Guha, "Literary Tropes and Historical Settings."

102 Iyengar, "Bakhair of Rama Raja." See also Herwadkar, *Forgotten Literature*, 12–13; Herwadkar, *Marāṭhī bakhar*, 40–41. For Mackenzie, see Robb, "Colin Mackenzie."

103 Sastri, *Further Sources*, vol. 3, 204–42. Note on p. 205 refers to the Mackenzie translation as India Office Mss no. X.

104 Rajpurohit, "Rākṣastangḍīcyā raṇāngaṇācā sthalanirṇaya," 17–22.

105 Meyer, Burn, Cotton, and Risley, *Imperial Gazetteer of India*, vol. 7, 371.

106 Gramopadhye, *Marathi bakhar gadya*. This little book was intended, he declares, to provide students with a quick introduction to this class of Marathi text. He titled his extract on the defeat of Vijayanagara "Rakshes Tagdicha Ranasamgrama" (The Battle of Rakshes Tagdi). Rajpurohit, "Rākṣastangḍīcyā raṇāngaṇācā sthalanirṇaya," 17–22; annotation 170–71.

107 Gramopadhye, *Marāṭhī bakhar gadya*, 18n.

108 Rao, *Textures of Time*, 2–5, 226–34. Gramopadhye's fragment was read with a naïve historicism by Rao et al. in 2001. They claimed that, being "at home" in the culture, they could analyze by "texture" alone. Then, of course, even a few pages of a text are sufficient to understand it. The *bakhar* extract under review is the only Marathi text that Rao et al. chose to "read" in the original Marathi. They did not find it necessary to consider *eighteen* other texts found in the same little reader.

109 Jaffrelot, *Hindu Nationalism*, 1–19.

110 Naipaul, *India: A Wounded Civilization*, 9.

111 Jaffrelot, *India's Silent Revolution*, 146, 490–95. Even in the late twentieth century, he observes the greater pull of "Sanskritization" in North India.

112 Prachi Deshpande, *Creative Pasts*, 177–202. In *Beyond Caste*, I outline how variations in social change at the all-India level structured this phenomenon.

113 See Talbot, *Last Hindu Emperor*; and Sreenivasan, *Many Lives of a Rajput Queen* for two studies of the countrywide transmission of motifs from Tod's narrative sources.

114 Azad, "Introduction to Surendranath Sen," xviii–xix. He also mentioned Henry M. Elliot as a contributor to this poisoning of initially amicable relations.

115 For example, the Padmini story. See Sreenivasan, *Many Lives of a Rajput Queen*.

116 Roman Catholics were, of course, present at the court of the Emperor Akbar (ruled 1556–1605) and his successors. But their evangelical efforts had little success, and some converts soon relapsed into Islam. This account is largely based on Powell, *Muslims and Missionaries*, 76–102.

117 Powell, *Muslims and Missionaries*, chs. 6–8. Powell has presented an erudite narration of these changes. She shows how discomfited the missionaries were when they found Muslim scholars equipped not only philosophical arguments but also historical critiques derived from Biblical text criticism, published only a few years earlier in Europe in works such as David Strauss' *Life of Jesus*. But Islamic scholars then felt that the weight of colonial power was pitted against them.

118 Syed Ahmed Khan, *Causes of the Indian Revolt*, 16–21.

119 India, Ministry of Education, *Selections from the Educational Records*, vol. I, 10–17, 364–65, 378–79.

120 India, Ministry of Education, *Selections from the Educational Records*, 53, 99–105.

121 Marshman, *History of India from Remote Antiquity*, ii–iv.

122 Marshman, *History of India Translated*. Mitra's protest is in his unpaginated introduction.

123 The fable of Ādiśūra (here termed Udīśvara) being exasperated by the sinful ignorance of the Bengali Brahmans and bringing in five learned Brahmans (along with five Kayastha servants) from Kanauj is not found in the 1836 English text of John C. Marshman's *History of India from Remote Antiquity*, but it occurs in the Hindi translation published in Agra in 1846. The Hindi edition is titled *Bhā Bhāratavarṣīya itihāsa arthāt Hindusthān kī kathā*.

124 Marshman, *History of India from Remote Antiquity*, 83, 121. This popular etymological invention was exploded when Sena epigraphs were found and deciphered. Not only where they not "physicians" but, like many dynasties of the time, they claimed to be Brahma-kshatri (or Brahmans who became Kshatriya). See Ramesh C. Majumdar, *History of Ancient Bengal*, vol. I, 219–21.

125 For the many translations of Marshman's *History of India from Remote Antiquity*, see Blumhardt, *Catalogue of Bengali Printed Books*.

126 Stark, "Knowledge in Context," 76–78.

127 Penner, "Elliot, Sir Henry Miers."

128 Elliot, *Bibliographical Index*, xx–xxxi.

129 Stark, "Knowledge in Context," and personal communication.

130 The bilingual title page of *Itihāsa timirnāśaka* declares that the first 1864 printing ran to 10,000 copies. There were to be several reprints. It was evidently widely used as a textbook and sold in every district by the Deputy Inspectors of Schools.

131 Urdu was adopted as the language of administration in the Panjab, even though the vast majority of its people spoke variants of Panjabi as a home language. But it would have been convenient for carpetbagger officials from the older British provinces.

132 My information on Raja Shiv Prasad and Karim al-Din derives from Stark, "Knowledge in Context" and Powell's extraordinarily rich essay, "History Textbooks."

133 These works (and especially the Mahabharata) had indeed been used by Mughal-era historians. But that did not impinge on the educated public in the way that school textbooks and missionary street polemic did.

134 Kenneth W. Jones, *Religious Controversy in British India*, especially Conlon, "Polemic Process," 5–29.

135 Ballantyne, *Christianity Contrasted with Hindu Philosophy*, 20–2. I was led to this source through Dalmia, *Nationalization of Hindu Traditions*.

136 Dalmia, *Nationalization of Hindu Traditions*, 349–53 (emphasis added).

137 Amin, *Conquest and Community*, 163–69.

138 My account of Vishnubawa and his publications is drawn from Conlon, "Polemic Process," quotes from 10, 22–23.

139 Krishna Kumar, "Hindu Revivalism."

140 Parulekar, *Literacy in India*, 16.

141 Kenneth W. Jones, *Arya Dharm*; Barbara Metcalf, *Islamic Revival*.

142 Barbara Metcalf, *Islamic Revival*, 235–38, 348, 352, 360.

143 Barbara Metcalf, *Islamic Revival*, 359.

144 Safi Ullah Khan, *Mugalkālin Bhārat*, 46–74.

145 Krishna Kumar, *Prejudice and Pride*, 229. Kumar found that a few students in a government-run school in Delhi actually thought that "Pakistan" had formerly ruled "India." They were, he perceptively observes, simply using "Pakistan" as a synonym for Muslims.

146 This paragraph is shaped by the analytically sharp and empirically rich work of Krishna Kumar, "Hindu Revivalism and Education," esp. 536-39

147 Amin, *Conquest and Community*, 159–62.

148 Jaffrelot, *Hindu Nationalist Movement*, 5–8.

149 Kenneth W. Jones, *Arya Dharm*, 30–36.

150 Leitner was a European Christian convert from Judaism who was well trained in European-style Oriental and especially Islamic studies. He was appointed principal of the Government College, Lahore, in 1864, at the age of 24. He helped reorganize the new Panjab educational system in the 1870s. See Rubinstein, "Leitner , Gottlieb Wilhelm."

151 Sarasvatī, *Laghu grantha samgraha*, 176–86 (emphasis added).

152 Sarasvatī, *Satyārtha Prakāśah*, 218–39.

153 Sarasvatī, *Laghu grantha samgraha*, 176–77.

154 Rai, *Arya Samaj*, 87. This is taken almost literally from *Satyārtha Prakāśah*.

155 Cited in Roy, *Emergence of Monarchy in North India*, 5.

156 Cited in Rai, *Arya Samaj*, 170. I have not sought out the source of this fiction.

157 Sarkar, "Historical Pedagogy of the Sangh Parivar," 54.

158 Krishna Kumar, "Hindu Revivalism and Education"; King, *One Language*.

159 Safi Ullah Khan, *Mugalkālin Bhārat*, 28–29.

160 *Times of India*, October 10, 1912, and July, 3 1876, via Proquest database.

161 Raychaudhuri, "India, 1858 to the 1930s," vol. V, 214–30.

162 Banerjea, *Nation in the Making.*

163 Garratt and Thompson, *Rise and Fulfillment*, 550, 655, viii. This ethical vision was the one that official India presented to the world through the 1950s, before external and internal shocks moved its stance toward realpolitik.

164 Lived 1861–1930. See his entry in Ghosh, *Sāhityasevak manjuṣā*, vol. 2.

165 Krishna Kumar, *Prejudice and Pride*, 15. He presents succinct view in "Peace with the Past," 47–50.

166 Nehru, *Discovery of India*, 52, 505–22; *Essential Writings*, vol. I, 24–30.

167 Reprinted in Philips, *Evolution of India and Pakistan*, 353–54.

168 Hasan, *India's Partition*, 57–68.

169 Krishna Kumar, *Prejudice and Pride*, 160.

170 Naoroji, *Poverty and Un-British Rule.*

171 Mohammad Habib, "Present and the Past, " 19–20, 25 (emphasis added).

172 Chand, *History of the Freedom Movement in India*, vol. 1, 499–502. The very next year, Ramesh C. Majumdar, who had already published an alternative reading of the 1857 uprising, published a polemic against this Nehruvian vision.

173 Krishna Kumar, *Prejudice and Pride*, 220–22.

174 Qureshi, *Muslim Community*, esp. 82–93, quote from 79. Qureshi issued an essentially unchanged version of his book from Karachi in 1977.

175 Qureshi, *Short History of Pakistan.*

176 Ansar Zahid Khan, "Pakistan Historical Society"; Husain, *History of the Freedom Movement.*

177 Nair, "Textbook Conflicts in South Asia," 29–45; Fuchs, "Introduction," 1–12.

178 Cited in Chakrabarty, *Calling of History*, 11.

179 Sumit Guha, *Beyond Caste*, 193–94.

180 Neeladri Bhattacharya, "Problem," 12–18; Nita Kumar, "History at the Madrasas," 57–62; Sarkar, "Historical Pedagogy of the Sangh Parivar," 51–56.

181 Partha Chatterjee, "History and the Nationalization of Hinduism," 112. "To the extent that the genealogy of modern historiography in India is deeply implicated in the encounter with British colonialism, these historical claims of political Hinduism are also a product of the contestations with the forms of colonial knowledge."

182 Chatterjee and Ghosh, *History and the Present*, 1–23.

183 *The Hindu*, "'For Indians, Smartphone Is Primary Source of News.'"

184 Rudolph and Rudolph, "Rethinking Secularism," esp. 37.

185 Nandy, *Intimate Enemy*, 58–62.

186 Kaviraj, *Imaginary Institution of India*, 34–35.

Conclusion

1 Gopal, *Anatomy of a Confrontation*, esp. 1–37.

Bibliography

Abbreviations

BISM	Bharata Itihasa Samshodhaka Mandala
BISMT	*Bharata Itihasa Samshodhaka Mandala Traimasika*
SSRPD	*Selections from the Satara Raja's and Peshwa Diaries*

Sources

Abu'l Fazl. Also cited as Abul Fazl Ạllámi. *The History of Akbar*. Vol. 1. Translated by Wheeler M. Thackston. Cambridge, MA: Harvard University Press, 2015.

Abul Fazl Ạllámi. *The Aín i Akbari*. Vol. 2. Translated by H. S. Jarrett. Calcutta: Asiatic Society of Bengal, 1891.

Adas, Michael. *Prophets of Rebellion: Millenarian Protest Movements against the Colonial Order*. Chapel Hill: University of North Carolina Press, 1979.

Aerts, Stijn. "Canon and Canonisation of Ḥadīth." In Encyclopaedia of Islam, THREE, edited by Kate Fleet, Gudrun Kramer, Denis Matringe, John Nawas, and Everett Rowson. http://dx.doi.org/10.1163/1573-3912_ei3_COM_27570.

Ahmed, Farzand. "Kalyan Singh woos influential caste groups by erecting statues of popular leaders." *India Today*. November 30, 1998. www.indiatoday.in/magazine/states/story/19981130-uttar-pradesh-cm-kalyan-singh-woos-influential-caste-groups-by-erecting-statues-of-popular-leaders-827432-1998-11-30.

Albiruni, Abu al-Rahyan Muhammad ibn Ahmad. *The Chronology of Ancient Nations: An English Translation of the Athâr ul Bâkiya of Albîrûnî*. Translated and edited with notes and index by C. Edward Sachau. London: W. H. Allen, 1879, 1910.

Ali, M. Athar. "Translations of Sanskrit Works at Akbar's Court." In *Akbar and His Age*, edited by Iqtidar Alam Khan, 171–80. Delhi: Indian Council for Historical Research, 1999.

Amarasimha. *Amarakośah*. 3 vols. Annotated by Vishvanatha Jha. Delhi: Motilal Banarsidas, 1999.

American Historical Association. "AHA Condemns Second Draft of Executive Travel Ban (March 2017)." April 11, 2017. www.historians.org/news-and-advocacy/statements-and-resolutions-of-support-and-protest/aha-condemns-second-draft-of-executive-travel-ban.

Amin, Shahid. *Conquest and Community: The Afterlife of Warrior Saint Ghazi Miyan*. Hyderabad: Orient Black Swan, 2015.

Anant, Krishnaji. *Sabhāsad bakhar*. Edited by Bhimrao Kulkarni. Pune: Anmol Prkashan, 1987.

Anonymous. "Aitihasik sphuta lekha." *Itihasa samgraha* 1, nos. 10–11 (1908–9): 21–29.

Apfelbaum, Erik. "Halbwachs and the Social Properties of Memory." In *Memories: Histories, Theories, Debates*, edited by Susannah Radstone and Bill Schwarz, 77–92. New York: Fordham University Press, 2010.

Arnold, David, and David Hardiman, eds. *Subaltern Studies VIII: Essays in Honour of Ranajit Guha*. Reprint, Delhi: Oxford University Press, 1999.

Assmann, Jan. *Cultural Memory and Early Civilization*. Cambridge: Cambridge University Press, 2011.

Athavale, Sadashiv. *Umājī Rāje: Mukkām ḍongar.* Pune: Continental Prakashan, 1991.

Atre, Trimbak N. *Gāṁva-gaḍā*. 3rd ed. [1915]. Pune: Varda Books, 1989.

Auber, Peter. *An analysis of the constitution of the East-India company, and of the laws passed by Parliament for the government of their affairs, at home and abroad : To which is prefixed, a brief history of the company, and of the rise and progress of the British power in India*. London: Kingsbury, Parbury and Allen, 1826.

Auer, Blain H. *Symbols of Authority in Medieval Islam: History, Religion and Muslim Legitimacy in the Delhi Sultanate.* London: I. B. Tauris, 2012.

Avalaskar, S. V. *Āngrekālina aṣṭāgār: Adhikārī śakāvalī*. Pune: Bharata Itihāsa Samsodhak Mandala, 1947.

Azad, Abul Kalam. "Introduction to Surendranath Sen." In *Eighteen Fifty-Seven*, by Surendrath Sen, i-xxi. Second reprint, Delhi: Publications Division, 1977.

Babur. *The Baburnama: Memoirs of Babur, Prince and Emperor*. Translated, edited, and annotated by Wheeler M. Thackston Jr. Washington, DC: Freer Gallery of Art: Arthur M. Sackler Gallery, Smithsonian Institution, 1995.

Bagg, Ariel M. "Palestine under Assyrian Rule: A New Look at the Assyrian Imperial Policy in the West." *Journal of the American Oriental Society* 133, no. 1 (2013): 119–144.

Ball, Terence. "Mill, James (1773–1836)." In Oxford Dictionary of National Biography (online). https://doi.org/10.1093/ref:odnb/18709.

Ballantyne, James R. *Christianity Contrasted with Hindu Philosophy: An Essay in Five Books, Sanskrit and English: With Practical Suggestions Tendered to the Missionary among the Hindus*. London: James Madden, 1859.

Balslev, Anindita N. *A Study of Time in Indian Philosophy*. Wiesbaden, Germany: Otto Harrasowitz, 1983.

Banerjea, Surendranath. *A Nation in the Making: Being Reminiscences of Fifty Years in Public Life*. Third reprint, London: Humphrey Milford, 1927.

Banglapedia. "Raja Rajendralal Mitra." Accessed February 1, 2018. http://en.banglapedia.org/index.php?title= Mitra,_Raja_Rajendralal.

———. "Ramaprasad Chanda." Accessed February 1, 2018. http://en.banglapedia.org/index.php?title=Chanda,_Ramaprasad.

Bankim Chandra a.k.a. Chatterji, Bankim Chandra. *Racanāvali*. Vol. 2, *Upanyās vyatita samagra Bāṁglā racanā*. Fourth reprint, Kalikata: Sahitya Samsad, [1969].

Barlow, Frank. "Becket, Thomas [St Thomas of Canterbury, Thomas of London] (1120?–1170)." In Oxford Dictionary of National Biography (online). https://doi.org/10.1093/ref:odnb/27201.

Bartlett, Robert. *Trial by Fire and Water: The Medieval Judicial Ordeal*. Oxford: Clarendon Press, 1986.

Basu, Girishchandra. *Sekāler dārogār kāhinī*. Reprinted in *Dushprāpya sāhitya saṁgraha*, part III, edited by Kanchan Basu. Kalikata: Riphlekt Pablikesan, 1991–92.

Basu, Ram Ram. *Rājā Pratāpāditya Caritra*. Serampore: Mission Press, 1801/1802.

Bates, Crispin, and Marina Carter. "An Uneasy Commemoration: 1957, the British in India and the 'Sepoy Mutiny.'" In *Mutiny at the Margins: New Perspectives on the Indian Uprising of 1857*, vol. 6, edited by Crispin Bates, 113–35 New Delhi: Sage Publications, 2013.

Baxter, Craig. *The Jana Sangh: A Biography of an Indian Political Party*. Philadelphia: University of Pennsylvania Press, 1969.

Bayly, C. A. "Elphinstone, Mountstuart (1779–1859)." In Oxford Dictionary of National Biography (online). https://doi.org/10.1093/ref:odnb/8752.

Bendre, Vasudeva Sitaram. *Māloji Rāje aṇi Śahāji Mahārāj yāncī vicikitsak caritreṅ*. Pune: published by the author, 1967.

Benett, W. C. *A Report on the Family History of the Chief Clans of Roy Bareilly District*. Lucknow: Oudh Government Press, 1870.

Beveridge, Henry. "Kennedy, Vans (1783–1846)." In Oxford Dictionary of National Biography (online). https://doi.org/10.1093/ref:odnb/15394.

Beverley, Thomas. *The Kingdom of Jesus Christ entering its Succession at 1697 according to the Calendar of Time*. 1689. Available at Early English Books Online, https://eebo.chadwyck.com/home.

Bhatia, Varuni. *Unforgetting Chaitanya: Vaishnavism and Cultures of Devotion in Colonial Bengal*. New York: Oxford University Press, 2017.

Bhattacharya, Jogendra Nath. *Hindu Castes and Sects*. Calcutta: Thacker, Spink and Co., 1896.

Bhattacharya, Neeladri. "Predicaments of Secular Histories." *Public Culture* 20, no. 1 (2008): 57–85.

———. "The Problem." In *Seminar (Re-Writing History)*, no. 522 (February 2003): 1–12.

Bickerman, Elias J. "Origines Gentium." *Classical Philology* 47, no. 2 (April 1952): 65–81.

BISM. *Vārṣika itivṛtta*. Shaka [year] 1835 [1912–13].

Blumhardt, James F. *Catalogue of Bengali Printed Books in the Library of the British Museum*. London: Printed by order of the Trustees of the British Museum, 1886.

Blumhardt, James F., and S. G. Kanhere. *Catalogue of the Marathi Manuscripts in the India Office Library*. Oxford: Clarendon Press, 1950.

Blyth, Elizabeth. *Karnak: The Evolution of a Temple*. London: Taylor and Francis, 2014.

Bolnick, Deborah A. "Individual Ancestry Inference and the Reification of Race as a Biological Phenomenon." In *Revisiting Race in a Genomic Age*, by Barbara A. Koenig, Sandra S. Lee, and Sarah S. Richardson, 71–85. New Brunswick, NJ: Rutgers University Press, 2008.

Boone, Elizabeth Hill. *Cycles of Time and Meaning in the Mexican Books of Fate*. Austin: University of Texas Press, 2007.

Boone, Elizabeth Hill, and Walter D. Mignolo, eds. *Writing Without Words: Alternative Literacies in Mesoamerica and the Andes*. Durham, NC: Duke University Press, 1994.

Bose, Sisir Kumar. *The Artist in Chains: The Life of Bankimchandra Chatterji*. Delhi: New Statesman Press, 1984.

Bosworth, C. E. "Abū 'Abdallāh al-Khwārazmī on the Technical Terms of the Secretary's Art: A Contribution to the Administrative History of Mediaeval Islam." *Journal of the Economic and Social History of the Orient* 12, no. 2 (April 1969): 113–64.

———. "The Heritage of Rulership in Early Islamic Iran and the Search for Dynastic Connections with the Past." *Iran* 11, no. 2 (1973): 51–62.

Breisach, Ernst. "From Ancient to Medieval Historical Thinking." In *Turning Points in Historiography: A Cross-Cultural Perspective*, edited by George Iggers and Q. Edward Wang, 45–57. Rochester, NY: University of Rochester Press, 2002.

Brown, Michael P. "Stewart, Dugald (1753–1828)." In Oxford Dictionary of National Biography (online). https://doi.org/10.1093/ref:odnb/26471.

Burke, Peter. *History and Social Theory*. 2nd ed. Ithaca, NY: Cornell University Press, 2005.

Carey, William, J. C. Marshman, and W. Ward. *Hints Relative to Native Schools together with an Outline of an Institution for their Extension and Management*. Serampore: Baptist Mission Press, 1816.

Carson, Penelope. "Grant, Charles (1746–1823)." In Oxford Dictionary of National Biography (online). https://doi.org/10.1093/ref:odnb/11248.

Chakrabarty, Dipesh. *The Calling of History: Sir Jadunath Sarkar and His Empire of Truth*. Chicago: University of Chicago Press, 2015.

———. *Provincializing Europe: Postcolonial Thought and Historical Difference*. Princeton, NJ: Princeton University Press, 2000.

Chand, Tara. *History of the Freedom Movement in India*. Vol. 1. New Delhi: Ministry of Information and Broadcasting, Publications Division, 1961.

Chanda, Ramaprasad. *Gauḍarājamāla*. New ed. Kalikata: Navabharata Publishers, 1975.

———. *The Indo-Aryan Races: A Study of Indo-Aryan People and Institutions – Part I*. Rajshahi: Varendra Research Society, 1916.

Chandra, Bipan. *Rise and Growth of Economic Nationalism in India*. Delhi: People's Publishing House, 1966.

Chatterjee, Kumkum. "The King of Controversy: History and Nation-Making in Late Colonial India." *American Historical Review* 110, no. 5 (2005): 1454–75.

Chatterjee, Partha. "History and the Domain of the Popular." In *Seminar* (*Re-Writing History*), no. 522 (February 2003): 31–34.

———. "History and the Nationalization of Hinduism." *Social Research* 59, no. 1 (1992): 111–49.

Chatterjee, Partha, and Anjan Ghosh, eds. *History and the Present*. Delhi: Permanent Black, 2002.

Chaudhuri, Sashi Bhusan. *Civil Rebellion in the Indian Mutinies, 1857–1859*. Calcutta: New World Press, 1957.

Chirol, Valentine. *Indian Unrest*. London: Macmillan, 1910.

Chou, Min-Chih. *Hu Shih and Intellectual Choice in Modern China*. Ann Arbor: University of Michigan Press, 1984.

Choueiri, Youssef M. *Modern Arab Historiography: Historical Discourse and the Nation State*. Revised ed. London: Routledge, 2003.

Coats, Thomas. "Account of the Township of Lony." In *Transactions of the Literary Society of Bombay*, vol. III, (1823), 172–264.

Cohn, Bernard S. "The Camars of Senapur: A Study of the Changing Status of a Depressed Caste." PhD diss., Cornell University, 1954.

"Collection of Songs Made by Radhakrishna for C. E. Luard Esq., ICS." BL Mss Hindi D.1 British Library. Unpublished manuscript, [1904].

Collingwood, R. G. *The Idea of History*. Edited by Jan van der Dussen. Oxford: Oxford University Press, 2005.

Collini, Stefan, and Bernard Williams. "Collingwood, Robin George (1880–1943)." In Oxford Dictionary of National Biography (online). https://doi.org/10.1093/ref:odnb/32503.

Conlon, Frank. "The Polemic Process in Nineteenth-century Maharashtra: Vishnubawa Brahmachari and Hindu Revival." In *Religious Controversy in British India: Dialogues in South Asian Languages*, edited by Kenneth W. Jones, 5–29. Binghamton, NY: SUNY Press, 1992.

Cort, John. "Jain Knowledge Warehouses: Traditional Libraries in India." *Journal of the American Oriental Society* 115, no. 1 (1995): 77–87.

Crick, Julia C. *The Historia Regum Britannie of Geoffrey of Monmouth IV: Dissemination and Reception in the Later Middle Ages*. Cambridge: D. S. Brewer, 1991.

———. "Monmouth, Geoffrey of [Galfridus Arturus] (d. 1154/5)." In Oxford Dictionary of National Biography (online). https://doi.org/10.1093/ref:odnb/10530.

Culbert, T. Patrick, ed. *Classic Maya Political History: Hieroglyphic and Archaeological Evidence*. Cambridge: Cambridge University Press, 1991.

Currie, P. M. *The Shrine and Cult of Mu'in al-din Chishti of Ajmer.* 1989 reprint, Delhi: Oxford University Press, 2007.

Dalmia, Vasudha. *The Nationalization of Hindu Traditions: Bharatendu Harischandra and Nineteenth-Century Banaras*. Indian ed. Delhi: Oxford University Press, 1999.

Danvers, Frederic Charles, M. Monier Williams, Stuart Colvin Bayley, Percy Wigram, and Brand Sapte, eds. *Memorials of Old Haileybury College*. London: Archibald Constable, 1894.

Dasgupta, Kalyan Kumar. *Indian Historiography and Rajendralal Mitra*. Calcutta: Satchidanand Prakashani, 1976.

Davies, Wendy. "Liber Landavensis: Its Construction and Credibility." *English Historical Review* 88, no. 347 (1973): 335–51.

Deshpande, Prachi. *Creative Pasts: Historical Memory and Identity in Western India, 1770–1960*. New York: Columbia University Press, 2007.

———. "Narratives of Pride: History and Regional Identity in Maharashtra, India, 1870–1960." PhD diss., Tufts University, 2002.

Deshpande, Y. Khu. "Vijayanagarce Rājānca ullekha." *BISMT* 10, no. 3 (1929): 113–15.

Devle, S. R., ed. *Mahipatibuvā Tahrabādkar racita śrībhaktavijaya.* Pune: Sarasvati Grantha Bhandara, n.d.

D'Hozier, Louis-Pierre, and Hozier de Sérigny. *Armorial général ou registres de la noblesse de France*. Reproduction Textuelle de L'Édition Originale de 1738–1768. Reprinted vols., Paris: Firmin Didot [et al.], 1865.

Dillery, John. *Clio's Other Sons: Berossus and Manetho*. Ann Arbor: University of Michigan Press, 2015.

Dirks, Nicholas B. "Colonial Histories and Native Informants: Biography of an Archive." In *Orientalism and the Postcolonial Predicament*, edited by Carol A. Breckenridge and Peter van der Veer, 279–313. Philadelphia: University of Pennsylvania Press, 1993.

———. *The Hollow Crown: The Ethnohistory of an Indian Kingdom*. New ed., 1987. Cambridge: Cambridge University Press, 2000.

Dodson, Michael S. "Contesting Translations: Orientalism and the Interpretation of the Vedas." *Modern Intellectual History* 4, no. 1 (2007): 43–59.

Donovan, Joan, Irene Pasquetto, and Jennifer Pierre. "Cracking Open the Black Box of Genetic Ancestry Testing." Proceedings of the 51st Hawaii International Conference on System Sciences, 2018. https://doi.org/10.24251/HICSS.2018.218.

Duara, Prasenjit. *Rescuing History from the Nation*. Chicago: University of Chicago Press, 1995.

Duff, James Grant. *A History of the Mahrattas*. [1826] reprint in 3 vols., Delhi: Cosmo Publications, 1999.

Durrant, Stephen Wai-Yee Li, Michael Nylan, and Hans Van Ess. *The Letter to Ren An and Sima Qian's Legacy*. Seattle: University of Washington Press, 2016.

Eaton, Richard M. *A Social History of the Deccan, 1300–1761: Eight Indian Lives*. Cambridge: Cambridge University Press, 2005.

Ehret, Christopher. *The Civilizations of Africa: A History to 1800*. Charlottesville: University of Virginia Press, 2016.

———. "Language and History." In *African Languages: An Introduction*, edited by Bernd Heine and Derek Nurse, 272–96. Cambridge: Cambridge University Press, 2000.

Elliot, Henry M. *Bibliographical Index to the Historians of Muhammedan India*. Vol. I [1850]. Reprint, Delhi: Idarah-i Adabiyat, 1976.

Elliott, Charles A. *The Chronicles of Oonao, A District in Oudh*. Allahabad: privately printed, 1862.

Elman, Benjamin A. *From Philosophy to Philology: Intellectual and Social Aspects of Change in Late Imperial China*. Cambridge, MA: Harvard University Press, 1984.

Elphinstone, Mountstuart. *Account of the Kingdom of Caubul*. London: Longman, Hurst, Rees, Orme, and Brown, 1815.

———. *The History of India*. Vol. I. London: John Murray, 1841.

———. *The History of India: The Hindu and Mahometan Periods*. 3rd ed. London: John Murray, 1849.

———. *Report on the Territories Conquered from the Paishwa*. Calcutta: Government Gazette Press, 1821.

Ernst, Carl W. "Muslim Studies of Hinduism?" *Iranian Studies* 36, no. 2 (2003): 173–95.

Evans, Richard J. *In Defence of History*. London: Granta Books, 1997.

Eysenbach, G. *Histoire du blason et science des armoiries*. Tours: A. Mame et Cie., 1848.

Falola, Toyin. "Nationalism and African Historiography." In *Historiography: A Cross-Cultural Perspective*, edited by Q. Edward Wang and G. G. Iggers, 209–35. Rochester, NY: University of Rochester Press, 2002.

Fereshte. *Târîkh-e Fereshte by Mohammad Qâsim Hindushâh Astarabâdi*. Edited and annotated by Mohammad Rezâ Nasîrî. Vol. I. Tehran: Society for the Appreciation of Cultural Works and Dignitaries, 2009.

Folkenflik, Robert. "Macpherson, Chatterton, Blake and the great age of literary forgery." *The Centennial Review* 18, no. 4 (1974): 378–91.

Forrest, George W., ed. *Selections from the Letters, Despatches, and Other State Papers in the Bombay Secretariat: Marátha Series*. Bombay: Government Central Press, 1885.

Fox, James J. "A Rotinese Dynastic Genealogy: Structure and Event." In *The Translation of Culture: Essays to E. E. Evans-Pritchard*, edited by T. O. Beidelman. 37–79. London: Tavistock, 1971.

Fry, Michael. "Dundas, Henry, first Viscount Melville (1742–1811)." In Oxford Dictionary of National Biography (online). https://doi.org/10.1093/ref:odnb/8250.

Fuchs, Eckhardt. "Introduction: Contextualizing School Textbook Revision." Special issue, *Journal of Educational Media, Memory & Society* 2, no. 2 (2010): 1–12.

Führer, Adolf. *The Monumental Antiquities and Inscriptions in the North-Western Provinces*. Allahabad: Government Press, 1891.

Furet, François. *In the Workshop of History*, translated by Jonathan Mandelbaum. Chicago: University of Chicago Press, 1984.

Gallagher, John, Gordon Johnson, and Anil Seal, eds. *Locality, Province, and Nation: Essays on Indian Politics 1870 to 1940*. Cambridge: Cambridge University Press, 1973.

García Hernán, David. *La nobleza en la España moderna*. Madrid: Ediciones Istmo, 1992.

Gash, Norman. 2008. "Wellesley [formerly Wesley], Arthur, first duke of Wellington (1769–1852)." In Oxford Dictionary of National Biography (online). https://doi.org/10.1093/ref:odnb/29001.

Gavli, P. A. *Pesv́ekālina gulamgirī va aspruśyata*. Third reprint [1981], Kolhapur, India: Prachar Prakashan, 1990.

Gerbet, Marie-Claude. *Les noblesses espagnoles au Moyen Âge: XIe- XVe siécles*. Paris: Arman Collin, 1997.

Ghosh, Śourindrakumar. *Sāhityasevak manjuṣā*. 2 vols. Kolkata: Sahityalok, 1983.

Glacken, Clarence. *Traces on the Rhodian Shore*. Berkeley: University of California Press, 1976.

Gokhale, Shobana. "Matwan Plates of the Traikutakas." In *Studies in Indology: Professor G. H. Khare Felicitation Volume*, by Gaṇeśa Harī Khare, Madhukar Shripad Mate, and G. T. Kulkarni, 86–95. Poona: Joshi & Lokhande Prakashan, 1974.

Gopal, Sarvepalli, ed. *Anatomy of a Confrontation: the Babri Masjid–Ramjanmabhumi Issue*. New York: Viking, 1991.

Gordon, David C. *Self-Determination and History in the Third World*. Princeton, NJ: Princeton University Press, 1971.

Gordon-Reed, Annette. *Thomas Jefferson and Sally Hemings: An American Controversy*. Charlottesville: University of Virginia Press, 1997.

Government of Bombay. *Source Material for the History of the Freedom Movement in India*. Vol. I. Bombay: Government Central Press, 1957.

Grafton, Anthony. *What Was History?: The Art of History in Early Modern Europe*. Cambridge: Cambridge University Press, 2007.

Graham, G. F. I. *The Life and Work of Syed Ahmed Khan, C. S. I.* Edinburgh: William Blackwood, 1885.

Gramopadhye, G. B., ed. *Marāṭhi bakhar gadya*. 3rd ed. Pune: Mehta Publishing House, 1988.

Guardian. "British war veterans condemn Hollywood's revisionist history." May 3, 2000.

Guenée, Bernard. "La culture historique des nobles: Le succés des *Faits des Romains* (XIIIe-XVe siècles)." In *La noblesse au Moyen Âge*, edited by Philippe Contamine, 261–88. Paris: Presses Universitaire des France, 1976.

———. "Les généalogies entre l'histoire et la politique: La fierté d'être Capétien, en France, au Moyen Âge." *Annales: économies, sociétés, civilisations* 33e année, no. 3 (1978): 450–77.

Guha, Ranajit. *An Indian Historiography of India: A Nineteenth-Century Agenda and Its Implications*. Calcutta: K. P. Bagchi, 1988.

Guha, Sumit. *Beyond Caste: Identity and Power in South Asia, Past and Present*. Leiden, Netherlands: E. J. Brill, 2013 and Delhi: Permanent Black, 2016.

———. "Conviviality and Cosmopolitanism: Recognition of 'East' and 'West' in Peninsular India, c. 1600–1800." *Cosmopolitismes en Asie du Sud. Collections Purusartha* 33 (2015): 275–92.

———. *Environment and Ethnicity in India*. Cambridge: Cambridge University Press, 1999.

———. "The Frontiers of Memory: What the Marathas Remembered of Vijayanagara." *Modern Asian Studies* 43, no. 1 (2009): 269–88.

———. "Literary Tropes and Historical Settings: A Study from Southern India." In *Rethinking a Millennium: India from the Eighth to the Eighteenth Centuries*, edited by Rajat Datta, 106–20. Delhi: Aakar Books, 2008.

———. "Lower Strata, Older Races and Aboriginal Peoples: Racial Anthropology and Mythical History, Past and Present." *Journal of Asian Studies* 57, no. 2 (1998): 423–41.

———. "Rethinking the Economy of Mughal India: Lateral Perspectives." *Journal of the Economic and Social History of the Orient* 58, no. 4 (2015): 532–75.

———. "Speaking Historically: The Changing Voices of Historical Narration in Western India, 1400–1900." *American Historical Review* 109, no. 4 (October 1, 2004): 1084–1103.

———. "Transitions and Translations: Regional Power and Vernacular Identity in the Dakhan c. 1500–1800." *Comparative Studies of South Asia, Africa and the Middle East* 24, no. 2 (Fall 2004).

Gune, Vitthala T. *The Judicial System of the Marathas*. Pune: Deccan College, 1953.

Gupta, Ashutosh. "Ruins and Antiquities of Rampal." *Journal of the Asiatic Society of Bengal* 58, no. 1 (1889): 12–27.

Gupta, Chitrarekha. *The Brahmanas of India: A Study Based on Inscriptions*. Delhi: Sundeep Prakashan, 1983.

Habib, Irfan, ed. *Cambridge Economic History of India*. Vol. I. Cambridge: Cambridge University Press, 1982.

Habib, Mohammad. "Chishti Mystic Records of the Sultanate Period." Reprinted in *Studies in Medieval Indian Polity and Culture*, edited by Irfan Habib. Delhi: Oxford University Press, 2016.

———. "The Present and the Past: Our Approach to History." Reprinted in *Studies in Medieval Indian Polity and Culture*, edited by Irfan Habib, 17–30. Delhi: Oxford University Press, 2016.

Halbwachs, Maurice. *On Collective Memory*. Edited, translated, and with an introduction by Lewis Coser. Chicago: University of Chicago Press, 1992.

———. *The Social Frameworks of Memory*. Translated by Lewis Coser. Chicago: University of Chicago Press, 1991.

Hamilton, Charles. *The Hitler Diaries: The Fakes That Fooled the World*. Lexington: University of Kentucky Press, 1991.

Haq, S. Moinul. *The Great Revolution of 1857*. Lahore: Pakistan Historical Society, 1968.

Hardy, Peter. *Historians of Medieval India: Studies in Indo-Muslim Historical Writing*. Reprint [1960], Westport, CT: Greenwood Press, 1982.

Hartog, François. "The Invention of History." In *Turning Points in Historiography: A Cross-Cultural Perspective*, edited by George Iggers and Q. Edward Wang, 19–30. Rochester, NY: University of Rochester Press, 2002.

Hasan, Mushirul, ed. *India's Partition: Process, Strategy and Mobilization*. Reprint, Delhi: Oxford India Paperbacks, 1999.

Hastings, Warren. *Memoirs Relative to the State of India*. New ed., with additions. London: J. Murray, 1786.

Henige, David. *Oral Historiography*. New York: Longman, 1982.

Heerenden, Wyman H. "Camden, William (1551–1623)." In Oxford Dictionary of National Biography (online). https://doi.org/10.1093/ref:odnb/4431.

Henneman, John B. "'Enquêteurs-Réformateurs' and Fiscal Officers in Fourteenth-Century France." *Traditio* 24 (1968): 309–49.

Herwadkar, Rajaram V. *A Forgotten Literature: Foundations of Marathi Chronicles*. Mumbai: Popular Prakashan, 1994.

———. *Marāṭhī bakhar*. Revised and enlarged ed. Pune: Venus Prakashan, 1975.

The Hindu. "'For Indians, Smartphone Is Primary Source of News.'" March 28, 2019. www.thehindu.com/news/national/for-indians-smartphone-is-primary-source-of-news/article26657612.ece.

Humphreys, R. Stephen. "Turning Points in Islamic Historical Practice." In *Turning Points in Historiography: A Cross-Cultural Perspective*, edited by George Iggers and Q. Edward Wang, 89–100. Rochester: University of Rochester Press, 2002.

Husain, Mahmud, ed. *A History of the Freedom Movement: Being the Story of Muslim Struggle for the Freedom of Hind-Pakistan, 1707–1947*. 4 vols. Karachi: Pakistan Historical Society, 1957.

Ibbetson, Denzil. *Tribes and Castes*. Reprint, Lahore: Sang-i-Meel Press, 2001.

Ibn Baṭṭūṭa. *The Travels of Ibn Battuta: 1325–1354*. Translated by H. A. R. Gibb. Delhi: Munshiram Manoharlal, 1999.

Iggers, George G. "What is so Uniquely Western about the Historiography of the West in Contrast to China?" In *Western Historical Thinking: An Intercultural Debate*, edited by Jorn Rusen, 101–10. New York: Berghahn Books, 2002.

Iggers, George G., Q. Edward Wang, and Supriya Mukherjee. *A Global History of Modern Historiography*. Harlow, England; New York: Pearson Longman, 2008.

Inden, Ronald. *Marriage and Rank in Bengali Culture: A History of Caste and Clan in Middle Period Bengal*. Berkeley: University of California Press, 1976.

India, Ministry of Education. *Selections from the Educational Records*. Vol. I. Delhi: Manager of Publications, 1960.

Innocence Project. Accessed September 12, 2016. www.innocenceproject.org.

Isenberg, Shirley B. *India's Bene Israel: A Comprehensive Inquiry and Sourcebook*. Bombay: Popular Prakashan, 1988.

Iyengar, S. Krishnaswamy. "The Bakhair of Rama Raja." In *Proceedings of the Indian Historical Records Commission*, Seventh Meeting, 53–63. Calcutta: Government Central Press, 1925.

———. *Sources of Vijayanagar History*. Madras: University of Madras, 1919.

Jackson, Peter. *The Delhi Sultanate: A Political and Military History*. Cambridge: Cambridge University Press, 1999.

Jaffrelot, Christophe. *Hindu Nationalism: A Reader*. Indian ed. Princeton, NJ: Princeton University Press, 2007.

———. *The Hindu Nationalist Movement and Indian Politics, 1925 to the 1990s*. New Delhi: Viking, 1996.

———. *India's Silent Revolution: The Rise of the Lower Castes in North India*. New York: Columbia University Press, 2003.

Jalal, Ayesha. "Conjuring Pakistan: History as Official Imagining." *International Journal of Middle East Studies* 27, no. 1 (1995): 73–89.

Jaschik, Scott. "Could Trump Cut Berkeley's Funds?" *Inside Higher Ed*, February 3, 2017.

Jenkins, Richard. *Report on the Territories of the Rajah of Nagpore*. Calcutta: Government Gazette Press, 1827.

Jog, Ramacandra S., ed. *Marāṭhī vangmayācā itihāsa*. 6 parts. 1963–1993 reprint ed., Pune: Maharashtra Rajya Sahitya ani Sanskriti Mandal, 1999.

Johnson, David G. "Communication, Class and Consciousness in Late Imperial China." In *Popular Culture in Late Imperial China*, edited by Johnson, Andrew J. Nathan, and Evelyn S. Rawski, 34–72. Berkeley: University of California Press, 1985.

———. "Epic and History in Early China: The Matter of Wu Tzu-hsü." *Journal of Asian Studies* 40, no. 2 (February 1981): 255–71.

Joiya, P. C. "Cāraṇīk abhilekha sāṁsan bahi, Bikaner, 1614 Isvi." In *Cāraṇ sāhitya paramparā: Prophesor Vīrendra Svarūp Bhaṭnāgar abhinandan granth*, edited by Shyamsingh Ratnawat and Krishna Gopal Sharma, 390–95. Jaipur: Rajasthan Adhyayana Kendra, 2001.

Jones, Kenneth W. *Arya Dharm: Hindu Consciousness in 19th-Century Punjab*. Berkeley: University of California Press, 1976.

———, ed. *Religious Controversy in British India: Dialogues in South Asian Languages*. Binghamton, NY: SUNY Press, 1992.

Jones, William. *Discourses Delivered before the Asiatic Society*. 2 vols. 2nd ed. London: W. H. Carpenter, 1824.

Joshi, Lakshamanasastri. *Rajvade lekhasangraha*. Reprint ed. 1958, Delhi: Sahitya Akademi, 1992.

Joshi, Shankar Narayana, and Ganesh Hari Khare, eds. *Śivacaritrasāhitya*. Vol. 3. Pune: Bharata Itihasa Samshodhaka Mandala, 1930.

Julien, Catherine. *Reading Inca History*. Ames: University of Iowa Press, 2000.

Kane, Pandurang Vaman. *History of Dharmaśāstra: Ancient and Medieval Religious and Civil Law*. Vol. IV. 3rd ed. Pune: Bhandarkar Oriental Research Institute, 1991.

Karim, Abdul. "Did Ibn Battuta Meet Sheikh Jalal al-Din Tabrizi in Kamrup?" *Journal of the Pakistan Historical Society* 8, no. 4 (1960): 90–96.

———. *Social History of the Muslims in Bengal (Down to A.D. 1538)*. Dhaka: Asiatic Society, 1959.

Karmarkar, Dattatreya P., and Rajaram V. Oturkar, eds. *Vijayanagara smāraka grantha (Marāthī avṛtti)*. Pune: BISM, 1936–37.

Kasturi, Malavika. *Embattled Identities: Rajput Lineages and Colonial State in Nineteenth-Century North India*. Delhi: Oxford University Press, 2002.

Kāvyetihās Saṁgraha 1 (1878).

Kaye, J. W. *The Lives of Indian Officers*. Vol. I. New ed. London: J. J. Keliher, 1904.

Kehimkar, Haeem S. *History of the Bene Israel of India*. Tel Aviv: Dayag Press, 1937.

Kennedy, Kenneth A. R. "Have Aryans been identified in the prehistoric skeletal record from South Asia?: Biological anthropology and concepts of ancient races." In *The Indo-Aryans of Ancient South Asia: Language, Material Culture and Ethnicity*, edited by George Erdosy, 32–66. Berlin: Walter de Gruyter, 1995.

Kennedy, Vans. "Remarks on the Sixth and Seventh Chapters of Mill's 'History of British India,'" respecting the religion and manners of the Hindus." *Transactions of the Literary Society of Bombay* III (1823): 117–70.

Kennicott, Philip, and Peggy McGlone. "Trump wants to cut the NEA and NEH. This is the worst-case scenario for arts groups." *Washington Post*, September 18, 2017.

Khan, Ansar Zahid. "Pakistan Historical Society." *Journal of the Pakistan Historical Society* 26, no. 1 (1978): 2–25.

Khan, Safi Ullah. *Mugalkālin Bhārat ke ādhunik Urdu itihāskār*. Delhi: L. G. Publishers, 2012.

Khan, Syed Ahmed. *The Causes of the Indian Revolt*. Reprint, 1873 translation, Lahore: The Book House, 1970.

Khare, Ganesh Hari. *Mahārāṣṭrācī cār daivaten*. Reprint, Pune: BISM, 2012.

———. *Persian Sources of Indian History*. 6 vols., with Marathi parallel text. Pune: Bharat Itihas Samshodhak Mandal, 1937–73.

———. *Saṁśodhakāca Mitra*. Edited by Gajanan Mehendale. New edition. Pune: BISM, 2012.

Khare, Ganesh Hari, and S. N. Joshi. *Aitihāsik Marāṭhī sādhane*. Pune: Bharat Itihas Samshodhak Mandal, 1983.

King, Robert D. *One Language, Two Scripts: The Hindi Movement in Nineteenth Century North India*. Bombay: Oxford University Press, 1994.

Kirtane, Janardan N. *Grānṭḍuphkṛta Marāṭhyānce bakharīvar ṭīkā*. Reprint of 1884 ed., Pune: Chitrashala Press, 1926.

Kodesh, Neil. "Obituary for Jan Vansina." *H-Net*, February 17, 2017. https://networks.h-net.org/node/28765/discussions/166559/obituary-jan-vansina.

Kuiters, Willem G. J. "Dow, Alexander (1735/6–1779)." In Oxford Dictionary of National Biography (online). https://doi.org/10.1093/ref:odnb/7957.

Kulkarni, Ananta R. *James Cunningham Grant Duff: Marāṭhyāncyā itihāskār va prakāśak*. Pune: Pune Vidyapitha, 1971.

———. ed. *Jedhe śakāvali-karīnā*. Pune: Mansamman Prakashan, 1999.

———. *Maharashtra: Society and Culture*. Pune: Books and Books, 2000.

———. *Maratha Historiography*. Delhi: Manohar, 2006.

Kulke, Hermann. *Kings and Cults: State Formation and Legitimation in India and Southeast Asia*. Delhi: Manohar, 2001.

———. "Some Observations on the Political Functions of Copper-Plate Grants in Early Medieval India." In *Recht, Staat und Verwaltung im klassischen Indien*, edited by Bernhard Kolver, 237–44. Schriften des Historischen Kollegs, Band 30. München: De Gruyter Oldenbourg; Auflage, 1997.

Kumar, Krishna. "Hindu Revivalism and Education in North-Central India." In *Fundamentalisms and Society*, vol. 2, 536–57. Chicago: University of Chicago Press, 1993.

———. "Peace with the Past." In *Seminar* (*Re-Writing History*), no. 522 (February 2003): 47–50.

———. *Prejudice and Pride: School Histories of the Freedom Struggle in India and Pakistan*. Delhi: Viking, 2001

Kumar, Nita. "History at the Madrasas." In *Seminar* (*Re-Writing History*), no. 522 (February 2003): 57–62.

Lahiri, Nayanjot. "Commemorating and remembering 1857: The revolt in Delhi and its Afterlife." *World Archaeology* 35, no. 1 (2003): 35–60.

Las Siete Partidas del Sabio Rey Don Alonso el Nono. Manuscript completed 1265 CE, printed in Salamanca, 1555. 3 vols. Facsimile reprint, Madrid: Imprensa Nacional, 1985.

Li, Huaiyin. *Reinventing Modern China: Imagination and Authenticity in Chinese Historical Writing*. Honolulu: University of Hawai'i Press, 2013.

Lieberman, Victor. *Strange Parallels: South Asia in Global Context, c. 800–1800*. Cambridge: Cambridge University Press, 2009.

Liguori, Guido. "Tre accezioni di 'subalterno' in Gramsci." *Critica marxista (nuova serie)*, no. 6 (November–December 2011): 33–41.

Lloyd, John E. "Geoffrey of Monmouth." *English Historical Review* 57, no. 228 (October 1942): 460–68.

Loftus, Elizabeth N. "Creating False Memories." *Scientific American* 277, no.3 (1997): 70–75.

Loftus, Elizabeth N., and James M. Doyle. *Eyewitness Testimony: Civil and Criminal*. 3rd ed. Charlottesville, VA: Lexis Law Publishing, 1997.

Lorenzen, David N. *Kabir Legends and Ananta-das's Kabir Parachai*. Albany: State University of New York Press, 1991.

Mackintosh, Alexander. *A Sketch of the History of the Ramoossies*. Published serially in the *Madras Journal of Literature and Science*, no. 3 (April 1834) to no. 8 (July 1835).

Mahikāvatīcī bakhar. British Library, London, Add Mss 26494 B.

Majumdar, Ramesh C. *Baṁgīya kulaśāstra*. Kalikata: Bharati Buk Stal, 1973.

———. *History of Ancient Bengal*. Calcutta: G. K. Bhardwaj, 1971.

———. *History of the Freedom Movement in India*. Vol. 1. Calcutta: Firma KLM, 1962.

———. *The Sepoy Mutiny and the Revolt of 1857*. 2nd ed. Calcutta: Firma KLM, 1963.

Majumdar, Rochona. *Marriage and Modernity: Family Values in Colonial Bengal*. Durham, NC: Duke University Press, 2009.

Malcolm, John. *A Memoir of Central India Including Malwa*. London: Parbury, Allen and Co., 1832.

Mann, E. A. "Religion, Money and Status: Competition for Resources at the Shrine of Shah Jamal, Aligarh." In *Muslim Shrines in India*. edited by Christian W. Troll, 145–71. New Delhi; Oxford: Oxford University Press, 2004.

Marriott, McKim, ed. *India Through Hindu Categories*. New Delhi: Sage Publications, 1989.

Marshman, John C. *Bhāratavarṣīya itihāsa arthāt Hindusthān kī kathā*. Translated by Father (*pādrī*) J. J. Moore. Calcutta: for the Agra School Book Society, 1846.

———. *The History of India from Remote Antiquity to the Accession of the Mogul Dynasty*. Serampore, India: Baptist Mission Press, 1836.

———. *History of India Translated into Bengali by Gopal Lall Mitra*. Calcutta: Anglo-Indian Press, 1840.

Martínez, María Elena. "The Language, Genealogy and Classification of 'Race' in Colonial Mexico." In *Race and Classification: The Case of Mexican America*, edited by Ilona Katzew and Susan Deans-Smith, 25–42. Stanford, CA: Stanford University Press 2009.

Marwar, Kingdom of . *Riporṭ mardumśumārī Rāj Mārwāṛ San 1891 Īsvī*. Edited by Sukhvir Singh Gahalot. Reprint, Jodhpur: Sri Jagdish Singh Gahalot Shodh Samsthan, 1987.

Mate, M. S. "Hero-Stones: the 'Folk' and the 'Classic.'" In *Memorial Stones: A Study of Their Origin, Significance, and Variety*, edited by S. Settar and Gunther D. Sontheimer, 79–82. Dharwad, India: Karnatak University, 1982.

Mehendale, Gajanan B. *Śrī Rājā Śivachatrapatī*. 2 vols. 2nd ed. Pune: Diamond Publications, 2008.

Meisami, Julie S. "The Past in Service of the Present: Two Views of History in Medieval Persia." *Poetics Today* 14, no. 2 (1993): 247–77.

———. *Persian Historiography to the End of the Twelfth Century*. Edinburgh: Edinburgh University Press, 1999.

Metcalf, Barbara D. *Islamic Revival in British India, 1860–1900*. Princeton Legacy Library ed., 2014. Princeton, NJ: Princeton University Press, 1982.

Metcalf, Thomas R. *The Aftermath of the Revolt*. Princeton, NJ: Princeton University Press, 1964.

Meyer, William Stevenson, Richard Burn, James Sutherland Cotton, and Herbert Hope Risley, eds. *Imperial Gazetteer of India*. Oxford: Clarendon Press, 1908–1931. Accessed via http://dsal.uchicago.edu/reference/gazetteer/.

Misra, Bankey Bihari. *The Judicial Administration of the East India Company in Bengal, 1765–1782*. Delhi: Motilal Banarsidass, 1961.

Molesworth, J. T. *Dictionary of Marathi and English*. 2nd ed. Corrected reprint, Pune: Shubhada Saraswat, 1982.

Monson, Andrew. *From the Ptolemies to the Romans: Political and Economic Change in Egypt*. Cambridge: Cambridge University Press, 2012.

Moon, Vasant. *Growing Up Untouchable: A Dalit Autobiography*. Translated by Gail Omvedt. Lanham, MD: Rowman and Littlefield, 2001.

Morris, Morris D., Toru Matsui, Bipin Chandra, and T. Raychaudhuri. *Indian Economy in the Nineteenth Century: A Symposium*. Delhi: Indian Economic and Social History Association, 1969.

Mujumdar, Gangadharrao N., and Dattatreya V. Apte, eds. *Sivacaritrapradipa*. Pune: Sivacaritra Karyalaya, 1925.

Mukherjee, S. N. "Class, Caste and Politics in Calcutta, 1815–38" In *Elites in South Asia*, edited by Edmund Leach and S. N. Mukherjee, 33–78. Cambridge: Cambridge University Press, 1970.

Mukta, Parita. *Upholding the Common Life: The Community of Mirabai*. Delhi; New York: Oxford University Press, 1994.

Nahata, Bhaṃvarlal, ed. *Ṭhakkura Pherū viracita Dravyapariksā aur dhatūtpatti*. Vaishali, India: Prakṛt Jainśastra Ahiṃsa Śodha Samsthāna, 1976.

Naipaul, V. S. *India: A Wounded Civilization*. New York: Knopf, 1977.

Nair, Deepa. "Textbook Conflicts in South Asia." Special issue, *Journal of Educational Media, Memory & Society* 2, no. 2 (2010): 29–45.

Nandy, Ashis. "History's Forgotten Doubles." *History and Theory* 34, no. 2 (1995): 44–66.

Naoroji, Dadabhai. *Poverty and Un-British Rule in India*. Reprint, Delhi: Publications Division, Ministry of Information and Broadcasting, Government of India, 1962.

Nehru, Jawaharlal. *The Discovery of India*. Reprint [1946], Delhi: Oxford University Press, 1985.

———. *The Essential Writings of Jawaharlal Nehru*. Edited by S. Gopal and Uma Iyengar. 2 vols. Delhi: Oxford University Press, 2003.

Nesfield, John C. *Brief View of the Caste System of the North-Western Provinces and Oudh*. Allahabad: Government Press, 1885.

Novak, Josef, ed. *On Masaryk: Texts in English and German*. Amsterdam: Rodopi, 1998.

Novetzke, Christian L. "The Laine Controversy and the Study of Hinduism." *International Journal of Hindu Studies* 8, nos.1–3 (2003): 183–201.

———. *Religion and Public Memory: A Cultural History of Sant Namdev in India*. New York: Columbia University Press, 2008.

Novick, Peter. "My Correct Views on Everything." *American Historical Review* 96, no. 3 (1991): 699–703.

———. *That Noble Dream: The "Objectivity Question" and the American Historical Profession*. Cambridge: Cambridge University Press, 1988.

Nutt, Alfred. "History, Tradition, and Historic Myths." *Folklore* 12, no. 3 (September 1901): 336–39.

Osborne, Claire. "Supporters, opponents of Georgetown's Confederate Statue talk options." *Austin-American Statesman*, September 14, 2017.

Ossio A., Juan M. "Guamán Poma: nueva corónica o carta al rey." In *Ideología mesiánica del mundo andino*, edited by Juan M. Ossio A., 153–213. Lima: Ignacio Prado, 1973.

Oturkar, Rajaram V. *Peśvekālīn ārthik va sāmājik patravyvahāra*. Pune: BISM, 1950.

Oxford Dictionaries. "Word of the Year 2016 is . . ." English Oxford Living Dictionaries. https://en.oxforddictionaries.com/word-of-the-year/word-of-the-year-2016.

Pagdi, Setumadhavrao. *Hindvī svarājya ani Mogal*. Pune: BISM, 1966.

Pant, Ramacandra. *Ājñāpatra*. Edited by S. N. Banhatti. 1961 reprint ed., Nagpur: Suvichar Prakashan, 1986.

Paramananda. *Śivabhāratam*. Pune: Ananda Ashram Press, 1930.

Paramashivan, S. "Vijayanagarakālīn citrakalā." In *Vijayanagara smāraka grantha (Marāthī avṛtti)*, edited by Dattatreya P. Karmarkar and Rajaram V. Oturkar. Pune: BISM, 1936–37.

Parasnis, Dattatreya Balvant. *Jhānśī saṁsthānacyā Mahārānī Lakṣmībāisāheba hyāṅce caritra*. Satara: Ramacandra Appaji Citale, 1894.

"Parasnis transcripts." Vol. 12. Pune: Maharashtra State Archives.

Parulekar, R. V. *Literacy in India*. London: Macmillan, 1939.

Pathak, Vishwambhar S. *Ancient Historians of India: A Study in Historical Biographies.* Bombay: Asia Publishing, 1966.

Pavar, Appasaheb, ed. *Tārābāīkalīna Kāgadpatre.* 2 vols. Kolhapur: Shivaji Vidyapitha, 1969.

Pearson, M. N., ed. *Legitimacy and Symbols: The South Asian Writings of F. W. Buckler.* Ann Arbor: University of Michigan, 1985.

Pendse, N. V. *Pendse Kulavṛttānta.* Bombay: The Author, 1938.

Penner, Peter. "Elliot, Sir Henry Miers (1808–1853)." In Oxford Dictionary of National Biography (online). https://doi.org/10.1093/ref:odnb/8663.

Phatak, N. R. *Nyāyamūrti Mahādeva Govind Rāṇaḍe yānce caritra.* 2nd ed. Pune: Nilkantha Prakasan, 1996.

Philips, Cyril H., ed. *Historians of India, Pakistan and Ceylon.* Vol. 1. Oxford: Oxford University Press, 1961–62.

Pindye, Jayarama. *Rādhāmādhavavilāsacampu.* Edited by Vishwanath K. Rajwade. Reprint [1923], Pune: Varda Books, 1993.

Pingree, David, "Hellenophilia versus the History of Science." *Isis* 83, no. 4 (December 1992): 554–563.

Platts, John T. *A Dictionary of Urdu, Classical Hindi and English.* 1884 reprint ed., Delhi, 1997.

Pollock, Sheldon, ed. *Literary Cultures in History: Reconstructions from South Asia.* Berkeley: University of California Press, 2003.

———. "Mīmāṃsā and the Problem of History in Traditional India." *Journal of the American Oriental Society* 109, no. 4 (1989): 603–10.

———. "Pretextures of Time." *History and Theory* 46, no. 3 (2007): 366–83.

Porten, Bezalel. "Exile, Babylonian." In *Encyclopaedia Judaica*, vol. 6, 2nd ed., edited by Michael Berenbaum and Fred Skolnik, 608–11. Detroit: Macmillan Reference USA, 2007. Accessed October 21, 2018, from the Gale Virtual Reference Library. http://link.galegroup.com.ezproxy.lib.utexas.edu/apps/doc/CX2587506183/GVRL?u=txshracd2598&sid=GVRL&xid=766e3338.

Potdar, Datto Vaman. "Anjanvela tālukyācī vahivaṭa." In *Vārṣika Itivṛtta Śake 1835*, 319–42. Pune: BISM, 1913.

———. "Maraṭhīt Vijayanagara". In *Vijayanagara smāraka grantha (Marāthī avṛtti)*, edited by Dattatreya P. Karmarkar and Rajaram V. Oturkar. Pune: BISM, 1936–37.

Potdar, Datto Vaman, and Gangadharrao N. Mujumdar, eds. *Śivacaritrasāhitya.* Vol. II. Pune: BISM, 1930.

Powell, Avril A. "History Textbooks and the Transmission of the Precolonial Past in North-Western India in the 1860s and 1870s." In *Invoking the Past: The Uses of History in South Asia*, edited by Daud S. Ali, 91–133. Delhi: Oxford University Press, 1999.

———. *Muslims and Missionaries in Pre-Mutiny India.* Richmond, Canada: Curzon Press, 1993.

Quilter, Jeffrey, and Gary Urton, eds. *Narrative Threads: Accounting and Recounting in Andean Khipu.* Austin: University of Texas Press, 2002.

Qureshi, Ishtiaq Husain. *The Administration of the Sultanate of Delhi.* 4th revised ed. Karachi: Pakistan Historical Society, 1958.

———. *The Muslim Community of the Indo-Pakistan Subcontinent, 610–1947: A Brief Historical Analysis*. 1st ed. 's-Gravenhage: Mouton & Co., 1962.

———, ed. *A Short History of Pakistan*. 4 parts. Karachi: University of Karachi, 1967.

Rabasa, José, Javier Sanjines, and Robert Carr, eds. "Subaltern Studies in the Americas." Special issue, *Disposition: American Journal of Cultural Histories and Theories* no. 46 (1994).

Rai, Lajpat. *The Arya Samaj: An Account of its Origins, Doctrines and Activities, with a Biographical Sketch of the Founder*. London: Longmans, Green and Co., 1915.

Rajnish, Govind. *Lok mahākāvya Ālhā*. Ilāhabād: Satyendra Prakāśan, 1995.

Rajpurohit, N. S. "Rākṣastangḍīcyā raṇāngaṇācā sthalanirṇaya." *BISMT* 10, no. 1 (1928–29): 17–22.

Rajwade, V. K. *Itihāsācārya Vi. Ka. Rājwāḍe: Samagra sāhitya*. Edited by M. B. Shaha. 10 vols. Dhule: V. K. Rajwade Itihasa Samshodhana Mandal, 1998.

———. *Mahikāvatīcī bakhar*. 1924 reprint ed. Reprint, Pune: Varada Books, 1991.

———. *Maraṭhyāncyā itihāsācī sādhane*. 13 vols. New ed. Dhule: Rajwade Itihas Samshodhak Mandala, 2002–.

Ranade, M. G. *Rise of the Maratha Power*. Bombay: Punalekar & Co., 1900.

Rao, V. Narayana, David Shulman, and Sanjay Subrahmanyam. *Textures of Time: Writing History in South India 1600–1800*. New Delhi: Permanent Black, 2001.

Rashid, Abdur. "The Treatment of History by Muslim Historians." In *Historians of India, Pakistan and Ceylon*, edited by C. H. Philips. 139–51. London: Oxford University Press, 1961.

Ratnawat, Shyamsingh, and Krishna Gopal Sharma, eds. *Cāraṇ Sāhitya paramparā: Prophesor Vīrendra Svarūp Bhaṭnāgar abhinandan granth*. Jaipur: Rajasthan Adhyayana Kendra, 2001.

Raychaudhuri, Tapan. "India, 1858 to the 1930s." In *Oxford History of the British Empire*, vol. V, *Historiography*, edited by Robin W. Winks, 214–30. Oxford: Oxford University Press, 1999.

Renan, Ernest. *Qu'est ce qu'une nation?* 2nd ed. Paris: Calmann-Levy, 1882.

Renfrew, Colin. *Archaeology and Language: The Puzzle of Indo-European Origins*. New York: Cambridge University Press, 1990.

Report of Mr. H. Rivett-Carnac Cotton Commissioner for the Central Provinces and the Berars on the Operation of His Department for 1867. British Parliamentary Papers, Commons no. 289 for 1868–69.

Ricoeur, Paul. *The Reality of the Historical Past*. Milwaukee: Marquette University Press, 1984.

Robb, P. G. "Colin Mackenzie (1753–1821)." In Oxford Dictionary of National Biography (online). https://doi.org/10.1093/ref:odnb/17573.

Robertson, John. "David Hume (1711–1776)." In Oxford Dictionary of National Biography (online). https://doi.org/10.1093/ref:odnb/14141.

Robinson, Chase F. *Islamic Historiography*. Cambridge: Cambridge University Press, 2003.

Rodríguez, Ileana, ed. *A Latin American Subaltern Studies Reader*. Durham: Duke University Press, 2001.

Rosenthal, Franz. *A History of Muslim Historiography*. 2nd revised ed. Leiden, Netherlands: E. J. Brill 1968.

Row, T. Sambamurti, ed. *The Marathi Historical Inscription at the Sri Brihadeeswaraswami Temple at Tanjore.* Tanjore, India: self-published, 1907.

Roy, Kumkum. *The Emergence of Monarchy in North India.* Delhi: Oxford University Press, 1994.

Roy-Burman, J. J. *Hindu-Muslim Syncretic Shrines and Communities.* Delhi: Mittal Publications, 2002.

Rubbee, Khondkar Fuzle. *The Origin of the Musalmans of Bengal.* Calcutta: Thacker, Spink and Co., 1895.

Rubinstein, W. D. "Leitner [formerly Sapier], Gottlieb Wilhelm (1840–1899)." In Oxford Dictionary of National Biography (online). https://doi.org/10.1093/ref:odnb/51109.

Rudolph, Lloyd I., and Susanne H. Rudolph. "Rethinking Secularism: Genesis and Implications of the Textbook Controversy, 1977–79." *Pacific Affairs* 56, no. 1 (Spring 1983): 15–37.

Salim, Ghulam Husain. *Riyažu-s-Salātin: A History of Bengal.* Translated by Maulavi Abdus Salam. Calcutta: The Asiatic Society, 1902.

Sankpal, Bapuji. *Bakhar vāngmaya: Udgama ani vikās.* Pune: Dastane Ramachandra, 1982.

Sarasvatī, Maharṣi Dayanand. *Satyarth: Laghu grantha saṁgraha.* Arya Samaj Centenary Edition edited by Yudhisthira Mimamasaka. Bahalgarh, India: Ramlal Kapur Trust, 1975.

———. *Satyārtha Prakāśah.* 1884 ed. Thirty-fourth reprint, Ajmer: Vaidik Pustakalay, 1998.

Sardesai, Govind S. *Marathi Riyasat.* 8 vols. Revised and annotated ed. Mumbai: Popular Prakashan, 1988.

———, ed. *Selections from the Peshwa Daftar.* 46 vols. Bombay: Government Central Press, 1931–35.

Sarkar, Tanika, "Historical Pedagogy of the Sangh Parivar." In *Seminar* (*Re-Writing History*), no. 522 (February 2003): 51–56.

Sastri, K. A. Nilakanta, and N. Venkataramanayya. *Further Sources of Vijayanagar History.* 3 vols. Madras: University of Madras, 1946.

Savarkar, Vinayak D. *The Indian War of Independence.* First Indian ed. [1908?]. Bombay: Phoenix Publications, 1947.

Scott, James C. *Seeing Like a State: How Certain Schemes for Improving the Human Condition Have Failed.* New Haven: Yale University Press, 1998.

Sen, Amartya. "India: The Stormy Revival of an International University." *New York Review of Books.* August 13, 2015.

Sen, Dinesh Chandra. *Banga sāhitya paricaya.* 2 vols. Calcutta: University of Calcutta, 1914.

———. *Chaitanya and His Companions.* Calcutta: University of Calcutta, 1917.

Sen, S. P., ed. *Historians and Historiography in Modern India.* Calcutta: Institute of Historical Studies, 1973.

Sen, Surendranath. *Eighteen Fifty-Seven.* Second reprint, Delhi: Publications Division, 1977.

Sewell, Robert. *A Forgotten Empire (Vijayanagar): A Contribution to the History of India.* London: Swann Sonnenschein, 1900.

Shastri, Hara Prasad. *Racanā samagra — dvitiya khanda.* Compiled by Sukumar Sen. Kolkata: West Bengal Government Book Committee, n.d.

Shejwalkar, Tryambak S. *Nivaḍak lekha saṁgraha*, edited by H. V. Mote. Published by H. V. Mote, n.d.

———. "Vijayanagara Sāmrājyāce Maraṭheśāhivarīla pariṇāma.." In *Vijayanagara smāraka grantha (Marāthī avṛtti)*, edited by Dattatreya P. Karmarkar and Rajaram V. Oturkar, 64–78. Pune: BISM, 1936–37.

———. "Vijayanagarceñ ṛn." In *Vijayanagara smāraka grantha (Marāthī avṛtti)*, edited by Dattatreya P. Karmarkar and Rajaram V. Oturkar, 3–7. Pune: BISM, 1936–37.

Shekhāvat, Saubhāgya Siṁha. "Rājasthānī itihāsa kā ek srot—Dantāl patra." In *Cāraṇ sāhitya paramparā: Prophesor Vīrendra Svarūp Bhaṭnāgar abhinandan granth*, edited by Shyamsingh Ratnawat and Krishna Gopal Sharma, 116–25. Jaipur: Rajasthan Adhyayana Kendra, 2001.

Sherlock, Peter. "The Reformation of Memory in Early Modern Europe." In *Memories: Histories, Theories, Debates*, edited by Susannah Radstone and Bill Schwarz, 31–40. New York: Fordham University Press, 2010.

Sicroff, Albert A. *Les controverse des statuts de pureté de sang en Espagne du XV au XVII siécle*. Paris: Didier, 1960.

Siddiqi, Iqtidar Husain. "Early Chishti Dargahs." In *Muslim Shrines in India: Their Character, History and Significance*, edited by C. W. Troll, 1–23. Delhi: Oxford University Press, 1989.

———. *Indo-Persian Historiography to the Fourteenth Century*. 2nd enlarged ed. Delhi: Primus Books, 2014.

Sircar, D. C. *Indian Epigraphy*. Delhi: Motilal Banarasidass, 1965.

Siu, Helen F., Pamela K. Crossley, and Donald S. Sutton, eds. *Empire at the Margins: Culture, Ethnicity and Frontier in Early Modern China*. Berkeley: University of California Press, 2006.

Siva [Shiv] Prasad, Babu. *Itihāsa Timirnāśaka: A History of India in Three Parts*. Allahabad: Printed for Government by J. J. Michael, 1864.

Skaria, Ajay S. "A Forest Polity in Western India." PhD diss., University of Cambridge, 1992.

Smith, Bonnie G. *The Gender of History: Men, Women and Historical Practice*. Cambridge MA: Harvard University Press, 1998.

Smith, John D. *The Epic of Pābūjī: A Study, Transcription and Translation*. Cambridge: Cambridge University Press, 1991.

Sohoni, Krsnaji Vinayak. *Peśvyāncī bakhar*. Edited by R. V. Herwadkar. Pune: Venus Prakashan, 1975.

Sontheimer, Gunther D. "Forest and Pastoral Peoples: Pastoralist Groups." In *Essays on Religion, Literature, and Law*, 100–29. Delhi: Indira Gandhi Centre for the Arts, 2004.

———. "Hero and Sati Stones of Maharashtra," in *Memorial Stones: A Study of Their Origin, Significance, and Variety*, edited by S. Settar and Gunther D. Sontheimer, 261–81. Dharwad, India: Karnatak University, 1982.

———. "On memorials to the dead in the tribal area of Central India." In *Memorial Stones: A Study of Their Origin, Significance, and Variety*, edited by S. Settar and Gunther D. Sontheimer, 87–99. Dharwad, India: Karnatak University, 1982.

———. "The Origin, Structure and Transformation of the Cults of Birobā, Mhaskobā and Khandobā." In *Essays on Religion, Literature, and Law*, 185–206. Delhi: Indira Gandhi Centre for the Arts, 2004.

———. *Pastoral Deities in Western India*. Translated by Anne Feldhaus. Delhi: Oxford University Press, 1993.

Sovani, Avinash, ed. *Aitihasika bakhari: khand pahila*. Pune: Shabdavedha Prakashan, 1998.

Spivak, Gayatri C. "Can the Subaltern Speak?" In *Marxism and the Interpretation of Culture*, edited by Cary Nelson and Lawrence Grossberg, 271–314. Urbana: University of Illinois Press, 1988.

Squibb, George D., ed. *Reports of Heraldic Cases in the Court of Chivalry, 1623–1732*. London: Harleian Society, 1956.

Sreenivasan, Ramya. *The Many Lives of a Rajput Queen: Heroic Pasts in India c. 1500–1900*. Seattle: University of Washington Press, 2007.

Sridhar, T. S., and T. S. Ravishankar, eds. *South Indian Inscriptions, vol. XV. Part II. Bombay-Karnataka Inscriptions*. Madras: Government Press, 1964.

Stark, Ulrike. "Knowledge in Context: Raja Shivaprasad as hybrid intellectual and people's educator." In *Transcolonial Modernities in South Asia*, by Michael S. Dodson and Brian A. Hatcher, 68-91. London: Routledge, 2012.

Steele, Arthur. *The Law and Custom of Hindoo Castes within the Dekhun Provinces subject to the Presidency of Bombay*. New ed., first published in 1827. London: W. H. Allen, 1868.

Stein, Burton. *Vijayanagara*. Cambridge: Cambridge University Press, 1989.

Stewart, Charles. *The History of Bengal from the First Mohammedan Invasions to the Virtual Conquest of the Country by the English in A. D. 1757*. London: Black, Parry and Co, 1813.

Stokes, Eric. *The Peasant Armed*. Edited by C. A. Bayly. Oxford: Oxford University Press, 1986.

Strachey, John. *India*. London: Kegan Paul, 1888.

Suskind, Ron. "Faith, Certainty and the Presidency of George W. Bush." *New York Times Magazine*, October 6, 2017.

Swain, Joseph W. "The Theory of the Four Monarchies: Opposition History under the Roman Empire." *Classical Philology* 35, no. 1 (January 1940): 1–21.

Talbot, Cynthia. *The Last Hindu Emperor: Prithviraj Chauhan and the Indian Past, 1200–2000*. Cambridge: Cambridge University Press, 2016.

Tedder, H. R. "Nutt, Alfrred Trübner (1856–1910)." In Oxford Dictionary of National Biography (online). https://doi.org/10.1093/ref:odnb/35269.

Thapar, Romila. *The Past Before Us: Historical Traditions of Early North India*. Ranikhet, India: Permanent Black, 2013.

Thompson, Edward. *The Other Side of the Medal*. 1st ed. London: The Hogarth Press, 1925.

Thompson, Edward, and G. T. Garratt. *Rise and Fulfillment of British Rule in India*. London: Macmillan, 1934.

Times of India. Bombay newspaper, available on Proquest.

Tinker, Hugh. "1857 and 1957: The Mutiny and Modern India." *International Affairs* 34, no. 1 (1958): 57–65.

Tobert, Natalie. *Anegondi: Architectural Ethnography of a Royal Village*. Vijayanagara Research Project Monograph Series, vol. 7. Delhi: Manohar for the American Institute of Indian Studies, 2000.

Tod, James. *The Annals and Antiquities of Rajasthan*. Vol I. New ed. Madras: Higginbotham, 1873.

Thomas, William. "Macaulay, Thomas Babington, Baron Macaulay (1800–1859)." In Oxford Dictionary of National Biography (online). https://doi.org/10.1093/ref:odnb/17349

Trautmann, Thomas R. *Aryans and British India*. Berkeley: University of California Press, 1997.

———. *India: Brief History of a Civilization*. New York: Oxford University Press, 2016.

———. "Indian Time, European Time." In *Time: Histories and Ethnologies*, edited by Diane Owen Hughes and Thomas R. Trautmann, 167–97. Ann Arbor: University of Michigan Press, 1995.

———, ed. *The Madras School of Orientalism*. Delhi: Oxford University Press, 2009.

Troll, Christian W., ed. *Muslim Shrines in India*. New Delhi; Oxford: Oxford University Press, 2004.

Truschke, Audrey. *Culture of Encounters: Sanskrit at the Mughal Court*. New York: Columbia University Press, 2016.

Twinam, Ann. *Purchasing Whiteness: Pardos, Mulattos, and the Quest for Social Mobility in the Spanish Indies*. Stanford, CA: Stanford University Press, 2015.

Vad, Ganesh C., P. V. Mawjee, and D. B. Parasnis, eds. *Sanads and Letters*. Bombay: P. V. Mawjee, 1913. (Marathi)

———. *Selections from the Satara Raja's and Peshwa Diaries (SSRPD)*. 8 vols. Poona: Deccan Vernacular Translation Society, 1903–11.

Vansina, Jan. "Afterthoughts on the Historiography of Oral Tradition." In *African Historiographies: What History, Which Africa?*, edited by Bogumil Jewsiewicki and David Newbury. Beverly Hills, CA: Sage Publications, 1986.

———. *Oral Traditions as History*. Madison: University of Wisconsin Press, 1985.

Verbrugghe, Gerald P., and John M. Wickersham. *Berossos and Manetho, Introduced and Translated: Native Traditions in Mesopotamia and Egypt*. Ann Arbor: University of Michigan Press, 1996.

Vidyalankar, Mrityuñjaya, and Brajendra Nath Banerjee. *Mrityuñjaya Granthāvalī*. Kalikata: Rañjana Pābliśiṃ Hāusa, 1939.

Vidyanidhi, Lalmohan. *Sambandhanirṇaya*. 2nd ed. N.p., 1898.

Wagner, Anthony R. *Heralds and Heraldry in the Middle Ages: An Inquiry into the Growth of the Armorial Function of Heralds*. 2nd ed. Oxford: Oxford University Press, 1960.

Wagoner, Phillip B. "Precolonial Intellectuals and the Production of Colonial Knowledge." *Comparative Studies in Society and History* 43 (October 2003): 783–814.

———. *Tidings of the King: A Translation and Ethnohistorical Analysis of the Rayavacakamu*. Honolulu: University of Hawaii Press, 1993.

Wang, Q. Edward. "China's Search for a National History." In *Turning Points in Historiography: A Cross-Cultural Perspective*, edited by George Iggers and Q. Edward Wang, 185–207. Rochester: University of Rochester Press, 2002.

Warder, Anthony K. *An Introduction to Indian Historiography*. Bombay: Popular Prakashan, 1972.

Wemple, Erik. "The Post's bizarre story on President Trump and a statue of Robert E. Lee at Antietam." *Washington Post*, September 1, 2017.

Wheare, Degory. *The Method and Order of Reading Both Civil and Eccleisastical Histories*, translated and enlarged by Edmund Bohun. London: printed by T. H. for R. Bonwicke, W. Freeman, et al., 1710.

Wilks, Mark. *Historical Sketches of the South of India: From the Earliest Times to the Last Muhammadan Dynasty*. Vol. I. New Delhi: Cosmo Publications, 1980.

Williams, Robert C. *The Forensic Historian: Using Science to Reexamine the Past*. Armonk, NY: M. E. Sharpe, 2013.

Wongcha-um, Panu. "Thai court drops royal insult case over ancient king." Reuters. www.reuters.com/article/us-thailand-lesemajeste/thai-court-drops-royal-insult-case-over-ancient-king-idUSKBN1F60FD.

Yano, Michio. "al-Biruni." In Encyclopaedia of Islam, THREE, edited by Kate Fleet, Gudrun Kramer, Denis Matringe, John Nawas, and Everett Rowson. Accessed February, 27, 2018. http://dx.doi.org.ezproxy.lib.utexas.edu/10.1163/1573-3912_ei3_COM_25350.

Yarshater, Ehsan, ed. *Cambridge History of Iran*. Vol. 3, pt.1. Cambridge: Cambridge University Press, 1983.

Yerushalmi, Yosef Hayim. *Zakhor: Jewish History and Jewish Memory*. New York: Schocken Books, 1989.

Younge, Gary. "New Roots." *Guardian*, February 16, 2006. www.theguardian.com/science/2006/feb/17/comment.columnists.

Zachariah, Benjamin. "Histories and National Memory: 1857." In *Mutiny at the Margins: New Perspectives on the Indian Uprising of 1857*, edited by Crispin Bates and Marina Carter, 84–112. 7 vols. New Delhi: Sage, 2014.

Zerubavel, Eviatar. *Time Maps: Collective Memory and the Social Shape of the Past*. Chicago: University of Chicago Press, 2003.

Zhang, Xupeng. "In and Out of the West: The Past, Present, and Future of Chinese Historical Theory." Special issue, *History and Theory* 54, no. 4 (2015): 46–63.

Ziegler, Norman P. "Marwari Historical Chronicles: Sources for the social and cultural history of Rajasthan." *Indian Economic and Social History Review*, (1976): 219-250.

Zuidema, Reiner T. *The Ceque System of Cuzco: The Social Organization of the Capital of the Inca*. Leiden, Netherlands: Brill, 1964.

Index

Abul Fazl, 54, 63, 72, 158
academic historical practices, 5, 8, 169, 174, 176
Adilshah sultans, 87, 92, 105, 146, 192n53
Ādiśūra/Adishura/Udīśvara, king of Bengal, 74, 77, 79, 132, 155, 199n123
Afghans, 66, 71–72, 134
Ahmadnagar Police Corps, 95
Ahmadnagar sultanate, 88, 104, 105, 191n34
Ain-i Akbari (part of the *Akbarnāma*), 62, 63, 73, 77
aitihāsika (historical) schools of Vedic learning, 23–24
Akbar, Mughal emperor, 54, 61, 62–63, 75, 94, 127, 149, 199n116
Akbarnāma, 62, 72
Alamgir (Aurangzeb). *See* Aurangzeb, Mughal emperor
Alauddin Khalji, 56, 69
Albiruni, Abul Rayhan, 16, 51, 53
All-India Muslim League, 108, 169
alternative historical narratives, 5, 7, 118–19, 167, 168–72, 173
Ambar, Malik, 105
Ambedkar, Bhimrao, 151
Amin, Shahid, 59, 60, 65
Ancestry.com, 4, 49, 179n3(Intro)
Anglicists, 121, 130
Anglosphere, 5, 166, 172–74, 176, 177
Annals and Antiquities of Rajasthan (Tod), 64, 125, 127, 129–30, 151, 152, 196n44
Arab conquests, 20, 50, 119, 169
Arab historiography, 54
archaeology/archaeologists, 11, 47
archives: colonial government control of, 143, 146, 177; Pune archives, 144; subalterns and, 93
Arya Samaj ("modernist Hindu" organization), 8, 159, 160, 161–65
Asiatic Society, 120, 135
Assmann, Jan, 15–17, 18
Astarabadi (Fereshte/Firishta), 54, 63, 72, 128–29, 158
astrology, 6, 25, 43, 84
astronomy, 19, 51
Aurangzeb, Mughal emperor, 61, 68, 75, 82, 106, 114, 148, 162, 186
authentication protocols: authenticated memories, 56; for hadith, 52, 53; of Indo-Persian histories, 53
Awadh region, 70, 72
Ayodhya, 174, 176
Azad, Abul Kalam, 152, 169

Babur, Mughal emperor, 59, 61, 62, 69, 77
Bahmani sultans, 191n34
Bahraich shrine, 59–61, 65, 162
bakhar genre, 83–84, 86–93, 105, 106–7, 108, 117, 144, 147, 149–50, 180n11(Intro), 198nn106,108
Balslev, Anindita, 10
Baṅgaja kāyastha society, 76, 80, 82
Banaras region, 66
Banaras Sanskrit College, 158, 164
banned books, 145
Baptists, 124–25, 131, 154–55
bards (*charan*), 56, 57, 64–65, 67, 69–70, 81–82, 129
Basu, Nagendranath, 82, 131
Basu, Ram Ram, 74–77, 78, 79, 81, 131, 134, 189n101
Bene Israel of Western India, 17–18, 26, 28
Bengal: overview, 7; Bengali Brahmans, 196n62; conquest of, 72, 121; early colonial history in Bengal, 69, 130–36; East

India Company and, 127; educational system, 152–53; educational systems, 154; family estates in, 80; Ganga delta, 71; Ghurids in, 54; government of, 155; histories of, 121, 131, 133–34; Mughal era, 61; Muslims in, 73, 132; Nawabs of, 80; Persian language, 128; Phadke and, 197n68; scholars in, 134; scientific history, 145; Sena kings, 72; social and political power in, 81; social history of, 189n108; Sultanate of, 75
Bengal Presidency, 130, 196n57
Bengal Sultanate, 72, 75, 78
Bengali Brahmans, 132, 199n123
Bengali language, 74, 131, 134
Bengali literature, 8, 81
Bhadra, Gautam, 104
Bhārāta Itihāsa Samśodhak Manḍal (BISM) (Society for the Study of Indian History), 142–43, 145, 146, 148–50
Bhattacharya, Neeladri, 173
Bhosle, Shahaji, 104–5, 111, 147
Bhosle, Shivaji Raje, 92
Bhosle dynasty, 104–5, 107, 111, 114, 115
biblical chronology, 47, 122, 124, 128
bilingualism, 199n130
BISM (Bhārāta Itihāsa Samśodhak Manḍal) (Society for the Study of Indian History), 142–43, 145, 146, 148
Bombay: Coats in, 190n10; Elphinstone College, 136; government of, 155; government records about Phadke, 197n67; government records in, 83; public religious debates, 159; university in, 154
Bombay Presidency, 125, 136, 137, 146
Bosworth, C. E., 52
boundary disciplines, 5, 45–49
Brahmans, 63, 68, 147; as administrators, 111; Bengali Brahmans, 132, 196n62; British fears of, 138; genealogical accounts of, 80; historical narratives of, 89, 107–8; Jāmadagnya Brahmans, 140; lineages of Rarha, 77–78; Maga/Shakadwipi Brahmans, 21–22; Marathi (language) dictionary and, 112–13; Pendses, 139–40; village endowments for, 21; in Western India, 85
Briggs, John, 54, 128–29
British Empire: civil service, 121, 122, 125; local society and, 152. *See also* colonial empires
British historians, 53–54, 83, 122; critics of, 168
British India: anglicization of, 123; British imperial rule, 80, 173; divergence of master narratives during, 170; early colonial history in Bengal, 130–36; education systems, 154; historians of, 141; historiographic reactions to, 8, 70; indigenist responses in colonial education, 160–68; Jinnah on, 169; Maratha history under, 136–47; schoolroom history in, 152–60. *See also* colonial India
Buckler, F. W., 146
Buddhist tradition, 27, 55, 57–58, 70, 71
Burke, Edmund, 177
Burke, Peter, 45

Calcutta, 74, 80, 120, 121, 122, 127, 130, 131, 154
Carey, William, 74, 124
Chakrabarty, Dipesh, 4, 5, 18, 145, 181n31
Chanda, Ramaprasad, 135, 196n61
Chandra, Bankim, 79, 132–35, 137, 165, 189n108, 196n57, 197n68
Chandra, Satish, 173
charan (bards), 56, 57, 64–65, 67, 69–70, 81–82, 129
charter myths, 43
Chatterjee, Kumkum, 82
Chatterjee, Partha, 6, 78, 125, 173, 201n181
Chatterji, Bankim Chandra, 132–35, 137. *See also* Chandra, Bankim
China, 119–20; *Annals* (Chinese), 27; Han dynasty, 25; historians, 4–5, 119–20; historical tradition, 25–26; national history, 119–20; pilgrim accounts, 70; Qin dynasty, 120; Qing dynasty, 25; scholarly classes, 119; Taiping Rebellion, 119

Christians/Christianity: cathedral chapter, 4; Christian Quarter (Jerusalem), 15; collective memory, 14, 181n17; Evangelicalism, 124, 125, 130; Hindu faith and, 123, 162; historical frame of, 45; iconoclasts in Egypt, 20; institutional response to, 160; Jesuits, 153; Jesus Christ, 14, 44, 184n115; missionaries, 130, 158–59, 161; monasteries, 4, 6, 20–21; narrative memory, 15, 121; in Palestine, 15; Protestant missions, 153; Protestant narrative, 124; Protestant Reformation, 29–30, 44; scientific history and, 159; as state religion, 20; theologians, 63; Western historians and, 44. *See also* Roman Catholic Church

civil service: British Civil Service, 121, 122, 125; Indian Civil Service, 81, 111, 146, 167

clan histories, 65–71

cloister metaphor, 4–5, 18–26, 181n31

cloisters metaphor, 18–26; Babylonian temples as, 19; Chinese traditions as, 25–26; Christian monasteries as, 20–21; Egyptian temples as, 19–20; Hellenic traditions as, 20; Iranian traditions as, 21–22; overview, 18–19

Coats, Thomas, 85, 98, 190n10

Cohn, Bernard, 66–67, 70

collective memory: overview, 9–18; Christian and Jewish, 181n17; first cloisters, 18–26; in Marathi-speaking regions, 117; Medieval West and, 34–45; oral traditions and, 30–34; production/authentication of, 5; social frame of, 7; socially constructed, 176; struggles of, 6; traditions and, 26–30; Yerushalmi on, 13; Zerubavel on, 14

College of Arms (England), 8, 38, 43

colleges/universities: Banaras Sanskrit College, 158, 164; in Bombay, 154; College of Fort William (Calcutta), 74, 131; college of temple priests, 4, 19; Deccan College, Pune, 136; Delhi College, 153; Elphinstone College, 136; English-speaking in, 173; Government College, 200n150; Haileybury (college), 121, 126, 195n32; Pune University, 151; in South Asia/southern Asia, 21

colonial empires: accepted regional traditions in, 8; collapse of, 168; colonial histories, 130, 151; colonial honorific system, 186n40; colonial intelligentsia, 158–59, 177; early colonial history in Bengal, 69, 130–36; genealogy of modern historiography in India and, 201n181; imposed uniformity of, 176–77; Islamic scholars on power of, 199n117; nationalism and, 175; record and archive access, 177. *See also* British Empire; British India

colonial India: early colonial history in Bengal, 130–36; indigenist responses in colonial education, 160–68; from Indomania to Indophobia, 120–30; Maratha history under, 136–47; schoolroom history in, 152–60. *See also* British India; East India Company

common knowledge, 46, 84–85

community memory, 90

Conlon, Frank, 159

conversions/converso ancestry, 40–41, 132

Cornwallis, Charles Cornwallis, Marquis, 121, 127

court historiographers, 62–63

Court of Wards, 135

cultural capital, 174, 175

cultural memory, 18

culture-brokers, 45

Dalhousie, James Andrew Broun Ramsay, Marquis of, 156

Dalit, 97–98

Dalits of Maharashtra, 97–98, 102, 104

Dalmia, Vasudha, 158

Dayanand, Swami, 153, 162–64

Delhi, India, 149, 153; Ghurids in, 54; Kalkaji shrine, 61; Maratha administration in, 137; Muslim conquest of, 77, 78; Turkic power elite in, 52

Delhi College, 153

Delhi Sultanate, 53, 55–61, 62, 69, 72, 74
Delhi sultans, 53, 55–61, 62, 69, 71, 72, 74, 113
deshmookhs (hereditary office), 57, 90–92, 93, 103, 137
deshmukh (hereditary office), 57, 90–92, 93, 103, 137
deshpande (hereditary office), 57, 90–92, 93, 103, 137
Deshpande, Prachi, 85, 108, 130, 143, 196n64
Dow, Alexander, 54, 128
Dowson, John, 157
Doyle, James, 12
Duara, Prasenjit, 119
Duff, Grant, 25, 107, 127–30, 136–37, 139–40, 142, 143, 193n69
Duncan, Jonathan, 66
Dundas, Henry, 195n25

East India Company, 72, 77, 111, 120–22, 124, 127, 129, 130, 146, 155–56, 195n19
East India/eastern India, 8; British colonial rule in, 8; patterns in historical memory, 71–82. *See also* East India Company
educational system: after Indian independence, 173; Arya Samaj and, 8, 160, 161–65; Christian missions and, 160; colonial textbooks, 161; critics of, 168; Dar al-Ulum in Deoband, 160; East India Company and, 120–21; Elliot's translations and, 157; funding sources, 160; as gateway, 177; imperial legitimacy and, 8; of independent India, 170; Indian history textbooks, 125, 171; indigenist responses in colonial education, 160–68; indigenous histories and, 131–35; intelligentsia and, 166; Islam and, 153; judicial systems and, 156; Marathi translations, 193n69; primary education expansion, 160; professional history and, 6; public sphere and, 8; schoolroom history in colonial India, 152–60; textbook controversy, 172; Urdu language, 160. *See also* colleges/universities; textbooks
Egypt/Egyptian civilization, 119, 148; Augustus Caesar and, 19–20; college of temple priests, 19; Egyptian hieroglyphic script, 6, 19; Egyptian historiographic tradition, 19; glyphic records, 16; Manetho, 20, 181n35; temples as first cloisters in, 19–20
elite classes: Classic Maya elites, 27; cultural capital and, 174; English-speaking elites and, 175; English-speaking elites in, 173; memories of, 28; Persian clerical elite in, 52; Rajput elite, 63–64, 73; subaltern class and, 104; Turkic power elite in, 52
Elliot, Henry M., 156–57, 160, 176, 183n81, 199n114
Elliott, Charles A., 67–68, 70, 192n41
Elphinstone, Mountstuart, 103, 109, 125, 127, 128, 130, 154, 155, 156, 195n32
England: College of Arms, 8, 38, 43; English cloister, 41; English historians, 142; English histories, 133; gentry status in, 38–39; Henry VIII, king of England, 30; heralds and, 35; Magna Carta, 42; Merlin legends, 42; Stuart Monarchy, 44; Stuart monarchy, 44; Tudor monarchy, 30. *See also* British Empire
English language usage, 130, 173, 177
English sources, 155
English translations, 149
English-language histories, 154
English-speaking elites, 173, 175
epigraphs, 72, 128, 199n124
Erikson, Eric, 45
Ernst, Carl, 62
eschatological events, 87
etymological (*nairukta*) school of Vedic learning, 23–24, 25
etymological analysis, 47
evidentiary processes, 13, 85, 92–93, 97, 178
eyewitness accounts, 12

Facebook, 174
factuality, 84, 176, 194n103

family history, 5, 25, 38–39, 90
Fereshte/Firishta (Astarabadi), 54, 63, 72, 128–29, 158
Firishta/Fereshte (Astarabadi), 54, 63, 72, 128–29, 158
folk traditions: contemporary impact, 45–49; of descent, 48–49; folk memory, 30, 104; folklore, 25, 57, 65, 73, 76; *kula-grantha* texts/tradition, 82; in North India, 65; on tax revenues, 116
forensic science, 47
forgeries, 21, 46, 92, 113, 118, 140, 191nn29–30
forms of memory, 28
foundation myths, 73, 79
frameworks of collective memory quote, 12–13
France: Capetian dynasty, 35–36; clerical oversight of scholarship in, 44; *franc fief* tax, 36; French Revolution, 118; Henry III, king of France, 37; Henry IV, king of France, 37; heralds and, 35; Hugh Capet, king of France, 35; Louis XIII, king of France, 37; Louis XIV, king of France, 37, 181n19; Louis XV, king of France, 37; status in, 35–37

Gandhi, Mohandas, 146, 167, 170, 174
Gangetic Plain, 55, 59, 61, 65, 69, 70, 161–62
genealogical records, 179n3(Intro); as arbiters of rank, 8; *Armorial général* (*The Register of the Nobility of France*), 35; in Bengal, 81–82; of Brahmans, 80; clan hierarchy and, 56; clan/family genealogy, 5; creation of, 22; of Incan rulers, 28; loss of, 55; masonry monuments and, 24–25, 90; New Christians equality and, 40–41; for parvenu monarchs, 53; patrimonial claims and, 90; pre-Islamic kings of Iran and, 53; Rajput lineages, 105; research methods, 4; Rigord's genealogy of French kings, 184n108; standardization of, 69; Thakurs and, 66
genealogists, 35, 45, 176; caste purity and, 74; lineage lore and, 79; in *Paṭivyākhyā* (manuscript), 81; in village society, 56–57. *See also* bards (*charan*)
genetics, 48–49
gentry status: in England, 38–39; in France, 35–37; gentry-literati class, 24, 26, 73, 127; in Spain, 39–41
Geoffrey of Monmouth, 42
geology, 46–47
ghaṭak (marriage broker), 78, 79, 176
Ghazi Miyan, 59, 60, 65, 68
Ghaznavids, 51, 53
Ghur sultans, 53
Ghurids, 53, 54
Giberne, George, 94–95, 96
Grafton, Anthony, 43
grammatical analysis, 47
Gramsci, Antonio, 93
Grant, Alexander, 136
Grant, Charles, 121, 122–24, 126, 127, 130
Grant, James, 195n39
great traditions: and little traditions, 26–30; oral traditions as, 30–34
Greek civilization: Alexander of Macedon, 19, 42; Greco-Roman historical narratives, 23; Greek language, 122, 123–24, 182n35; Greek Orthodox Church, 15; Hellenic conquests, 19; Hellenic dynasty, 19; Hellenic Greeks, 20; Hellenic traditions, 16, 20, 21; Herodotus, 183n81; history of Babylonian civilization by Berossos, 20; Homer, 20
Griffith, R. T. H., 164
Guha, Ranajit, 133, 134, 196n58

Habib, Mohammad, 171
hagiographic tradition, 74, 85, 104
Haileybury (college), 121, 126, 195n32
Halbwachs, Maurice, 11–15, 18, 45, 60, 90, 180nn8–9(ch1), 181nn13,17,19, 187n52
Hardinge, Governor-General Lord, 156
Hardy, Peter, 195n41
Harishchandra, Bharatendu, 153
Hastings, Warren, 109, 126
heraldic study, 6, 29, 35, 43, 183n84
heralds, 29, 35, 37, 38, 45, 49

hereditary offices, 57, 90–92, 93, 103, 137
hero-stones, 24–25, 29
hieroglyphic tradition, 6, 20
Hindi language, 166, 199n123; Hindi poets, 62; histories, 65; literature, 65; sacred texts, 158; texts, 155
Hindi-Urdu controversy, 158
Hindi-Urdu textbooks, 156–57
Hindu dynasties/rulers, 69, 77, 78, 94, 103, 114
Hindu literati, 26
Hindu nationalism, 151; emergence of, 173; narrative of, 176, 177; politics of, 8, 147–52, 174, 197n83; Rajwade on, 147. *See also* nationalists, Indian
Hindu scholars, 156, 158
Hindu/Muslim divide: Hindu critics, 155; Jinnah on, 169; political tensions, 147; Qureshi on, 171, 172
Hindu-pad-padshahi (Savarkar), 150–51
Hindutva, 151
historians: African historians, 47, 119; British historians, 53–54, 83, 122, 168; in British India, 141; Chakrabarty on, 18–19; Chinese historians, 4–5, 119–20; Christianity and, 44; English historians, 142; English language usage, 173; exclusion from social memory shaping, 174; grand historian, 25; Indian historians, 170–71; legitimization and, 45; of Maharashtra, 91, 141, 146, 147; Maratha historians, 89, 147; in Mughal era, 200n133; North African historians, 119; official establishment of, 26; official historians, 177; Persianate historians, 53–54; Perso-Indian historians, 54; professional historians, 6, 197n64; secular European historians, 43; of South India, 116, 147; of Western civilization, 128
historical (*aitihāsika*) school of Vedic learning, 23–24
historical memory: bards (*charan*) and, 56; in Bengal, 81; claims centered on, 6; colonial renderings of, 177; comparative study of, 168, 200n145; contestation and, 190n14; under Delhi sultans, 55–61; differing patterns of, 8; Eastern India patterns in, 71–82; Marathi-speaking peoples and, 111–12, 151; overview, 4–5; social frame of, 188n94; social memory and shaping of, 9; structured by sociopolitical organizations in eastern, northern, western India, 7
historical narrative in Western India: overview, 8, 83–86, 117; authors of, 89; evidentiary processes and, 97; forgetting Vijayanagara, 109–17; social frame of *Bakhar* genre, 86–93; subaltern class, 97–109
historical novels, 144
history (term usage), 9
history and memory through 19th and 20th centuries: overview, 118–20; alternative historical narratives, 168–72; Anglosphere and, 172–74; early colonial history in Bengal, 130–36; early colonial India, 120–30; Hindu nationalist project, 147–52; indigenist responses in colonial education, 160–68; Maratha history under colonialism, 136–47; popular and professional in India, 174–75; schoolroom history in colonial India, 152–60; Vijayanagara Empire and, 147–52
History of Bengal (Stewart), 127
History of England (Hume), 122
History of India (Elphinstone), 125, 127
History of India from Remote Antiquity to the Accession of the Moghul Dynasty (Marshman), 155, 158, 199n123
History of India (Mill), 124–26
History of Orissa (Stirling), 72
History of the Freedom Movement in India (Chand), 171
History of the Mahrattas (Duff), 127, 129–30, 136–37, 143, 193n69
History of the Mahrattas (Waring), 83
History of the Rise of the Mohammedan Power in India (Briggs), 128–29
Hitler diaries case, 46

Holkar, Jaswant Rao, 109
honor claims, 66, 97; colonial India honorific systems, 186n40; historical memory and, 6, 7–8
Humayun, Mughal emperor, 61, 69
Hume, David, 122

Ibbetson, Denzil, 57
Idilshahs, 93
Iggers, Georg, 26
illiteracy, 161, 173
immigrant literati, 55
Inden, Ronald, 134
India, Republic of, 136, 152, 169, 172–73, 177. *See also* nationalism
Indian administration, 154
Indian Civil Service, 81, 111, 146, 167
Indian Education Service, 146, 166
Indian historians, 170–71
Indian historiographies, 133
Indian History Congress, 170–71
Indian history textbooks, 171
Indian independence, 177
Indian languages: basic education in, 124; printing, 131; public sphere for, 174; textbooks in, 158; usage, 177
Indian National Congress, 135, 136, 169
Indian subcontinent pasts: overview, 50–55; Eastern Indian patterns of historical memory, 71–82; historical memory under sultans of Delhi, 55–61; Mughal integration in culture and narrative, 61–65; parganas and clan histories in North India, 65–71
The Indian War of Independence (Savarkar), 144–45, 146, 150
Indic tradition: contemporary, 21; first cloisters, 22–25; four-yuga cosmological cycle in, 54; *itihāsa* (history), 22; Yama (god of death), 27
indigenes, in North Africa, 119
indigenist responses, 134–35, 160–68
indigenous histories, 131
indigenous learning, 120–21
indigenous memory, 28
indigenous scholars, 121
indigenous sources of history, 147
Indo-European language family, 47
Indomania, 120–30
Indo-Persian historiography, 50, 51, 53
Indophiles, 126
Indophilia, 123, 160
Indophobia, 120–30
information enclaving, 174
Innocence Project, 48
inscriptions, 71; in Arabic, 72; in Bengal, 72; donative inscriptions, 29; New Persian historiography, 52; Pendse lineage and, 140; in Persian, 72; temple inscriptions, 19
intelligentsia, 21, 44, 51, 78, 161, 162, 166; in Algeria, 119; of Calcutta, 130, 131; in China, 120; colonial intelligentsia, 158–59, 177; in East India, 120–22; local Islamic intelligentsia, 153; Maharashtrian, 136, 139; postcolonial metropolitan, 173
Iran/Iranian civilization, 148; after Arab conquest, 51, 54; Iranian dynasty, 52; Iranian traditions, 21–22, 51, 53; New Persian historiography, 53; Persianate dynasties of eastern, 52
Islam: Azad on, 169; conversion to, 57, 73, 132, 134; Habib on, 171; historical success of, 185n2; Islamic chronography, 51; Islamic conquest, 147; Islamic empire in Palestine, 14–15; Islamic narrative histories, 50–51; Islamic rule in India, 97, 103–4; Islamic scholars (ulema), 18, 52, 85, 153, 199n117; Islamicate Persian traditions, 53; Nehru on, 170; rise of, 50; universalism of, 51
Ismail, Kazi, 85
Ismailis, 172
itihāsa (history), 10, 24; defined, 22; historical novels and, 144; Sanskrit tradition and, 25
Itihāsa timir nāśaka (Dispeller of Historical Obscurity) (Prasad), 157, 199n130

Jackson, Peter, 69
Jaffrelot, Christophe, 151, 162
Jagannātha of Puri, 71–72
Jahangir, Mughal emperor, 75, 105
Jains, 56, 63, 70, 186n34
Jalal, Shah, 73
Jessore, 74, 76. *See also* Yaśahara (modern Jessore)
Jewish people/Judaism: Bene Israel of Western India, 17; diaspora of, 16–17; in India, 17; Jewish clerical classes, 17; Jewish collective memory, 14, 181n17; Jewish festivals, 17; Jewish kingdoms, 16–17; Jewish sites of memory, 15; Jewish Temple, 14; Judaic traditions, 16; Mosaic chronology, 122; Nuh (Noah), 54; rabbinical tradition, 182n47; rabbis, 18; in Spain, 40–41; Torah, 17
Jinnah, M. A., 169, 171
Jones, Kenneth, 160
Jones, William, 122–24, 185n121
judicial systems, 131, 156; East India Company and, 120; legal texts, 131; in South Asia/southern Asia, 21; in Western India, 84–85, 88–89
judicial verdicts, 84, 113, 190n6
juges d'armes, 37
Julien, Catherine, 28, 193n78
Juzjani, Minhaj al-Siraj, 51, 53

karaṇam (clerk) historian, 115
Karim, Abdul, 73
Kasturi, Malavika, 67
Kautiliya arthaśāstra, 22
Kaviraj, Sudipta, 175
Kayasthas of Jessore, 76–77, 78, 80, 81, 132
kayath (scribe) caste, 73, 81
Kaye, J. W., 144
Kehimkar, Haeem S., 181n27
Kennedy, Vans, 125
Kesarī (periodical), 141–42
khabar (news), 83
Khalji sultans, 56, 113
Khandoba shrine, 60–61
Khare, Ganesh Hari, 60, 145–46
Khare, Vasudev Vaman, 143–44
khipus/quipus (knotted bundles of dyed cord), 28
Khobrekar, V. G., 141
Khomne, Umaji Naik, 93–97
Khwârizmî (Pahlavi) writing, 16, 21, 51
King Arthur legends, 42
Kings of Arms, 37
kinship ties, 66, 67–68, 69
Kirtane, N. J., 136–39, 142
knowledge: debates on, 159; defeating colonial knowledge, 143; God's knowledge, 180n2; of past, 9; production of, 4, 5; Veda and, 159
Kolis, 96–97, 104, 191n36
Kolis, Chivhe, 93
kulagrantha texts/tradition, 82, 135
kulaji genealogical traditions, 131
kulin (aristocratic) system, 77, 79, 134
Kulkarni, A. R., 89, 136–37, 151
Kulke, Hermann, 71–72, 188n93
Kumar, Krishna, 159–60, 161, 166, 168, 171, 172, 200n145
Kumar, Nita, 173

Lakshmana Sena, king of Bengal, 73, 74, 79
Lakshmibai, rani of Jhansi, 141
land claims, 68–69, 72, 74, 76, 84, 85, 189n115, 190n13; copper plate transcripts, 94–95, 97; historical memory and, 6, 7–8; local assemblies and, 86; Mahars and, 98
The Last Hindu Emperor (Talbot), 70, 186n34
Latin language/texts, 42, 44, 122, 123
legends: adoption of, 53; holy men/holy sites associated, 5; Vijayanagara Empire, 110–11
legitimatization: of British India, 168, 170; of French rule, 119; historians and, 45; subaltern class and, 104
Leitner, Gottlieb W., 163, 200n150
Liang Qichao, 120
Lieberman, Victor, 26
lineage (term), 179n4(Intro)

lineages, 56, 76, 78, 79, 89, 91–92, 93–94; kingly lineages, 72, 182n35; Maratha lineages, 114, 136; Rajput lineages, 105; representatives of, 99; struggles of, 93–94; of subaltern classes, 102
linguistics, analytic ideas from, 45, 47
literacy, 153, 160, 161
literati, 56; in Bengal, 73; in China, 26; Hindu literati, 26; historical narratives of, 89; immigrant literati, 55; in India, 26, 55; literati-gentry class, 24, 26, 73, 127; Marathi-speaking literati, 84, 107; Muslim literati, 26, 73, 132; Persianate literati, 52, 63, 83–84
lithic inscriptions, 131
little traditions, and great traditions, 26–30
local assemblies, 84–85
local histories, 151, 173
local memory, 24–25
local tradition, 38–39
Loftus, Elizabeth, 12
Lorenzen, David, 58
lost texts, 16
Lyell, Alfred, 47

Macaulay, T. B., 126–27, 131, 154, 167, 177, 183n81, 195n37
Mackenzie, Colin, 110, 115, 116
Mackintosh, Alexander, 94–96, 191n33
Madhwu, 112
Madras, 121, 125, 130, 149, 154, 155
Madras Presidency, 111, 116, 198n95
Magadha, 133
Maga/Shakadwipi Brahmans, 21–22
Magians, 21–22
Mahabharata, 54, 62, 128, 200n133; as *itihāsa* (history), 22; oral traditions and, 24; rewriting of, 23; Yudhisthira of the, 77
Mahabharata War, 162, 165
Mahanadi (Odisha), 71
Mahar community, 98
Maharashtra, 57; overview, 7; *bakhar* genre and, 88, 107; *bakhar* genre in, 84; boundary issues in, 98; British military occupation in, 83; defined, 194n104; historians of, 91, 141, 146, 147; identity of, 108; legendary history of, 103; precolonial, 7; public religious debates, 159; resistance in, 151; rise of Shivaji, 104; scientific history, 145; Yadava dynasty, 113
Mahars (hereditary village servants), 98, 99, 100, 102, 103
Mahipati, 191n35
Mahmud of Ghazni, 51, 54, 59, 68
mahzar (collective attestation/judicial award), 86
Maimonides, Moses, 17
Majumdar, Ramesh C., 81, 131, 171, 201n172
Malcolm, John, 67, 69
Malik Ambar, 88, 92
Mallari (deity), 60–61
Malleson, G. B., 142, 144
Mandal (Bhārāta Itihāsa Samśodhak Manḍal) (Society for the Study of Indian History), 142–43, 145, 146, 148–50
Manetho, 20, 181n35
Maratha Empire, 67, 83–84, 115, 129, 191n37; founding of, 148; Maratha administrations, 137; Maratha castes, 194n104; Maratha community, 194n104; Maratha historians, 89, 147; Maratha historical memory, 111; Maratha history under colonialism, 136–47; Maratha identity, 86, 106; Maratha rulers, 111; Marathas, 105, 107, 136, 149
Maratha kingdoms, 138
Maratha lands, 128
Maratha lineages, 114, 136
Maratha nationalism, 143
Marathi historical narratives, 84, 113–14, 136–37
Marathi historical novels, 86, 107, 141, 144, 145, 151
Marathi historical traditions of Vijayanagara Empire, 7
Marathi language, 83, 101, 130, 180n11 (Intro), 194n104; Bene Israel of

Western India, 17; dictionary of, 112; family histories in, 114; *keriyath Shema*, 181n27; Marathi translation as required schoolbook, 193n69; Marathi-speaking area, 7, 83; Marathi-speaking literati, 84, 107; Marathi-speaking public sphere, 151; Marathi-speaking region, 108–9; poems in, 84; texts in, 198nn106,108
Marathi texts, 95, 113–14, 115–16, 129, 148–50
Marriage and Rank in Bengali Culture (Inden), 134
marriage broker (*ghaṭak/kulajña*), 78, 79, 176
marriage patterns, 67–68, 69, 77, 79, 82, 162
Marshal of Arms office, 37
Marshman, John C., 54, 124, 127, 131, 133, 154–55, 158, 199n123
Marshman, Joshua, 154–56
Marwar, kingdom of, 56, 64
Marwari chronicles, 64
Marxism, 135
maṭha (Indic), 4
mathematics, 19, 51
Maya civilization, 16, 27
Mehendale, Gajanan, 91, 92, 191n29, 197n89
Meisami, Julie, 52–53
memorandum books, 89–90, 115
memory, erasures of, 109–17, 181n13, 193n78
memory fabrication, 7, 171, 180n9(ch1)
Mesoamerica record systems, 27–28
Mesopotamia, 19, 20
Metcalf, Barbara, 160, 166
microhistories, 48–49
Middle East, 52
Mill, James, 124–27, 195n26, 195n37
mīmānsā (analytic) approach to Vedic texts, 23–24
Minhaj al-Siraj Juzjani, 51, 53
miracles, 46, 158–59
mīrāsī (Arabic, literally "hereditary"), 57
miscegenation, 41
missionaries, 130, 153, 158–59, 161, 162, 199n117, 200n133
Modi (script), 101, 115, 193n72
Moin, Azfar, 182n57
monasteries: Buddhist monastic libraries, 55; Jain monastic organizations, 56, 186n34; in South Asia, 21
monotheism, 52
monuments, 152; hero stones, 24–25; to Mughal rule, 161; reworking of, 29; rock carvings, 24–25; sati stones, 24–25; use of, 103, 104
Mosaic chronology, 122
Mueller, Max, 165
Mughal emperors, 105, 146, 148. *See also specific emperors*
Mughal Empire: administrative practices of, 127; Babur, 61; Bengal conquest by, 72; decline of, 115; East India Company and, 120–22; ecumenical histories, 129; historical culture of, 128; Humayn, 61; imperial enterprise of, 62; indigenous traditions in, 62; Marathas and, 105, 115; Mughal rule, 130; Rajput elite in, 63–64; Sarkar on, 166; Shibananda and, 75
Mughal era: Babur, 59; historians in, 200n133; imperial memory unification in, 50; imperial patronage in, 58; integration in cultural and narrative, 61–65; Mughal histories, 63; Mughal integration in culture and narrative, 61–65; Mughal invasion, 91; Mughal retreat, 111; Mughals in East India, 71
Muin al-Din Chishti, 58
multilingualism, 175
Munro, Thomas, 125, 126, 154
Muslims: anti-Muslim attitudes, 197n68; in Bengal, 73; brotherhoods (*barādarī/qaum*), 66; conquest of Delhi, 77; converts to, 132; depictions of Muslim rule, 157–58, 160; invasion of, 147, 163; Jinnah on, 169; Muslim Arabs, 50; Muslim League, 169; Muslim literati, 26, 73, 132; Muslim scholars, 156, 199n117; Muslim shrines, 57–58; Muslim sites of memory, 15; Muslim sultans, 136; Qureshi on, 171–72; rulers in Delhi, 78; Urdu

language, 160; Yazid (Umayyad caliph), 52. *See also* ulema (Islamic scholars)
mythic past, 66–67

nairukta (etymological school of Vedic learning), 23–24
Nandy, Ashis, 174, 175, 176
nationalism: in Bengal, 134; in China, 119–20; crafting vision of, 170; Maratha nationalism, 143; memory fabrication and, 7; narrative of, 170; in Southern Africa, 119
nationalism, Indian: all-India narrative, 108; colonialism and, 175; historical research and, 146, 177; national essence, 120; national history, 175; national identities, 8, 119, 169, 170; national language, 166; national narratives, 151, 170; national projects, 104–9; national unification, 8
nationalist histories, 144, 173
nationalists, Indian: BISM and, 142–43; historical research and, 177; history recovery by, 118–19; nationalist scholars, 146
Nehru, Jawaharlal, 167, 168, 170–71, 174, 175
Nehruvian ideology: consensus, 177; early period, 136, 172–73; economics, 174; government, 171; history, 177; vision, 201n172
New Christians, 40–41
noble status: in England, 38–39; in France, 35–37; historic status of, 36; historical writing and, 21; in Spain, 39–41; symbols of, 37
nonconformism, 155
nonprofessional history, 6
Nora, Pierre, 152, 183n69
North India/northern India: Ahir caste, 59; parganas and clan histories in North India, 65–71; Persianate dynasties of, 52; Sanskritization in, 198n111; uprising in, 137; vernacular historical traditions of, 61
Northwest India, 65
North-Western Provinces, 128, 154
Novetzke, Christian L., 181n30, 186n34
Novick, Peter, 3–4, 185n130

Oḍiyā people, 133
officeholders (*watandars*), 97, 100, 107, 139
oral traditions, 63; bards (*charan*) and, 56; Bengali history residing in, 8; as great tradition, 30–34; historical novels and, 144; interactions with text, 24; Iranian epics, 21; noble status in Spain and, 40; in pre-Islamic Arab world, 50; as sources, 119; vernacular traditions and, 25
"Oriental learning," 131, 154
origin myths, 132, 134
Orissa (Odisha) region, 27, 61, 71–72, 188n94
Oxford, 6, 43–44

padshaha, 114
Pagdi, Setu Madhavrao, 92
Pakistan, 168, 169, 171, 172, 200n145
Pakistan Historical Society, 172
Pala dynasty, 80, 134
Panjab province, 153, 158, 163; British annexation of, 128; language use in, 128, 200n131; Panjab educational system, 166, 200n150; Panjabi language in, 200n131; Urdu language in, 200n131
parallel memories, 60, 74, 176
Parasnis, Dattatreya Balwant, 140–42
parganas (village clusters), 56, 65–71, 86, 87, 97
past (term): definition/usage, 9; grammatical past, 9; historical narration of past, 9–10; narrative past, 9–10
Pathak, V. S., 22–23, 24, 55
patrimonial claims, 89, 90–91, 93–95, 97, 102
patronage, 69; to learning in China, 25; of Muslim officials, 80; official historians, 177; pressure of, 176; radical nationalist history and, 144
peasant consciousness of China, 27

pedigree system, 79
performative memory, 181n30
Persian (Sassanid) kings, 14
Persian canon, 65
Persian chronologies, 51, 72
Persian clerical elite, 52
Persian histories, 55, 57–58, 61, 63, 65, 72, 74, 84, 127, 129, 152, 157, 158, 161
Persian language, 72, 74, 125, 185n1; in India, 127–28; in Mughal Empire, 62
Persian literary traditions, 128, 158
Persian sources, 145, 147, 155
Persianate dynasties of eastern Iran and North India, 52
Persianate historians, 53–54
Persianate historical tradition, 72
Persianate literati, 52, 63, 83–84
Persian-speaking Islamic peoples, 53
Peshwa dynasty, 108, 137, 140, 143, 149, 151
Phadke, Wasudeo Balwant, 137–38, 197nn67–68
Philips, C. H., 117, 180n11(Intro)
philology/philologists, 46, 196n64
philosophy, 10, 159, 180n1
pilgrimages: Bahraich shrine, 65; Chinese pilgrim accounts, 70; Ghazi Miyan shrine, 65; pilgrimage spots, 24; in South Asia/southern Asia, 57–58, 59–60
places of memory, 174
Pollock, Sheldon, 23–24, 117, 194n103
Portuguese empire, 72, 121
post-truth era, 176–78
Potdar, Datto Vamana, 116
Powell, Avril, 54, 156, 158, 199n117
Prasad, Raja Shiv, 153, 156, 157–58, 164, 176, 200n132
pre-Hispanic manuscripts, 27–28
pre-Islamic Arab chronologies, 51
pre-Islamic Iranian world, 21, 53
pre-Islamic kings of India, 62
pre-Islamic kings of Iran, 53
pre-Islamic rule in Bengal, 77
print technology, 8, 152–53, 159
Prithviraj (king), 61, 64, 66, 70
Prithviraj Chauhan (Chahamana), 58, 78, 151, 152
Prithviraj legend, 78, 186n34
Prithvirajraso (long poem), 61, 65
professional historians, 6, 197n64
professional history, 3–4, 6, 7
property claims, 6, 7–8, 28, 180n7(ch1)
public life in the Medieval West, 34–45
public memories, 14, 70
public sphere: Indian language usage, 174, 177; social memory and shaping of, 6; subcontinental influence on, 50
Pune district, 83, 85, 90, 93, 94, 95, 103, 136, 139, 141, 143, 144, 145, 190n10
Puranas, 24, 25, 72, 108, 129, 164–65
Puranika succession of dynasties, 64, 77, 78
Puri, 71–72
purity of blood criterion, 40–41
pursuivants (investigators), 35, 37

qanungo, 91
qasba settlements, 69
qazi (Islamic judge), 86, 99, 103
Qureshi, I. H., 171–72, 201n174
Qutbuddin Aybeg/Aibak, 68, 97

radiocarbon dating, 47
Rajaram, king of the Marathas, 91
Rajasthan, 7, 55, 64, 69, 105, 151, 186n34
Rajasthani chronicles, 64
Rajatarangini, 186n29
Rajnish, Govind, 65
Rajput kingdoms, 61, 69, 129, 151
Rajputana, 55. *See also* Rajasthan
Rajputs: annals of, 125; bardic genealogists and, 56–57; clans, 64/69, 69; elites, 63, 73; land claims, 66; lineages of, 70, 105; marriage patterns, 67, 69; oral traditions, 63; traditions of, 152
Rajwade, Vishwanath Kashinath, 101, 142, 146–47, 192n53
Ramaraja, 110–11, 113, 114, 115
Ramdas, Samartha, 85–86
Ramoshi tribe, 93–94, 97, 104, 137, 191
Ranade, Mahadev Govind, 136, 138, 144

Ranke, Leopold von, 46, 143
Rao, V. Narayana, 198n108
Ray, Nikhilnath, 74, 76–77, 80, 189n103
Ray, Rammohan, 74
record chronicles: Andean, 28; creation of, 22, 27; deeds and charters, 46; earliest, 19; subaltern classes and, 97
Redfield, Robert, 26–27
regional identities, 8
regional languages, 7, 175
religious debate, 159
religious identities, 8, 17
religious nationalism, 151, 175
religious violence narrative, 177
Renan, Ernest, 110
revivalism, 160, 161, 166
Ricoeur, Paul, 10–11
Rise of the Christian Power in India (Basu), 167
Rise of the Mahomedan Power (Briggs), 54
Rise of the Maratha Power (Ranade), 144
Risley, H. H., 132, 135, 189n110
Rivett-Carnac, Harry, 57
rock carvings, 24–25
Roman Catholic Church, 30; Council of Trent, 41; court of Akbar and, 199n116; as Fourth Monarchy, 44; Greek traditions and, 20; on Hindu gods, 155; preaching orders of, 153; process of sainthood, 46; Roman Catholic conversions, 199n116
Roman Empire, 14, 20, 42, 44, 67, 119, 157
Rosenthal, Franz, 50, 53

Sabhasad, Krishnaji Anant, 105, 106, 109
sacred sites, 57–58, 59–60
sacred/secular distinction, 85
Salar Masud Ghazi, 58–59, 61
sanctity claims, 6
Sane, K. N., 139, 140
Sanskrit language, 51, 62–63, 122, 123–24, 128, 147, 150, 152, 159
Sanskrit texts, 72, 73, 112–14, 129, 136
Sanskrit thesaurus, 83
Sanskrit tradition, 23, 72
Sanskritization, 151, 166, 198n111
Sardesai, G. S., 146, 147
Sardesai family, 113
Sarkār, Dineścandra, 135
Sarkar, Jadunath, 135, 146, 166
Sarkar, Tanika, 173
Sassanid (Persian) Iran, 14, 21, 51
sati stones, 24–25
Satyartha prakash, 163, 164–65
Satyashodhak Samaj, 151
Savarkar, Vinayak Damodar, 144–45, 146, 147, 150, 197n83
scientific history, 145, 159, 175, 197n64
Scott, James, 61
Scottish Enlightenment, 124
scribes, 21, 75, 76, 80, 130
scripts, 24, 26
secularism, 174, 176
Sena kings, 72, 73, 74, 77, 78, 80, 134, 155, 199n124
Senji (Jinji) in southern India, 91
Serampore, 74, 131, 155
Sewell, Robert, 111, 147, 193n84, 198n95
Shah Jalal shrine in Sylhet, 73
Shahaji Raje, 105, 107, 111, 148
Shahid Amin, 159, 162
Shahnama (Persian epic), 71
Shahu, Chatrapati, 99
Shakadwipi Brahmans/Maga, 21–22
Sharqi kings of Jaunpur, 68, 69
shastris, 18
Shejwalkar, Tryambak S., 143, 148
Shibananda, 75
Shivaji, Chatrapati, 87–88, 97, 105, 106–7, 108, 148, 151
Shivaji, king of the Marathas, 83, 87, 102, 104, 145, 191n37
shrines, 24; Ajmer shrine, 58; Bahraich shrine, 59–61, 65, 162; Bu Adam shrine in Bikrampur, 73; Buddhist tradition and, 57–58; of East India, 71; Ghazi Miyan shrine, 59, 60, 65; Kalkaji shrine, 61; Khandoba shrine, 60; Muin al-Din Chishti shrine, 58; Muslim shrines,

57–58; Shah Jalal shrine in Sylhet, 73; Sufi shrines, 85
shripats (temples), 74
Shulman, David, 116, 198n108
Sisodiya Ranas of Mewar, 105
sites of memory, 14–15, 30, 102, 152, 183n69
slave-raiding, 72, 73
smartphones, 174
Smith, Vincent, 167
social frame(s), of *bakhar* genre, 86–93
social frames, 177; Lieberman on, 26; of memory, 18
social media, 174
social memory: academic historians exclusion from shaping of, 174; Assmann on, 15–17; in Bengal, 81; creation of, 9, 176; diverse forms of, 6; in East India, 72; ethno-nationalist project and, 162; Halbwachs on, 11–16; of Hindi-speaking North India, 70; of Marathi-speaking area, 7; modification of, 12–13; production/authentication of, 5; Puranas and, 24; regional languages and, 7; socio-political frame and, 83; within societal setting, 6
Sontheimer, Gunther D., 59
South India/southern India: historians of, 116, 147; Padshah of Bidar (Padshaw/Patsah/Padsah), 191n34; Sewell on, 147; sultanates of, 104; Vijayanagara Empire, 147
Southwest Asia, 7
Spain, 28, 35, 39–41, 183n93
Spencer, Edward, 38
Spivak, Gayatri, 98–99, 192n48
Stephens, James F., 127
Stewart, Dugald, 123–24, 127, 129, 133, 195n26
Strachey, John, 126–27, 177, 195n37
subaltern classes, 7, 93–94, 97–104, 192n48
Subaltern School, 192n48
Subaltern Studies, 133
Subrahmanyam, Sanjay, 116, 198n108
Sufism, 73, 85, 186n34
Suleiman Karrani, Sultan of Bengal, 75
Sultanate of Bengal, 72, 75, 78
Sultanate of Bijapur, 105
Sultanate of Delhi, 53, 55–61, 62, 69, 72, 74. *See also* Delhi sultans
Sumeria, 20, 148

ṭabaqāt genre (study of successive generations), 51
Tagore (Thakur) family, 80, 154, 189n110
Talbot, Cynthia, 61, 64, 70, 129, 151–52, 186n34
taluqdars (landlord class), 69–70
Tamil region, 60, 147, 188n93
ta'riẖ (*tārīkh* in Persianate form), 51, 53
taxation, 66, 134; bards (*charan*), 56; under Delhi sultans, 55–56; East India Company and, 120, 127; exemptions from, 111; folk traditions on, 116; *franc fief* tax, 36; historical memory and, 6; historical narratives and, 87–88; military class and, 39–40; in Mughal Empire, 62; noble status and, 36; racialization of, 40; Ranade on, 136; salt tax collection, 77; taxation claims, 51
Telangana, 60, 114
Telugu, 147
temple-centered histories, 19, 188n93
textbooks, 200n133; colonial textbooks, 161; Hindi-Urdu textbooks, 156–58; Indian history textbooks, 125, 171; mass production of, 8, 199n130; religious objections to, 158; subcontinental influence on, 50; textbook controversy, 172
texts: biblical text criticisms, 199n117; folklore, 25, 82; foundational texts, 16; foundational texts of, 16; German text-critique tradition, 136; Hindi texts, 155, 156–58; Kannada text, 149–50; *kulagrantha* texts/tradition, 82, 135; legal texts, 131; lost texts, 16; Marathi texts, 95, 113–14, 115–16, 129, 144–45, 148–50, 198nn106,108; medieval texts, 118; Nagari text, 149; oral traditions and, 24; perishability of, 24; Persian texts,

75; Sanskrit texts, 72, 73, 112–14, 136; Sumerian texts, 20; Vedic texts, 23–24, 158, 164
Thakurs (lords), 57, 66. *See also* Rajputs
Thanjavur, 111, 114, 137
That Noble Dream (Novick), 185n130
Thompson, Edward J., 167
three-epoch sequence, 54
Timur, Amir, 55, 68, 77
Tod, James, 64, 70, 125, 127, 129–30, 151, 152, 196n44
Torah, 17
traditions: foundational texts and, 16; great and little, 26–30; regional differences of, 8; traditional scholars, 108, 156
translation projects, 62, 155, 157
Trautmann, Thomas, 52, 122–24, 185n1
tribalism, 97–98, 174
Trojan descent claims, 42–43
Truschke, Audrey, 62, 63
Tughlaq, Feroz Shah, 195n41
Tughlaq, Muhammad bin, 55
Tughlaq, Sultan Ghiyasuddin, 58
Tughlaq sultans, 56, 69
Tungabhadra River, 111, 112, 128
Turani (Central Asian), 73
Turkic power elite, 52
Turkish conquest, 94, 155
Turkish sultanates, 127
Turkish-speaking Islamic peoples, 53
Turko-Afghan regional centers, 69
Tusaran-Bihar site, 70
23andMe, 49

Udīśvara/Ādiśūra/Adishura, king of Bengal, 74, 77, 79, 132, 155, 199n123
ulema (Islamic scholars), 18, 52, 85, 153, 199n117
universal history, 50–51, 62, 77
universal time, 45, 51, 52, 53, 159
University Grants Commission, 173
Urdu language, 128, 153, 157, 158, 160, 166, 200n131
usurpation of French titles, 37
Utilitarianism, 124
Utkala, 133
Uttar Pradesh, 7, 57, 70, 156, 159, 192n41, 196n62

Vaidya (physician) caste, 77, 80, 155
Vansina, Jan, 183n71
Varendra Research Society, 135
varṇa, 77
Vedas, 23, 159, 163–65
Vedic knowledge, 162–63, 164, 165
Vedic texts, 23–24, 158, 164
Vega, Garcilaso de la, 28
vernacular historical traditions, 7, 25, 42, 121, 174, 176
Vidyalankar, Mrityuñjaya, 74, 77, 78, 79, 112
Vidyanagara, 113. *See also* Vijayanagara Empire
Vidyanair, 111. *See also* Vijayanagara Empire
Vijayanagara Empire: erasure of, 109–17; Hindu nationalist project and, 147–52; Marathi historical traditions of, 7
village clusters (parganas), 56, 65–71, 86, 87, 97
Vīraśaiva, 101–2
Vishnubawa Brahmachari, 159

Wagoner, Phillip, 108, 110, 115
Wang, Edward, 119–20
Warangal, 110–11
Ward, John, 124
Waring, Edward Scott, 83
warrior caste, 66, 67, 73, 109, 111
watan (hereditary patrimony), 102
watandari (hereditary estates), 96
watandars (officeholders), 100
Weber, Max, 45
West Asia, 132–33, 171. *See also* Indian subcontinent pasts
Western civilization: church institutions in, 45; domination of writing, 119; early modern to modern era, 5; European feudal society, 29; European historical narrative, 161; European medieval history, 183n71; feudalism, 29; France,

35–37, 44, 118, 181n19; Greece, 15, 20, 23, 122, 123–24, 182n35, 183n81; historians of, 128; histories of, 165; Holy Roman Empire, 21; medieval public life, 34–45; medieval texts, 118; monarchies of, 184n112; monasteries, 4, 6, 20–21; narrative of power, 119; political decentralization in, 26; Renaissance Europe, 21; Roman Empire, 14, 20, 42, 44, 67, 119, 157; roots of, 16; Spain, 28, 35, 38–41, 183n93; tenets of, 7; traditions, 20; Westernization, 160; Western-style schools, 131, 153–54; writings about Indian intellectual history, 22. *See also* England

Western India, 70; overview, 83–86, 117; *Bakhar* genre in, 86–93; Bene Israel of, 17; histories of, 141; judicial verdicts/process, 84; Khomne and, 93–97; Marathi-speaking area of, 83; national projects, 104–9; subaltern class in, 97–104; subaltern classes in, 97–104; uprising in, 137; Vijayanagara Empire and, 109–17

WhatsApp, 174

Wilks, Mark, 128

William of Malmesbury, 41

Yadava dynasty, 113

Yadavas, 93, 113

Yarshater, Ehsan, 21

Yaśahara (modern Jessore), 76. *See also* Jessore

Yazdigird III, king of Sassanid Iran, 21

Yazid (Umayyad caliph), 52, 76

Yerushalmi, Yosef, 13, 182n47

yuga, 54

Yusufzai tribe, 66

Zakaullah, Munshi, 153, 161

zamindari rights, 68, 76, 101

zamindars (landholders), 65, 74

Zerubavel, Eviatar, 14

Ziegler, Norman, 63–64

GLOBAL SOUTH ASIA

Padma Kaimal
K. Sivaramakrishnan
Anand A. Yang
SERIES EDITORS

GLOBAL SOUTH ASIA takes an interdisciplinary approach to the humanities and social sciences in its exploration of how South Asia, through its global influence, is and has been shaping the world.

A Place for Utopia: Urban Designs from South Asia, by Smriti Srinivas

The Afterlife of Sai Baba: Competing Visions of a Global Saint, by Karline McLain

Sensitive Space: Fragmented Territory at the India-Bangladesh Border, by Jason Cons

The Gender of Caste: Representing Dalits in Print, by Charu Gupta

Displaying Time: The Many Temporalities of the Festival of India, by Rebecca M. Brown

Banaras Reconstructed: Architecture and Sacred Space in a Hindu Holy City, by Madhuri Desai

Mobilizing Krishna's World: The Writings of Prince Sāvant Singh of Kishangarh, by Heidi Rika Maria Pauwels

The Rebirth of Bodh Gaya: Buddhism and the Making of a World Heritage Site, by David Geary

Making New Nepal: From Student Activism to Mainstream Politics, by Amanda Thérèse Snellinger

High-Tech Housewives: Indian IT Workers, Gendered Labor, and Transmigration, by Amy Bhatt

Privileged Minorities: Syrian Christianity, Gender, and Minority Rights in Postcolonial India, by Sonja Thomas

Creating the Universe: Depictions of the Cosmos in Himalayan Buddhism, by Eric Huntington

Mountain Temples and Temple Mountains: Architecture, Religion, and Nature in the Central Himalayas, by Nachiket Chanchani

Gandhi's Search for the Perfect Diet: Eating with the World in Mind, by Nico Slate

Marrying for a Future: Transnational Sri Lankan Tamil Marriages in the Shadow of War, by Sidharthan Maunaguru

Bhakti and Power: Debating India's Religion of the Heart, edited by John Stratton Hawley, Christian Lee Novetzke, and Swapna Sharma

Climate Change and the Art of Devotion: Geoaesthetics in the Land of Krishna, 1550–1850, by Sugata Ray

History and Collective Memory in South Asia, 1200–2000, by Sumit Guha